Work and Power
in Maale, Ethiopia

Studies in Cultural Anthropology, No. 8

Conrad Phillip Kottak, Series Editor

Professor of Anthropology
The University of Michigan

Other Titles in This Series

Work and Power in Maale, Ethiopia

by
Donald L. Donham

UMI RESEARCH PRESS
Ann Arbor, Michigan

Produced and distributed by
UMI Research Press
an imprint of
University Microfilms International
A Xerox Information Resources Company
Ann Arbor, Michigan 48106

Library of Congress Cataloging in Publication Data

Donham, Donald L. (Donald Lewis)
Work and power in Maale, Ethiopia.

(Studies in cultural anthropology ; no. 8)
"A revision of the author's dissertation, Stanford
University, 1979"—Verso t.p.
Bibliography: p.
Includes index.
1. Maale (African people)—Economic conditions.
2. Economic anthropology—Ethiopia.   3. Communism and
anthropology—Ethiopia.   I. Title.   II. Series.

DT380.4.M32D64   1984   330.963'3   84-22223
ISBN 0-8357-1557-4 (alk. paper)

Contents

Figures

Maps

Plates

Tables

Preface

Since this book was completed in 1979, I have continued to develop many of the ideas contained in the following chapters. A fuller discussion of neoclassical method and particularly the assumptions made here in relation to Chayanov's and Sahlins' works is contained in Donham (1981). Also, the political significance of cooperative labor—particularly its cultural idiom—is discussed in a forthcoming essay, "History at One Point in Time: 'Working Together' in Maale, 1975." Finally, as I point out in the introductory chapter, I use Marxism here more as a guide to the structure of society than as a subject for analysis in its own right. Much more can be done along the latter lines, and I am currently engaged in such a project.

The fieldwork on which this study is based began in early May 1974 and ended in late December 1975. The "creeping coup," as it was soon to be called, had begun a few months before my wife and I arrived in Ethiopia. It was not until the following September, however, that Haile Selassie was finally deposed. I spent most of my twenty months of fieldwork in Maale, except for sometimes uneasy, two-week visits to Addis Ababa every three or four months. In a house I had built by local *mol?o* and *dabo* work parties (cf. Chapter 4), I lived in Dofo hamlet in Bola chiefdom—part of the locale that is the focus of following chapters (Map 6). I saw other areas of Maale through short trips and through one-month stays in Bio chiefdom and in southern Bunka chiefdom (Map 5).

One of my first tasks on arriving was to construct an elementary grammar of the language and to collect a vocabulary, since almost no linguistic research had been done on Maale. In these as well as in other projects, my assistant Yekade Kelibo, one of the very few Maale who had learned English in school, provided invaluable and remarkably conscientious help. By the middle of my field stay, I had learned enough to carry out most of my research in Maale, though even at the end I still sometimes became lost when Maale spoke among themselves.

Most of my research methods will become obvious in following chapters. Here I will make two comments. The census of the Maale locale that is my main subject was carried out over almost the entire period of fieldwork. With cross-checking and revision, its accuracy is probably fairly high. Second, the historical analyses of Chapter 2 (when not based on published sources) depend on interview material with Maale, Muslim, and northern informants. (The choice of these categories of people will become clear in Chapter 2.) Almost all of the incidents or episodes that I report are based on interviews with persons of opposing points of view. Interviews were conducted and transcribed in Maale; since Muslim traders and northerners living in Maale generally spoke Maale, this choice of language posed few problems. At times, Yekade Kelibo translated difficult questions into Amharic, another language in which he was fluent.

I would like to acknowledge the roles that a number of people played in the making of this study. Nancy Powelson Donham shared in every phase of the research, sometimes disproportionately in its difficult aspects. Her emotional support, critical intelligence, and editing skills have all been crucial. This is her work too. Frank Cancian, Bridget O'Laughlin, and G. William Skinner also contributed in very substantial ways to my work. Others offered their assistance by reading and commenting on individual chapters: Donald Crummey, Paul Diener, Michael Dove, Joseph Greenberg, Renato Rosaldo, and Ivo Strecker. I want to thank Hal Fleming whom I visited in the field on my first trip to southwestern Ethiopia in the summer of 1972 and Jean Lydall who offered her hospitality as well as a last-minute course in field methods when I arrived in Addis Ababa in 1974.

I am grateful for generous funding and other kinds of support from the following institutions and people: the National Science Foundation for a research grant from 1974 to 1976; the Institute of Ethiopian Studies in Addis Ababa for sponsorship of my research in Ethiopia; the Mabelle McCloud Lewis Foundation for a grant to write up; the Stanford African Studies Program and its executive secretary, Emily Hallin, for grants for a summer field trip to Ethiopia in 1972 and for the translation of Amharic documents; and finally the Stanford Department of Anthropology for five years of fellowship support. I am indebted to Benjamin Paul for his role in making the latter possible.

Finally, it is difficult to acknowledge adequately my neighbors and informants in Maale, who tolerated many tedious and sometimes bad-mannered questions and who yet offered me their companionship and friendship. For the former, I apologize, and for the latter, I express my special gratitude. I thank in particular Yekade Kelibo, Makarso Kansira, Arregude Sulunge, and Dulbo Tonna. *maalesa məli maom. insi 'ditsi 'ditsi nangom. ts'osi nuna kamisom.*

December 1983

Plate 1.   A Maale Elder

1

Introduction: Images and Theories

> Though we find in the current anthropological literature information on technology or, at best, on exchange, we have hardly any information on the social organization of production: Who is working with whom and for whom? Where does the product of the laborer go? Who controls the product? How does the economic system reproduce itself?
>
> Claude Meillassoux (1972: 98)

Perhaps a historian of science would call them "paradigms" or a philosopher might say "stances"—I want to begin by focusing on what I will call dominant "images" in anthropological work (cf. Rosaldo 1975; Levine 1974). Specifically, I want to recount how two very different images of the Maale of southwestern Ethiopia guided my research (often in only half-conscious ways) and how I came to see one as considerably more useful than the other.

The first image is one of a traditional African kingdom which has somehow survived into the present, an isolated society, uninfluenced by social forces like Western colonial governments, cash cropping, or migrant labor that long ago transformed the lives of other peoples. This image calls up notions of well-integrated, "primitive" communities of kinsmen and of divine kings who magically ensure the fertility of crops and people. The second image, in contrast, is a great deal less exotic and, at first glance, perhaps less arresting: this is the idea of a peasantry, neither isolated nor self-contained, but a constituent part of a larger, stratified social system. Located toward the lower economic and political rungs, most peasants today play a role in the world economic system. One immediately thinks of hard work, factionalism, and domination by "outsiders."

I went to Ethiopia more or less expecting to find the first kind of people. The available literature certainly pointed me in that direction. Almost every work on Ethiopia starts with the idea of a mountain fortress inhabited by fierce people who have managed to maintain their independence, their traditions, and their Orthodox Christianity for centuries. Few Ethiopianists have neglected to quote Gibbon's famous phrase in *The Rise and Fall of the Roman Empire* describing Ethiopia after the Muslim conquests of the seventh century:

"Encompassed on all sides by the enemies of their religion, the Aethiopians slept near a thousand years, forgetful of the world by whom they were forgotten."

In the nineteenth century, Ethiopia, unlike most of the rest of Africa, managed to defeat her would-be European master and to remain free. Sociological studies of twentieth-century Ethiopia speak still of feudalism, of an imperial regime, and of the almost divine status of Haile Selassie in the eyes of his people. Here indeed was a faraway place, a place where one could apparently step back in time:

> [Traditional life in northern Ethiopia] offers a gate through time to a state of being that is richly medieval. Such sights and sounds! A minstrel singing his subtle lyrics as he bows a one-stringed fiddle; in the dark interiors of church, barefoot deacons holding beeswax candles...; the pomp of a nobleman moving cross country with his crowded entourage; a young girl washing the feet of her father's guests...(Levine 1965:vii-viii).

If Ethiopia itself was thought to be isolated and traditional, the southwest of the country—where I was to do fieldwork—was doubly so. The southwest, although strongly influenced by the northern Christian empire around the fourteenth century, had developed independently since the sixteenth century. By the late 1890s, the region was again conquered and incorporated into the expanding Ethiopian empire, but since only a weak system of indirect rule was established, many of the traditional kings and chiefs of the area maintained their powers. According to a major study carried out in the 1950s, "The archaic peoples of southwestern Ethiopia live in far-off and inaccessible settlements— typical areas of retreat—and are as yet little affected by the more highly developed peoples of northern and western Ethiopia" (Jensen 1959: 419). The southwest—archaic and traditional—was isolated from the rest of Ethiopia, and Ethiopia—uncolonized and free—was as independent of the rest of the world as possible in the twentieth century.

When I arrived in Maale, these expectations were initially reinforced to some extent. The trip into Maale seemed enough to convince me of its isolation. For the first half of the way, there was an old Italian road in disrepair and passable for trucks only during four months of the dry season; for the rest of the way, there were overgrown footpaths over a steep mountain pass. The whole trip from Jinka, the subprovincial capital, took two days by mule. Once we arrived, my wife and I camped close to the king's compound. We were there two weeks when a group of elders arrived from the southernmost region of Maale. From what I could make out of their animated conversation, the Banna, the people just to the south of Maale, had raided Maale and many Maale people had been killed in the fighting.

When the men were telling their story to the mother of the king, the "queen-mother" (an important role in many African kingdoms), I was surprised when the men suddenly gathered around the old woman, extended their hands toward her, palms up, and began a rhythmic recitative chant—first the queen-mother, then the elders, then the queen-mother. I was later to identify this as something like prayer. This experience and others like it, as well as the fact that there was no labor migration from Maale, that no cash crops had been introduced, that customs like labor tribute to the king continued, all reinforced my image of the Maale as a traditional people living in a small and mostly bounded social unit, "forgetful of the world by whom they were forgotten."

Now it is true that from the beginning I distrusted this rather romantic image. And there were a number of awkward facts: the king turned out to be a young man in his early twenties with an eighth-grade education who could speak English. He wore fashionable suits, an expensive Seiko watch, and preferred to live outside Maale in Jinka, the subprovincial capital. And on my very first day in Maale, an old man came up to me, saluted smartly, and said with a smile across his face, "*bon giorno.*" During the occupation of Ethiopia, he had been a servant to one of the Italian soldiers. Finally, my assistant was a Maale Protestant from one of the first families to convert when missionaries began their work in Maale in about 1962.

Details such as these certainly contradicted the image of a traditional Maale. But the decisive event that finally forced me to see Maale differently and to ask new questions was the revolution in 1974. In September of that year, four months after I arrived in the field, Haile Selassie was deposed. A new government was established. Newspaper reports said that the people of Addis Ababa sang in the streets. At the very least, there was no effective opposition to the political change.

The events in Addis Ababa were quickly felt in Maale. By November an odd coalition of disaffected Maale had formed, including a disinherited son of the richest chief, a group of Protestant converts, and a group of traditional Maale living in the cattle-raising south. These people temporarily united and formally accused the king, the richest chief, and northern landlords living in Maale of misdeeds and, in their words, "oppression." (The Amharic word for oppressor, *ak'ork'waj,* was immediately adopted into the Maale vocabulary from radio broadcasts from Addis Ababa.) Their accusation to the subprovincial court was dated 21 November 1974 and reads in part as follows:

> During the time Haile Selassie was Emperor of Ethiopia, there were rich and powerful people who lived in many places in our country. They were the *bālābbāt, c'ek'āshums,* and *grāzmāches*[1] appointed by Haile Selassie. Most of these people did us much damage: The *bālābbāt* whose name is Tinke Bailo has done many bad deeds at market and elsewhere. When we bring our things to market to sell them, he forces us to sell them to him at a very low price. Because we are poor people, we sell in the market to earn money. But he upsets the market and makes the country poor by buying something worth five dollars for two, something worth ten dollars for five. If anyone argues with him about the price, then that

man is sent away from the marketplace, and his goods are simply confiscated ... In addition, the *bālābbāt* has taken away land from Maale people who have paid their land taxes since 1950. He has taken these lands for himself, his relatives, and for northerners living in Maale. He has conspired with one of the *c'ek 'āshum,* Babo Guadari, and the two of them together have instigated quarrels among the people about land. Since Tinke and Babo are *bālābbāt* and *c'ek 'āshum,* they force the people to elect their relatives to government positions. The people would like to elect someone else but they cannot ...

Suddenly, political cleavages were a great deal more evident. The "king" of Maale began to look much more like a rich Ethiopian landlord. The national system of land law and the way it was applied in Maale became a more obviously important issue. The history of the Ethiopian conquest of the southwest and the subsequent administration became a relevant topic. Instead of being marginal outsiders, landlords from the north and Muslim traders living in Maale began to appear as integral parts of the Maale social system. Instead of being a "primitive" society, a fairly bounded social unit where primordial traditions survived into the present, Maale was arguably a subunit of a larger stratified society.[2] It became clear that almost any topic in Maale economics or politics would have to include a consideration of Maale's involvement in the encompassing social system of Ethiopia.

While the study that follows concentrates on the period just before the revolution (the Maale *bālābbāt* was removed and new farmers' cooperatives were established only in mid-1975), the revolution itself, with its revelation of quick and varied response to change and with its unmasking of underlying tensions, was a formative influence on the general interpretative stance I have adopted. Throughout I have attempted to present my material so as to make clear (1) spatial variation and the fact that local spatial units fit into and are conditioned by larger units up to and beyond the Ethiopian state, and (2) temporal variation and the fact that Maale communities are and probably always have been in a process of continuous change, sometimes revolutionary change. This image of Maale, surely as "complex" in its own way as any so-called complex society, precludes any loose talk of *the* Maale pattern of production or of kinship or of anything else. Quite simply, what I have to present is data from one rather small locale in the Maale highlands during one rather brief period of time in 1974 and 1975. It is only by recognizing this specificity, I think, that more general questions about Maale society and about how local units relate to more inclusive ones can be posed, much less satisfactorily answered.

Traditional primitive Maale—that simple, static, and self-contained whole—probably never existed. Indeed, it could be argued that the anthropological concept of primitive societies had mroe to do with covering up methodological difficulties (with concentrating study on one small locality during one short time frame when in reality all localities are conditioned by their placement in larger social systems, the whole being in continual flux) than with advancing social theory. Within African studies in particular, these issues have proven difficult to resolve. In 1965, Aidan Southall observed:

> One of the worst biases in the African material is the tendency to a simple dichotomy between supposedly primeval systems, stated in the ethnographic present, and the contemporary situation... Schapera actually states, 'by a political community I mean a group of people organized into a single unit managing its own affairs independently of control (except that exercised nowadays by European governments).' What sort of a universal definition is it that depends upon such an exception? A breath of reality must be introduced by recognition that African peoples have often passed through a number of significant phases... (Southall 1965: 135).

Varieties of Theory in Economic Anthropology

Anthropological theories are, in a sense, extended and elaborated images. They direct and shape one's vision of social reality. My object in this monograph is to analyze one crucial aspect of Maale social organization—the production process. As the quotation from Claude Meillassoux at the beginning of this chapter noted, studies of production in noncapitalist societies are few. Substantivist, neoclassical, and Marxist writers have made various contributions. Below I will review the major issues in the literature and attempt to develop an internally consistent and empirically useful standpoint from which to analyze Maale production.

To understand any of the schools of economic anthropology requires some attention to the fact that they have generally developed their approaches to noncapitalist societies in interaction with the much larger and more comprehensive body of theory on capitalism. Often, the influences have been only indirect, yet almost every theory of noncapitalist economies has contained at least some implied contrast with and therefore some notion of the structure of capitalist economies. (The simple designation, "noncapitalist," reveals this tendency.) While, therefore, I will concentrate on theories of noncapitalist economies below, it is important to realize that such theories cannot be evaluated in complete isolation from satisfactory theories of capitalist economies.

If economic anthropology has often been influenced by economics proper, theoretical developments within the two disciplines have proceeded largely at their own pace and in relation to their own problems. Both Marxian and neoclassical theory—the two grand schools of present-day economics—developed in the nineteenth-century, neoclassicism somewhat later and in some ways in reaction to Marxism (see Dobb 1973).

The progression in economic anthropology has been different. Self-consciously Marxist approaches have developed late, mostly since the late

1960s, while the bulk of neoclassical (in anthropological terminology, "formalist") studies began in the 1950s. Substantivism, which has no exact counterpart within economics (except perhaps institutional economics), is a variety of the functionalist theory that dominated social anthropology from the 1930s to the 1950s and combines elements of both neoclassicism (acceptable to most substantivists for capitalist economies) and Marx's fragmentary writings on noncapitalist economies. All three schools—substantivism, neoclassicism, and Marxism—are presently active in economic anthropology, and below I will review each of their contributions to a theory of production in noncapitalist economies.

I will pay particular attention to the relative emphasis these different schools give to individual versus institutional factors. A common understanding of the variety of theories goes something like this: According to substantivists, different institutional complexes make economic systems fundamentally incomparable so that it is institutions that must receive the greatest stress in analyses. Neoclassical writers, on the other hand, maintain that institutions are not so different that all economies cannot be analyzed with the postulate that persons act so as to maximize their individual gains. In other words, neoclassical works depend on the universal presence of a psychological inclination to selfishness, an inclination "to truck and to barter." Finally, Marxists are closer to substantivists than to neoclassical writers since they also emphasize the primacy of institutions. Marxists, however, give priority to productive institutions while substantivists concentrate on institutions that facilitate the circulation of goods.

None of these conventional notions is any more than a half-truth, it seems to me. Together, these ideas present a major obstacle to developing a logically consistent and empirically useful standpoint from which to analyze the Maale case. Below, I attempt to cut a path through the underbrush that has grown up about these issues.

Let me begin with substantivism. Of the three schools in economic anthropology, it is probably the substantivists who have given least attention to production; indeed, it is sometimes said that their work is concerned only with circulation (Meillassoux 1972: 96). Such an assertion is false, however, for it is clear that analysts like Karl Polanyi and others intend their major theoretical concepts—mainly "reciprocity" and "redistribution"—to apply both to circulation and to production in noncapitalist economies (Polanyi 1957: 255; Dalton [1962] 1971).

If substantivists have a theory of production, what is it? And specifically, what are Polanyi's principles of reciprocity and redistribution? As a preliminary, it must be understood that the whole substantivist enterprise is founded on a negative premise—what primitive economies are not. Such economies are not capitalistic; they are not dominated by the motive of individual material gain. (Notice particularly the stress that Polanyi places on the profit motive as the defining feature of capitalism.)

> All types of societies are limited by economic factors. Nineteenth century civilization alone was economic in a different and distinctive sense, for it chose to base itself on a motive only rarely acknowledged as valid in the history of human societies, and certainly never before raised to the level of a justification of action and behavior in everyday life, namely, gain. The self-regulating market system, was uniquely derived from this principle (Polanyi 1944: 30).

Having delimited the subject of noncapitalist economies in negative terms, Polanyi sought a more positive specification. Intended to serve that purpose, the concepts of reciprocity and redistribution refer, first of all, to motives of individual action—what Polanyi calls principles of behavior—which contrast with that of individual gain in capitalist economies (i.e. "exchange"). Reciprocity, as the word suggests, is mutually motivated action as when a person gives a gift and then receives one in return. Redistribution covers a variety of motives but is mainly action motivated by the value of sharing; when a group pools its resources, redistribution has taken place. Polanyi went on to insist that these motives or principles of behavior become economically dominant only when they are "supported" by particular kinds of social institutions:

> Reciprocity behavior between individuals integrates the economy only if symmetrically organized structures, such as a symmetrical system of kinship groups, are given. But a kinship system never arises as the result of mere reciprocating behavior on the personal level. Similarly, in regard to redistribution. It presupposes the presence of an allocative center in the community, yet the organization and validation of such a center does not come about merely as a consequence of frequent acts of sharing as between individuals (1957: 251).

In sum, reciprocity is a mutual give and take between symmetrically placed social persons or groups, while redistribution is sharing or pooling which takes place in groups with allocative centers:

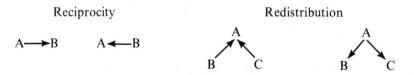

With regard to production, reciprocity would appear to apply to those forms of labor cooperation (like the Maale *dabo* described in Chapter 4) in which neighbors work for one another on the understanding that help will eventually be returned. Redistribution, in contrast, would cover cases like labor tribute: The subjects of a chief work in the latter's fields, after which the produce of their labor is given back to them through feasts and gifts.

As a starting point for empirical analyses, any analytical framework such as the one above must have some minimal degree of coherence and clarity. The substantivist scheme, however, appears to involve a number of ambiguities from the very outset. First, there is the question of whether reciprocity has been clearly differentiated from redistribution or from capitalist exchange. At one point in his discussion, Polanyi writes,

> Reciprocity as a form of integration gains greatly in power through its capacity of employing both redistribution and exchange as subordinate methods. Reciprocity may be attained through a sharing of the burden of labor according to definite rules of redistribution as when taking things "in turn." Similarly, reciprocity is sometimes attained through exchange at set equivalencies for the benefit of the partner who happens to be short of some kind of necessities. In nonmarket economies these two forms of integration—reciprocity and redistribution—occur in effect usually together (1957: 253).

The pertinent question is not whether the two principles occur together but whether they have been unambiguously defined in the first place. Consider Polanyi's example above of a group that takes things in turn. In one kind of Maale work group (the *helma* described in Chapter 4) three or four persons work on each others' fields by turn. Shall we say that this is redistribution achieved through reciprocity or vice versa?

This issue recurs in Marshall Sahlins' work on reciprocity where he writes:

> On an even more general view, the two types [reciprocity and redistribution] merge. For pooling [redistribution] is an organization of reciprocities, a system of reciprocities—a fact of central bearing upon the genesis of large-scale redistribution under chiefly aegis (1972: 188).

But Sahlins concludes that reciprocity and redistribution must be distinguished since they occur in different kinds of social relationships. "Pooling is socially a *within* relation... Reciprocity is a *between* relation... Thus pooling is the complement of social unity and, in Polanyi's term, 'centricity'; whereas, reciprocity is social duality and 'symmetry'" (1972: 188-89).

While specifying the type of social relationships in which economic action takes place would clarify the substantivists' scheme (indeed, it would be in line with their insistence that the economy is a socially instituted process), Polanyi's and Sahlins' distinctions between centricity and symmetry, "within" and "between" relations, do not appear adequate to the task. Social boundaries—on which any ideas of within or between depends—are often relative to the social actor's point of view. Ethnic boundaries, for example, tend to depend upon exactly whom is asked and for what purposes. Boundaries, moreover, vary from extremely distinct ones to very fuzzy ones. Sahlins' simple distinction, within versus between, leaves a large grey area unanalyzed.

Polanyi's concepts of symmetry and centricity appear more promising at st sight, but upon inspection, they turn out to be strictly formal (and fore empty) categories. Consider the idea of social symmetry. To be this concept would have to be specified further. Symmetrical with o what? Wealth? Power? Ethnic identity? George Dalton ([1965] 1971: several examples of symmetrical, reciprocal economic relationships— kinship, friendship, and master-client ties. In what sense are father-son and master-client relationships symmetrical? The only symmetrical property that all of Dalton's examples possess is some kind of "give and take"—that is, some kind of social relationship—between two people filling some kind of social roles.

In the face of these confusions and in spite of their programmatic aims to analyze the social relationships underlying the economy, substantivists have in practice fallen back to stress the role of motives in economic action and how these motives are conditioned by cultural values. And their great theme has been that primitive cultures, unlike capitalism, do not inculcate individuals with the value of material gain. In some ways, this result is a logical outcome of substantivists' acceptance of neoclassical theory as adequate for capitalism: If capitalism is defined by the individual quest for profit, then it would seem that noncapitalist economies must be defined by contrasting motives or values.

Briefly, I will consider two examples in the substantivist literature where an emphasis on individual preferences is critical and where, on the contrary, attention to social institutions would have indicated other lines of analysis. The first case is George Dalton's discussion of the effects of colonialism on African societies. Dalton writes:

> The destructive aspect of colonialism was not *economic* exploitation of Africans in the conventional Marxist sense; it could hardly be so, considering that material poverty was already the common lot before Europeans arrived...The destructive colonial impact consisted in forcing socio-economic change which was not meaningful to Africans in terms of their traditional societies...European enterprise was devoid of social meaning for Africans because it required work which was not part of social obligation to kin, friends, or rulers ([1962] 1971: 135).

What is crucial, according to Dalton, is that colonial rule was not legitimated by indigenous cultural values. (By implication, before the Europeans, rulers in African societies were always seen as legitimate.) But we are told nothing about colonial institutions, the level of wages offered by Europeans compared to their profits, the incidence of taxation on Africans, the coercive power of colonial governments, or the terms of trade for African cash crops. Economic exploitation, if that concept is to have any value (as Dalton writes elsewhere, it is a difficult idea to use precisely), must be specified in institutional terms. Moreover, it is a concept that applies internally to the colonial order. The relevant comparison is not the well-being of Africans before and after colonial rule but the kinds of systematic economic inequality that colonial institutions did or did not foster between African workers and European capitalists.

A second example of the lack of institutional analyses in substantivists' works is Marshall Sahlins' use of the distinction between production "for use" and "for exchange." This distinction goes back to Aristotle, and Marx himself incorporated the concepts into his work. (Below I will have occasion to examine Marx's views on the subject.) With a Marxian ring to these phrases and with the substantivists' insistence on the primacy of institutions, we expect that Sahlins will analyze these concepts in terms of contrasting kinds of economic institutions. Instead, he gives us an analysis based entirely on individual preferences.

In societies in which production for use dominates, "... wants are finite and few, and technical means unchanging but on the whole adequate" (1972: 2). Thus Sahlins calls hunting and gathering society "the original affluent society." But "affluence" here does not carry the usual dictionary meaning of level of wealth (an institutional factor, after all, intimately bound up with systems of stratification) but of psychological satisfaction. Hunters and gatherers are poor but satisfied. "We should entertain the empirical possibility that hunters are in business for their health, a finite objective, and that bow and arrow are adequate to that end" (Sahlins 1972: 5).

Production for exchange, in contrast, is based on unlimited needs, an insatiable quest for profit, for "as much as possible." "The sky is the limit" (Sahlins 1972: 84). According to Sahlins, the whole apparatus of neoclassical theory reflects the properties of economic systems based on exchange but not those oriented toward use. He does not seem to understand that since he has defined production for use in terms of individual preferences—the starting point of all neoclassical analyses—it takes only a minor alteration of ordinary neoclassical assumptions (i.e. that in X society, individuals prefer leisure to work above a certain level of production, Y) to cover any possible system of production for use.[3] In fact, neoclassical economists have done just that; in their felicitous phrase, individuals in such societies are said to have reached their "bliss point"—they have satisfied all their wants and needs (Stent and Webb 1975).

It is mainly the substantivists' retreat from institutional analysis, as in these two examples, and their emphasis on motives and cultural values, a line of thought entirely compatible with neoclassical theory, that made the substantivist-formalist debate in anthropology (LeClair and Schneider 1968) of minor theoretical importance. The only issue between the two sides turned on the relative importance of individual material gain versus the value of social acceptability in motives of economic action. Polanyi stressed the latter to such degree that he produced (curiously enough for a historian) a completely static theory of primitive economies caught, as it were, in a cultural *rigor mortis:*

> Symmetry and centricity will meet halfway the needs of reciprocity and redistribution; institutional patterns and principles of behavior are mutually adapted. As long as social organization runs in its ruts, no individual economic motives need come into play; no shirking of personal effort need be feared; division of labor will be duly discharged; and, above all, the material means of an exuberant display of abundance at all public festivals will be provided (1944: 49).

Polanyi's view comes close to the "myth of Merrie Africa" that historian A.G. Hopkins has parodied. We are asked to believe, Hopkins says, in a precolonial Golden Age "in which generations of Africans enjoyed congenial lives in well-integrated, smoothly functioning societies. The means of livelihood came easily to hand . . . and this good fortune enabled the inhabitants to concentrate on leisure pursuits, which, if some sources are to be believed, consisted of interminable dancing and drumming" (1973: 10).

It was mainly in reaction to substantivists' idea of whole societies rigidified by cultural values that neoclassical or formalist studies in economic anthropology began in the late 1950s. Two problems seem to have turned anthropologists and others toward neoclassical theory—analyzing conflict and understanding social change, particularly economic development. Neoclassical anthropologists maintained that all of these problems required a new theoretical framework. The first chapter of Harold Schneider's monograph on the Turu begins with the following incident:

> In 1959 in Tanzania, while I was studying the people of a village of the subtribe of Wahi in the country of the Turu, I was startled one day by the refusal of a group of brothers to help their ancient mother cultivate her field. The old lady, Nyankambi . . . was so agitated by the danger of permanent damage to her crops that she prevailed upon me to carry to a mill five miles away a load of grain she wanted ground. With the flour she planned to make some beer with which to pay her sons and others to help her cultivate her field. This incident and others of the same type raised questions in my mind about the theory I was working with—a theory based on the assumption of cooperation and mutual aid among the members of the family and the larger community (1970: 1).

Schneider goes on to develop what he calls a competitive approach to African societies, one in which persons are seen as maximizing their own individual interests. Instead of being confined to capitalist societies (as substantives held), the motive of individual gain is universal according to Schneider and other neoclassical anthropologists.

The concern for economic change that the new school of analysis evinced shows most clearly in the work of economic historians of Africa. Both A.G. Hopkins (1973) and Philip Curtin (1975) stress the value of a cautious neoclassical approach in analyzing change. Hopkins flatly states, " . . . the substantivist case fails to meet the empirical test: the economy of precolonial West Africa simply did not function in accordance with principles which are supposed to characterize 'traditional' societies" (1973: 6). According to Curtin, "The substantivist position was strongly antihistorical, although Polanyi and his school took many of their examples from past societies" (1973: 236). With regard to changes entailed by economic development in particular, William Jones (1960) pointed out that the very possibility of development, *whether* along capitalist or socialist lines, depended upon the response of Africans to economic incentives. According to Jones' reading of the evidence, that response—the motive of individual gain—had always existed in Africa.

It is not my primary purpose here to inquire into the social backgrounds from which theoretical systems sprang. But to understand substantivism and formalism even on their own terms, it is important to notice that formalism originated in and the ensuing substantivist-formalist debate was played out against the backdrop of the decolonization of Africa. Some Marxists as well as others (cf. Jones 1960) have maintained that approaches like those of substantivism (and functionalism generally) with their emphasis on smoothly functioning societies in which noneconomic motives reign supreme were simply an apology for colonialism. Such arguments are misleading at best. Substantivism was, in fact, a romantic critique (perhaps "rejection" is more accurate) of Western capitalism and colonialism.

In Polanyi's first statement of substantivism (1944), noncapitalist societies were held up as the standard from which *laissez faire* capitalism had departed, and according to Polanyi (who was writing during World War II) the outcome of that departure was finally the horror of fascism. Anthropologists like Malinowski aimed their critique at missionaries and colonial administrators, and insisted that everything that had been done to improve "native" life had only disrupted the smooth working of well-integrated societies. Speaking of the attitude of British anthropologists at the time, Lucy Mair writes,

> We all made ourselves the defenders of African custom against its critics, and against policies aimed at radical change. We all assumed that colonial rulers were both self-righteous and self-interested. But we did not at that time see the end of colonial rule as a possibility, so we contented ourselves with advocating the kind of policy that seemed likely to be least disruptive of African society... ([1965] 1969: 136).

Whether the romanticism of anthropologists of the period allowed colonialism to continue unconfronted by any radical challenge is another question (like all counter-factuals, a very difficult question) but in terms of their own intentions, many anthropologists aimed their work against colonialism.[4]

The decolonialization of Africa in the late 1950s and the early 1960s decisively changed the social context in which economic theory was applied to African societies. Lucy Mair, again a clear-headed observer of the times, noted the almost complete about-face on the part of many social scientists ([1965] 1969: 135). Instead of protection from change instigated by self-interested colonial overlords, encouragement of change and of economic development demanded by Africans themselves became the order of the day. In the new social order, the substantivists' old emphasis on traditional noneconomic values and preferences became something of an embarrassment. To analyze the problems that decolonization highlighted—conflict, change, and development—formalists turned to neoclassical economic theory.

At first glance, it is curious that anthropologists and historians would have sought help for these particular problems from neoclassical economic theory. Within economics, neoclassicism has been criticized repeatedly for its inability to analyze the origin of systematic social conflict and for its limited value in discussing problems of economic change, development in particular (cf. Rowthorn 1974). Upon further inspection, however, it becomes clear—as Frank Cancian (1966) showed—that what formalists tended to borrow from neoclassical economics was not a theory at all but a magnificent tautology: that individuals in all societies act so as to maximize their individual gains. How do we know what a gain is for any particular individual? Basically, by what he or she does. If a person gives up extra income to help a friend, then his altruistic satisfaction is greater than the gain from the foregone income. If the person does the reverse, then the gain from the extra income is greater than that to be derived from helping a friend. There is no way to falsify the proposition that the person acted so as to maximize his gain.[5]

Looking back over the formalist-substantivist debate, it is difficult to understand how a tautology could have inspired such criticism. Surely other windmills would have been more vulnerable to attack. As late as 1972, Sahlins wrote, "... it is a choice between the perspective of Business, for the formalist method must consider the primitive economies as underdeveloped versions of our own, and a culturalist study that as a matter of principle does honor to different societies for what they are" (xi-xii). Many Marxists have followed substantivists in this line of criticism. Meillassoux, for instance, writes that the application of neoclassical concepts to noncapitalist economies "...is more than mere error or sheer ethnocentrism; it betrays the impact of ideology on social science; it betrays the imperialism of the science of Imperialism which wants to submit 'development' to the universal laws of capitalist exploitation..." (1978: 128).

Notice briefly the form these criticisms take. Typically, they accept the argument on neoclassical grounds—that of individual choice—and maintain that people in noncapitalist societies have relatively few choices to make:

In subsistence (non-market) economies, the question of choice among real alternatives does not arise in such explicit fashion [as in capitalism]. A Trobriand Islander learns and follows the rules of *economy* in his society almost as an American learns and follows the rules of *language* in his (Dalton [1969] 1971: 78).

... in a *contractual* society such as ours, men, except within the narrow range of their family, choose, to a certain point, their partners in work or business. But in a kinship or a feudal society, where rank and status are determined by birth, the choice of possible social relationships is extremely limited ... (Meillassoux 1972: 95).

But, of course, if choice were so limited in feudal society, then it is difficult to understand how feudalism ever changed over the centuries, much less went through a revolutionary transformation into capitalism.[6] If these positions be accepted, therefore, we are faced with a theory that is helpless to comprehend economic change.

To return to the formalists, their use of the maximization tautology led to several interesting results in practice. If substantivists began with an emphasis on social institutions and ended by stressing individual motives, the reverse was generally true of formalists. Starting with a postulate that every individual action is reasonable when seen in its proper context (something or other is being maximized), formalists were almost forced to inquire into the institutional forms of noncapitalist economies. Thus, while early Marxists were still preoccupied with kinship or with exegeses of Marx's texts, formalist-inspired studies such as those of Frank Cancian (1972), Polly Hill (1972), and Martin Orans (1968) revealed forms of economic inequality in peasant societies that had theretofore been overlooked or inadequately analyzed by anthropologists. These forms of inequality turned out to be a pervasive aspect of economic organization, a decisive influence on the rate of economic change, and often a critical variable for understanding how local communities responded to development programs.

With regard to the problem of production in noncapitalist economies, the basic formalist work was done not by an anthropologist but by an agricultural economist, Alexander Chayanov. Although Chayanov wrote in the early part of our century, his major work was translated from Russian into English in only 1966. Chayanov's empirical materials were drawn from Russian peasant communities, but he intended his theoretical scheme developed in relation to those data to apply more widely to noncapitalist economies in which peasant households are dominant units of production.

Chayanov began with psychological assumptions typical of neoclassical economics. He argued that the value of the return to an hour of labor declines as more and more hours of labor are expended. The threat of starvation makes the return from the first hours very valuable indeed, but as more and more is produced from more and more hours of labor, psychological satisfaction declines. Conversely, as the value of the return to each additional unit of labor declines, the "cost" of the labor increases. As a person works longer and longer hours, he finds each additional hour more difficult and more tiring. The level of production, according to Chayanov, is determined by the balance of these two forces of cost and gain.

To apply these psychological concepts, Chayanov had to inquire into the institutional setting in which production is carried out. He came to conclude that the distinctive feature of peasant production compared to capitalist is that the former contains no category of wage labor. That fact—given his starting psychological assumptions—is critical since it means that the expansion of any household's production must come, as it were, from the sweat of their own brows. Capitalist enterprises, by contrast, can expand almost indefinitely by hiring more and more workers as long as capital is available.

If households are the "firms" of peasant economies, then household composition determines the relative strength or weakness of the enterprise. The ratio of household consumers to workers (C/W), the "dependency ratio," is a crucial variable according to Chayanov. A high dependency ratio reflects a high relative proportion of consumers (typically many children). That means, in turn, a relatively weak household enterprise in which each adult worker has to produce more just to provision his household. In other words, for households with high dependency ratios, the psychological balance that Chayanov postulates between the cost and gain of an extra hour of labor shifts in favor of working extra hours.

Following this line of reasoning, Chayanov noted that over time Russian households generally went through a number of phases with respect to the dependency ratio. Consider what happens to a household as it moves through the developmental cycle. A new household is established at the time of marriage. As children are born and added to the family, food requirements increase. But children, initially at least, do not add to the household work force, and that is where the pinch comes. As subsistence requirements increase, the number of workers remains constant and the dependency ratio rises. According to Chayanov, there is only one possible outcome: Each household worker has to work longer hours. As more and more children are born, the burden on the household increases until the eldest child begins to work. At that point, the dependency ratio begins to decrease so that each household worker can begin to work fewer hours. Of course, the exact pattern of Chayanov's phases varies from society to society and depends on the particular kind of household developmental cycle; still, decades before anthropologists devised the concept of developmental cycle, Chayanov had hit on its essentials for the Russian peasant case.

Stated formally then, "Chayanov's rule" as it has become known (cf. Sahlins 1972) says that the amount of time a household worker works is proportional to the dependency ratio, the number of household consumers divided by the number of workers. As the relative proportion of consumers increases, each worker has to work longer hours. As the relative proportion of consumers decreases, then each worker can work shorter hours.

In view of the confusions in the literature (and, admittedly, the ambiguities in Chayanov's work itself, cf. Harrison 1975), it must be emphasized that Chayanov is not proposing a subsistence theory of peasant production, i.e. that peasants are interested only in producing for their own use and that they do not respond to opportunities to produce a surplus above subsistence (Millar 1970). Such an interpretation would rest upon an argument about peasant motives contrary to Chayanov's psychological assumption that peasants seek their own gain.

Characteristically, this reading of Chayanov is that presented by substantivists like Sahlins (1972: 82-92). Sahlins interprets Chayanov's system as one of "production for use," "an economic system of determinate and finite objectives," an economy in which "needs are limited." Compare what Chayanov has to say:

> Of course, our critics are free to understand the labor-consumer balance theory as a sweet little picture of the Russian peasantry in the likeness of the moral French peasants, satisfied with everything and living like birds of the air. We ourselves do not have such a conception and are inclined to believe that no peasant would refuse either good roast beef, or a gramophone, or even a block of Shell Oil Company shares, if the chance occurred. Unfortunately, such chances do not present themselves in large numbers, and the peasant family wins every kopek by hard, intensive toil. And in these circumstances, they are obliged not only to do without shares and a gramophone, but sometimes without the beef as well ([1925] 1966: 47-48).

> Any economic unit, including the peasant farm is acquisitive—an undertaking aiming at maximum income. In an economic unit based on hired labor, this tendency to boundless expansion is limited by capital availability and, if this increases, is practically boundless. But in the family farm, apart from capital available expressed in means of production, this tendency is limited by the family labor force and the increasing drudgery of work if its intensity is forced up ([1925] 1966: 119).

The distinctive differences between peasant and capitalist production do not stem from contrasts in economic psychology but from contrasts in the social organization of the production process. Specifically, according to Chayanov, the presence or absence of wage labor is crucial.

As I mentioned, Chayanov intended his theory to apply more widely than just to the Russian case, and later I will consider it in relation to Maale data. As it turns out, Chayanov's rule—by its apparent negation in Maale—offers a useful avenue of approach to specifying more precisely the institutional setting of Maale production. Chapter 3 will present data on Maale labor time in relation to household dependency ratio and will assess the relevance of Chayanov's theory to the Maale economy.[7]

As formalist studies began to accumulate into the late 1960s, the mood out of which they had originated—the optimistic hopes for economic development of poor countries—changed decisively. Instead of narrowing, the gap between rich and poor nations widened, and the leading theoretical and political issue gradually turned from one of how to promote development to how to account for the persistent lack of development. It was in this context of disillusion (augmented by the war in Vietnam and by the economic crises of the world capitalist system in the 1970s) that an increasing number of anthropologists and others turned to Marx for inspiration. And it was in this context, I will argue, that a romantic critique of capitalism—rather similar to the one that developed under colonialism—reappeared in Marxian guise.

As with the paradox in the rise of formalism, it is in some ways curious that social scientists should have invoked Marx in their search for the causes of underdevelopment. One has only to recall the stirring words of the Communist Manifesto to see that Marx apparently believed that capitalism would proceed apace, unhindered, to envelop the whole world:

> The bourgeoisie...draws all, even the most barbarian, nations into civilization. The cheap prices of its commodities are the heavy artillery with which it batters down all Chinese walls...It compels all nations, on pain of extinction, to adopt the bourgeois mode of production; it compels them to introduce what it calls civilization into their midst, i.e. to become bourgeois themselves. In one word, it creates a world after its own image (Marx and Engels [1848] 1965: 38).

The tension of bringing Marxian theory to bear on a set of problems that Marx himself hardly posed has led to innovative and stimulating works such as those of Meillassoux ([1960] 1978) and Wallerstein (1974). Both these works are the inspiration, in part, for following chapters; both, however, also contain a number of confusions and perhaps dead-ends. In particular, I will argue, both tend to resurrect the substantivist practice of distinguishing capitalist and noncapitalist production primarily in reference to differing motives of economic action.

According to Wallerstein, the distinguishing feature of capitalist economy is "...production for sale in a market in which the object is to realize the maximum profit. In such a system, production is constantly expanded as long as further production is profitable, and men constantly innovate new ways of producing things that will expand the profit margin" (1974: 398). Notice that Wallerstein's definition highlights two conditions: developed trade (a widespread feature of economic history) and production for profit (an individual orientation in economic action). Moreover, the expansiveness of capitalism is directly tied to the motive of profit—not, for example, as Chayanov maintained, to the institutional context of production with wage labor.

Wallerstein's definition of capitalism has direct implications for a theory of noncapitalist production. If capitalist production is for profit, then noncapitalist production must be motivated by other aims. Thus Wallerstein utilizes Polanyi's concepts of reciprocity and redistribution to describe those contrasting kinds of economic motives (1974: 390). But within such a framework, trade in noncapitalist economies becomes problematic. Wallerstein writes, "...in an exchange of preciosities [in noncapitalist economies], the importer is 'reaping a windfall' and not obtaining a profit. Both exchange-partners can reap windfalls simultaneously but only one can obtain maximum profit, since the exchange of surplus-value within a system is a zero-sum game" (1974: 398).

Wallerstein's distinction between the forms of circulation in capitalist and noncapitalist economies contains a number of confusions in terms of Marxian theory. First of all, it is not correct to say that exchange within capitalist economies is necessarily a zero-sum game. (For a discussion of this characteristic assertion of dependency theorists including Wallerstein, see Hopkins 1976.) On the contrary, according to Marx, it is not circulation but production and the resulting distribution of product between wages and profits that is zero-sum. Second, it is difficult to understand the distinction between (noncapitalist) windfalls and (capitalist) profits except in terms of individual intentions. Windfalls are apparently unintended consequences of actions motivated by other ends; these unintended "profits" fall, as it were, like manna from heaven. But Marxists repeatedly point out that individual intentions—the starting point of neoclassical analyses—cannot be taken as the basis for fundamental analytical distinctions within Marxian theory.

Meillassoux's work shares Wallerstein's emphasis on circulation and on individual motives. In an early theoretical article in 1960, which has been very influential since, Meillassoux attempts to develop a theory of closed, noncapitalist horticultural economies. Despite, however, an appeal to Marx's ideas, production itself is hardly examined. Meillassoux begins by noting a characteristic pattern of circulation of goods—prestations "from juniors to seniors" and "redistribution from seniors to juniors" ([1960] 1978: 135).

Elders

Juniors

What accounts for this pattern and for the structure of inequality behind it? Meillassoux has two answers. The first is a functional explanation:

At this point in our argument, the seniors' authority is based on the possession of knowledge which justifies their control over the product of the juniors' labor. By taking on the task of redistribution, the seniors therefore carry out a useful function which socially legitimizes this authority ([1960] 1978: 139).

As with a great many functional explanations, Meillassoux's is not convincing. To make it so, he would have to show (1) that the social reproduction of all closed horticultural economies requires some kind of redistribution of goods and (2) that this function can be performed only by elders by virtue of their greater knowledge (cf. Francesca Cancian 1968).

The second part of Meillassoux's answer relates to a complementary pattern of circulation, that of bridewealth transactions. Elders are dominant, according to Meillassoux, because they control bridewealth goods and therefore younger mens' access to wives:

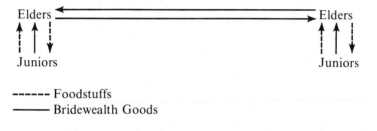

------ Foodstuffs
———— Bridewealth Goods

> Staple goods are basically the object of prestations by the juniors to the seniors and of redistribution by the seniors to the juniors; marriage goods are the object of transfer and imply both alliance and reciprocity. [Marriage goods] are the object of prestations when they are given by the juniors to the seniors... When they circulate between peers, they imply reciprocity ([1960] 1978: 145).

Now if one assumes the fact that elders somehow control the goods needed for bridewealth transactions, their dominance appears to follow. Meillassoux, however, nowhere explains how elders come to control those goods. Why are juniors, who apparently produce bridewealth goods, willing to turn them over to elders? We are simply told that the circulation of goods from juniors to elders is a part of a "redistributive" pattern and that between elders is a "reciprocal" one. Conforming to substantivist practice, Meillassoux differentiates these modes of economic action from capitalist exchange primarily in relation to individual intentions:

> There is reciprocity because the parties regard each other as of equivalent social rank... This is not strictly speaking an 'exchange' but *two movements with different intentions* (first alliance, then preservation of social prestige) (Meillassoux's emphasis, [1960] 1978: 143).

If we follow Meillassoux's argument to its conclusion, the only explanation he offers for the inequality of elders and juniors is that the juniors are somehow "prestation-minded"—whether from their internalization of traditional cultural values or from what we are not told. This line of argument is hardly compatible with Meillassoux's expressed aims, much less with those of Marx.

As I pointed out, Meillassoux's article was written very early in relation to the development of Marxian studies in anthropology. One might expect, especially after his empirical study of production in Guro society, that Meillassoux would have later clarified the role of production in his model. In 1972, however, he still writes, "These relations of production [seniors versus juniors] are materialized through a redistributive system of circulation, close to Polanyi's description" (1972: 100). But, of course, relations of production become manifest principally with the production process.[8] Marx stressed again and again the different views of capitalism to be gained by different avenues of approach, whether by circulation or by production:

> The sphere of circulation or commodity exchange, within whose boundaries the sale and purchase of labor-power goes on, is in fact a very Eden of the innate rights of man. It is the exclusive realm of Freedom, Equality, Property, and Bentham ... When we leave this sphere [and enter that of production] a certain change takes place, or so it appears, in the physiognomy of our *dramatis personae.* He who was previously the money-owner now strides out in front as a capitalist; the possessor of labor-power follows as his worker. The one smirks self-importantly and is intent on business; the other is timid and holds back, like someone who has brought his own hide to market and now has nothing else to expect but—a tanning (Marx [1867] 1976: 280).

If Marxist works like those of Meillassoux and Wallerstein tend to reproduce the major theoretical categories of substantivism, they also tend to replicate the same kind of romantic critique of capitalism, though with somewhat different emphases. If capitalism is to be defined by production for profit, then it is but a short step to a rejection of capitalist society because it turns all individuals into entrepreneurs and turns all human relationships into commodities. (Wordsworth: "Getting and spending, we lay waste our powers.") Of course, this is part of Marx's own critique, but always a part set within a fundamental critique of institutionalized inequality in capitalist societies.

I pointed out earlier that substantivists and functionalists generally tended to maintain that *everything* that Western governments and missionaries had done to colonized peoples had only tainted and destroyed well-integrated societies. The same theme reappears in Meillassoux's writings:

> [Self-sustaining horticultural societies] represent comprehensive, integrated, economic, social, and demographic systems ensuring the vital needs of all the members—productive and nonproductive—of the community. A change towards a material productive end, the shift from production for self-sustenance and self-perpetuation to production for an external market, must *necessarily* bring a radical transformation, if not the social destruction of the communities, as indeed we witness the process nowadays (my emphasis, 1972: 102).

Again, within the dependency literature that inspired Wallerstein's work on the rise of capitalism, it is frequently maintained that capitalist development for poor countries as a group is currently *impossible,* given the structure of the world economic system. *All* exchange is unequal exchange that transfers surplus from poor countries to rich. Some critics have maintained that this simple stress on adjectives like "necessarily" and "impossible" reflects more the current sense of powerlessness to effect any radical changes (not unlike that felt apparently by many anthropologists under colonialism in the 1930s and 1940s) than any sustained theoretical analysis of actual empirical tendencies (cf. Warren 1973).

At this point one is tempted to proceed under the banner of "back to Marx." One does not get very far, however, before he or she discovers that Marx himself is the source of some of the confusions that I have noted so far. In his discussion of capitalism, Marx often discusses individual motives of gain as they are conditioned by a particular institutional background; with respect to noncapitalist economies, however, Marx's brief analyses hardly reach the institutional level.

Consider Marx's distinction between noncapitalist and capitalist production, "production for use" and "production for exchange," a problem that has already arisen in this discussion. Marx's famous formulas, C-M-C versus M-C-M', refer first of all to contrasting motives of individual economic action. In the first case, production for use, the actor exchanges a commodity C for money M in order to buy another commodity C. The actor's aim is to obtain the second commodity for his own use.

Production for exchange is different. An individual begins with money M and exchanges it for commodity C in order to obtain a greater quantity of money M'. But Marx did not rest his analysis on economic psychology. As Robert Brenner has carefully shown, production for exchange, according to Marx, can only take place in a particular institutional context defined by the presence of a class separated from the means of production and from means of subsistence—the proletariat—who must sell their labor-power in order to survive:

> It is only with the emergence of free wage labor, labor power as a commodity, that there is the separation of the producers from the means of subsistence and production . . . [Then] there is, in a true sense, production for exchange. Only then is there predominance of exchange value, leading to systematic pressure to accumulate and thus develop the forces of production. As Marx puts it, "The domination of exchange value itself, and of exchange-value-producing production, presupposes alien labor capacity itself as an exchange value [i.e. wage labor]" (Brenner 1977: 50).

In other words, the dynamism of capitalism compared to noncapitalist modes of production springs from (1) the ability of capitalists to hire and fire workers as the developing technology of the production process requires, all the while workers producing more than they receive in wages, and (2) competition between capitalists to increase production and to expand their profits, principally by introducing more efficient means of production.

Given this view of capitalism, Marx could in contrast distinguish noncapitalist production by (1) the different kind of social relationships in which production is carried out, and/or (2) the different kind of economic psychology, the lack of competition, etc. In practice, Marx stresses the second aspect. Often we are told that there is no competition for material gain in noncapitalist societies or that, indeed, the range of individual choice is limited or even nonexistent:

> Wealth [among the ancients] does not appear as the aim of production, although Cato may well investigate the most profitable cultivation of fields, or Brutus may even lend money at the most favorable rate of interest. The enquiry is always about what kind of property creates the best citizens. Wealth as an end in itself appears only among a few trading peoples— monopolists of the carrying trade—who live in the pores of the ancient world like the Jews of medieval society (Marx [1953] 1964: 84).

> Hence, in one way the childlike world of the ancients appears to be superior; and this is so, in so far as we seek for closed shape, form, and established limitation. The ancients provide a narrow satisfaction, whereas the modern world leaves us unsatisfied, or, where it appears to be satisfied with itself, is vulgar and mean (Marx [1953] 1964: 85).

> Cooperation in the labor process, such as we find it at the beginning of human civilization, among hunting peoples or, say, as a predominant feature of the agriculture of Indian communities, is based on the one hand on the common ownership of the conditions of production, and on the other hand on the fact that in those cases the individual has as little torn himself free from the umbilical cord of his tribe or community as a bee has from his hive (Marx [1867] 1976: 452).

There are a number of reasons for Marx's relative neglect of the institutional features of noncapitalist production. First, there was a simple lack of empirical information on noncapitalist societies during Marx's time. Little was known in the nineteenth century compared to the present, and what information there was tended to be overlaid with bourgeois prejudices (some of which Marx incorporated, as his reference to the "childlike" ancients shows). Also, Marx's rhetorical aim, even when discussing noncapitalist societies, was to demonstrate the "historicity" of capitalism—that capitalism had arisen and would disappear at particular historical moments (Meillassoux 1972: 96). Very often, therefore, Marx stressed contrasts, the lack of private property in some noncapitalist societies (one institutional feature that Marx did note), or more frequently, as we have just seen, the lack of individual motives for gain and enrichment. But negative concepts, the absence of some feature, cannot serve as the basis for a positive theory of noncapitalist economies (Meillassoux 1972: 97; O'Laughlin 1975: 354). Despite some tentative beginnings, Marx has no developed theory of noncapitalist varieties of production.

Once again, we are pushed a step backwards. With one of the most influential sections of current Marxists sliding into a kind of substantivism and with Marx himself silent, what would a "Marxian" theory of noncapitalist societies look like? Is a Marxian theory of noncapitalist societies in fact possible? One line of Marxists including Lukács ([1923] 1971) have remained agnostic about the very possibility.

A Theoretical Stance for Examining Maale Production

My goal in previous sections has been to approach, by way of critical examples, a theoretical point of view that would take productive institutions—not individual psychologies—as problematic. For that purpose, the most relevant and the most elaborated body of theory is Marxian theory. Substantivism is not well formulated enough to reach its aim of institutional analysis, and neoclassical theory, as I will explain more fully below, typically takes institutional arrangements into account only as assumptions, not as variables to be explained.

Attempts to extend Marx's approach to noncapitalist societies, however, have raised serious problems. At this point in the evolution of Marxian studies, there seem to be me to be at least two principal difficulties: first, specifying the essentials of a Marxian approach, the distinctive contributions it can make to the analysis of noncapitalist economies, and second, clarifying the relationship between Marxian theory and neoclassical theory (for misguided criticisms, we have seen, have a way of introducing the supposed deficiencies of other approaches into one's own).

Let me begin with the second problem. Marxist after Marxist in ritual succession has felt called upon to refute the very possibility of neoclassical theory by attacking the proposition that all individuals in all societies maximize. Ironically, as I have attempted to show, that attack has often led to arguments carried out on neoclassical not Marxist grounds—individual motives in economic action—and to conclusions far from the spirit of Marx's work taken as a whole. In this respect, neoclassical writes like Chayanov have come to more profoundly "Marxist" conclusions than some Marxists.

At the outset, the structure of neoclassical arguments must be appreciated. As Oskar Lange (1934-35: 192) noted, neoclassical theory typically assumes the following as data: (1) psychological preference scales of consumers, (2) the level of technology or the "production function," and (3) the institutional forms of property distribution. To jump ahead of myself, the last two of these are close to the heart of what Marx sought to explain. But since neoclassical theory usually assumes all of these factors as given, it can offer no explanation of them. In other words, neoclassical theory refers to a certain range of problems, a range to some extent merely different from Marxian theory.[9]

There are some problems before which Marxian economics is quite powerless, while "bourgeois" economics solves them easily. What can Marxian economics say about monopoly prices?... What apparatus has it to offer for analyzing the incidence of tax, or the effect of a certain technical innovation on wages? And (irony of Fate!) what can Marxian economics contribute to the problem of the optimum distribution of productive resources in a socialist economy (Lange 1934-35: 191)?

According to Lange again, the distinctive range of problems that Marx addressed (and what neoclassical theories tended to take for granted) was the technological and institutional context in which economic processes occur:

It is not the specific economic concepts used by Marx, but the definite specification of the institutional framework in which the economic process goes on in capitalist society that makes it possible to establish a theory of economic evolution different from mere historical description. Most orthodox Marxists, however, believe that their superiority in understanding the evolution of capitalism is due to the economic concepts with which Marx worked, i.e. to his using the labor theory of value. They think that the abandonment of classical labor theory of value in favor of the theory of marginal utility is responsible for the failure of "bourgeois" economics to explain the fundamental phenomena of capitalist evolution. That they are wrong can be easily shown by considering the economic meaning of the labor theory of value. It is nothing but a static theory of general economic equilibrium (Lange 1934-35: 194).

As I argued above, when neoclassical theory was finally applied to noncapitalist economies, anthropologists like Frank Cancian (1972) and Martin Orans (1968) found that they had to take into account the institutional context of the economic processes they were studying—in particular, the distribution of property—in order to "balance their equations." In that respect, neoclassical theory proved extremely useful in highlighting forms of economic inequality in noncapitalist societies that previous anthropologists had tended to overlook. At the same time, however, these studies took institutional factors as given and used them to explain patterns of individual action. While certain of these patterns (such as differential rates of economic innovation) react back and influence institutional patterns (like stratification systems), the changing forms of economic institutions themselves are not taken as problematic. For that purpose, Marxian theory should be of particular relevance:

The general conclusion at which I arrived and which, once reached, became the guiding principle of my studies can be summarized as follows. In the social production of their existence, men inevitably enter into definite relations, which are independent of their will, namely relations of production appropriate to a given stage in the development of their material forces of production. The totality of these relations of production constitutes the economic structure of society, the real foundation, on which arises a legal and political superstructure and to which correspond definite forms of social consciousness. The mode of production of material life conditions the general process of social, political, and intellectual life. It is not the consciousness of men that determines their existence, but their social existence that determines their consciousness (Marx [1959] 1970: 20-21).

Marx's reader is thankful for such a clear and lucid passage; yet the simplicity of the statement above is perhaps more misleading than the prolixity of many others. What exactly does Marx mean? At the outset it is best to specify what Marx did *not* mean. He did not mean that the "base" one-sidedly determines or causes the "superstructure." This, of course, is what one strand of Marxism has insisted Marx meant, that base and superstructure are separate social systems and that the first determines the second just as A causes B. Any number of recent writers have contested this interpretation of Marx. Bertell Ollman, for example, shows that such a view does not square with Marx's own theoretical writings nor with his empirical analyses. Rather, according to Marx's usage, terms like base and superstructure, forces and relations of production are aspects of a single interacting social structure, not separable substructures. "... the mutual dependence of all elements in the world is conceived of in terms of a constant, multi-faceted interaction. This does not rule out causal relationships, where one element or structure or event is primarily responsible for a change in the form or function of others, but simply qualifies them" (Ollman 1976: 274).

What then does Marx mean by "determination?" And a prior question: What does he mean "forces of production," "relations of production," and "superstructure?" I want briefly to consider these terms and how they can be used to analyze production processes and to formulate historically specific models for understanding how forms of inequality are generated and transformed over time.

For Marx, the production process is a privileged entryway into the analysis of interacting social systems. Man is a part of nature and subject to natural laws, but as a conscious being man also struggles against and ultimately transforms nature (and himself) through human labor (Dobb 1973: 143-44). Work, therefore, and the various forms in which people relate to one another in the work process set human societies apart from animal ones and, at the same time, provide the key to, the groundplan for the distinctive periods of human history.

Marx analyzed the production process with two master concepts: "forces of production" and "relations of production." Rather than separable components of the production process, these are two interrelated aspects of one organic whole. The first, forces of production, is not only "technology" as that word is commonly understood but also the various social organizations in which production is carried out: "... relations between people and relations between people and their means of production in the production process" (O'Laughlin 1975: 360). Within advanced capitalist economies, for example, the organization of assembly lines would be a crucial part of the forces of production. In horticultural societies like Maale, the demographic composition of households, the organization of cooperative labor, the knowledge of the proper sequencing and duration of various horticultural tasks in the swidden cycle are all aspects of the forces of production.

Forces of production specify the total social and technological context in which goods are produced. As goods are produced, how and by what means are they distributed among different categories of people? Marx's answer is that power determines distribution, power or "relations of production." In a capitalist society, relations of production are those between capitalists on the one hand and workers on the other. The total product (after replacement of used-up means of production) is divided between wages to workers and profits to capitalists. During any period of production, the higher wages are, the lower profits will be. Marx's genius in *Capital* was to show the complex ways in which distribution is determined by power differences, by the state of workers' political consciousness, the reserve army of the unemployed, technological progress, and so forth. Whatever the particular historical conjuncture, capitalists are able to reap their profits for the fundamental reason that they hold power, they own the means of production. Without such access to land or machines, workers enter the employment of capitalists or they starve (at least in the nineteenth-century capitalism that Marx analyzed).

In noncapitalist economies, of course, relations of production comprise different kinds of power relations. Consider the following example which, as we shall see, is characteristic of part of the Maale pattern: Adult household members all cooperate in the production of food; all share in its consumption; but male household heads alone enjoy the power of controlling the household's surplus above consumption. The head has authority to use the extra grain to become a bond friend with one of his neighbors, or to make marriage gifts for another wife, or to help an adult son marry. Neither wives nor younger dependent members of the household fully control the fruits of their own labor. In this case, relations of production are those between men and their wives and between household heads and their younger male and female dependents.

Relations of production are said, then, to determine the superstructure—dominant forms of consciousness, the organization of political coercion, and "law" in the widest sense. As I have said, determination for Marx did not mean linear causation. Rather, as G.A. Cohen (1978) has argued, determination for Marx most often meant a kind of functional determination. Functional explanations have a distinct logical form in which the *effects* of a trait enter into the explanation of the presence of that trait. The effect of the superstructure is to define and uphold systems of power, relations of production. In other words, trait Y's presence is partly explained by the "positive" consequence it has for X. In such a schema, we can say that X "determines" Y in as much as the existence of Y is partially dependent upon X. X selects Y.

This interpretation has a great many merits among which I will mention two: (1) It combats any notion that the superstructure is somehow secondary.

If production relations require legal expression for stability, it follows that the foundation requires a superstructure. This seems to violate the architectural metaphor, since foundations do not normally need superstructures to be stable. We must be careful if we are looking for a visual image to go with the metaphor. One slab resting on another would be inappropriate. One correct picture is the following. Four struts are driven into the ground, each protruding the same distance above it. They are unstable. They sway and wobble in the wind... Then a roof is attached to the four struts, and now they stay firmly erect in all winds... Of this roof one can say: (i) it is supported by the struts, and (ii) it renders them more stable. There we have a building whose base and superstructure relate in the right way (Cohen 1978: 231).

(2) It does not require that the superstructure comprehend all forms of consciousness or that it perfectly stabilize relations of production. Indeed, just the opposite, we expect that fundamental power relations, relations of production, will provide the fault lines of any social formation, the lines along which tension *can* build up. In as much as the superstructure performs its functions, these tensions are deflected, misrepresented, and dissipated. But oppositional forms of consciousness and of political practice always exist, even if they are dampened, drowned out by dominant forms of the superstructure.

It is this image of society as a set of poised contradictions that I have found most useful about Marxism. Indeed, it is one that adds definition to the historical image of Maale that I discussed at the beginning of this chapter. Work and power, forces and relations of production, in a particular historical context—these are the organizing ideas that stand behind the ethnographic description that follows. I am not, of course, using Maale data to "test" Marxism. "Evidence can be used to help solve any problem except how this same evidence should be viewed" (Ollman 1976: 239). Rather, Marxist ideas, broadly interpreted, provide the lens for seeing Maale.

Since the following chapters proceed within their own terms and since I have found it difficult to refer repeatedly to Marx's Germanic phrases (terms like work and power seem much more direct), I should map the route I will follow in succeeding chapters in relation to the theoretical concepts just discussed. Chapter 2 attempts to set out the larger regional and historical context in which Maale society existed. First of all, I note a certain pattern of trade and conquest in northeastern Africa and try to show how it was connected with (as a necessary but not sufficient cause of) the changing form of relations of production between the Maale king and chiefs and their subjects. The exact shape that these relations of production took in different periods was always the direct outcome of internal events and causes and, at the same time, wider conditions that extended far beyond Maale. In Chapter 3 the spatial and temporal framework narrows to one particular Maale vicinity in 1974 and 1975, and I briefly outline certain aspects of local forces of production—the swidden cycle and the annual horticultural cycle. Following sections focus on household organization among the various social categories that made up the local vicinity that I studied, and my major theme here is the interaction between the demographic composition of households (local forces of production) and the social relationships between male household heads and their domestic dependents (local relations of production). After a consideration of the inadequacies of Chayanov's and Sahlins' theories of domestic production for the Maale case, Chapter 4 describes the various forms of cooperative labor arrangements into which households entered. Changing relations of production between the Maale king and his subjects (described in Chapters 2) turn out to be one of the determinants of the social forms in which labor cooperation occurred. Chapter 5, in conclusion, considers the previous analysis in terms of Marxian and neoclassical theory.

2

The Long-Term History of Ethiopia and of Maale

The idea of "isolated traditional" societies, commonly agreed to be a false one for twentieth-century Africa, has been pushed back by some writers and applied instead to an earlier period before colonialism or before European commercial expansion (cf. Dalton 1972). But for what we now know as southwestern Ethiopia, such a notion is still misleading. For 2,000 years and possibly longer, southwestern Ethiopia has been a component part, located at the farthest periphery, of the vast and complex Mediterranean-Indian Ocean trading network (see Map 1). When, moreover, the world configuration of wealth and power made the Red Sea (rather than the Persian Gulf or the Cape of Good Hope) the major commercial link between Mediterranean and Indian civilizations, southwestern Ethiopia was drawn ever more tightly into the world economy and, at times, politically incorporated into northern Ethiopian empires. At their zeniths, these northern empires grew rich and powerful by feeding products found mainly in the south and southwest—gold, animal hides, ivory, and slaves—into the Red Sea trade. This more comprehensive historical context, what Fernand Braudel has called *la longue durée*, provides a background for understanding nineteenth-century Maale political economy, the earliest period for which I can reconstruct Maale history.

In the more inclusive spatial and temporal framework that I have adopted, Ethiopia—unlike most other African states, or at least the presently accepted notion of African states—is not a jumble of disparate peoples and lands whose fates converged only as a result of the policies and compromises of colonial powers. The Ethiopian high plateau—drained to the north, west, south and east by the great river systems of the Awash, Atbara, Blue Nile, Sobat, Omo, Juba, and Webi Shebelle—forms a single if varied ecological zone.

As Map 1 suggests, the well-watered Ethiopia highlands stand in contrast to the lower, drier savannah which surrounds it on all sides. This highland zone and parts of the immediately surrounding lowlands, what Donald Levine (1974) called Greater Ethiopia, has provided a common arena in which

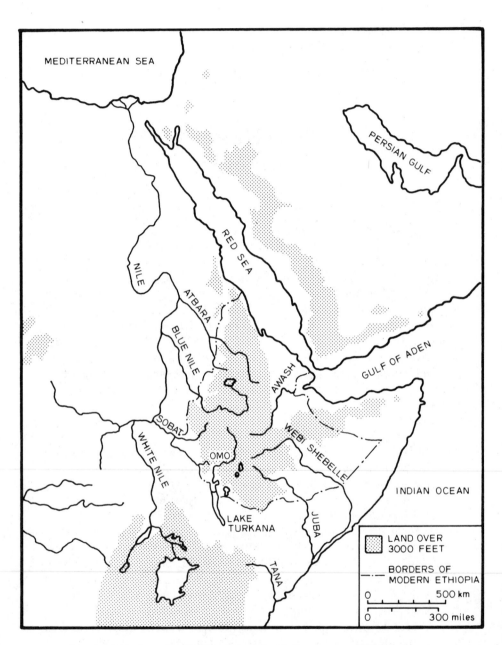

Map 1. Ethiopia and its Red Sea link to the Mediterranean and Indian Oceans

different but related peoples have interacted, each affecting the others, over tens of centuries. Trade, warfare, migration, and intermarriage have created, according to Levine, a single "... relational network, now thin and localized, now extensive and profound, but never absent..." (1974: 40).

The physiography of the highlands has had long and pervasive influence on the network of connections among Ethiopian peoples. In contrast to regional patterns in many parts of the Eurasian world (for China, see Skinner 1977), river valleys are not grand avenues of social intercourse in Ethiopia. They tend, in fact, to form barriers and to demarcate social boundaries. Commenting on this contrast, the writer of a British Foreign Office handbook noted:

> In Switzerland, the heights are barren peaks, the valleys are fairly broad and fertile. In Abyssinia, all this is reversed. The heights are mostly open plateaux, the valleys jungle-choked or canyons of great depth. The population lives on the plateaux, and the lines of communication follow the high ground, the valleys being formidable obstacles to traffic (quoted in Trimingham 1952: 2).

As a result, the principal thoroughfares of interchange and contact have tended to follow the contours of watersheds shown in Map 2. The trade, warfare, and migration that Levine argues have united Greater Ethiopia have all been "channeled" over the centuries by the lines of highest ground.

The interconnections among Ethiopian peoples can best be followed into the distant past through linguistic data. Almost all of the languages spoken in the highlands today belong, according to Joseph Greenberg's classification (1966), to one grand language family, Afro-Asiatic. After a modification of Greenberg's original classification by Harold Fleming (1969; 1976), Afro-Asiatic is thought to consist of six major branches: Semitic, Cushitic, Omotic, Chadic, Berber, and Ancient Egyptian (now extinct).

All of these linguistic stocks apparently evolved from a single language community somewhere in northeastern Africa, perhaps in Ethiopia, that began to break up as early as the seventh millennium B.C. Proto-Chadic, Proto-Berber, and Proto-Ancient Egyptian speakers supposedly moved to the west, northwest, and north, respectively, leaving little traces on Ethiopian history. At the same time, Proto-Cushitic and Proto-Omotic speakers began populating the Ethiopian highlands, while Semitic speaking groups spread eastward into Asia. Even though recently questioned (Hudson n.d.), the commonly accepted view seems to be that Proto-Semitic speakers migrated perhaps via Suez to Asia where they split into several language subgroups, and that one of these returned to Ethiopia from South Arabia. In any case, almost all scholars agree that for at least 3,000 years and probably longer, Semitic, Cushitic, and Omotic languages, all of which are genetically related, have been spoken in the highlands of Ethiopia.

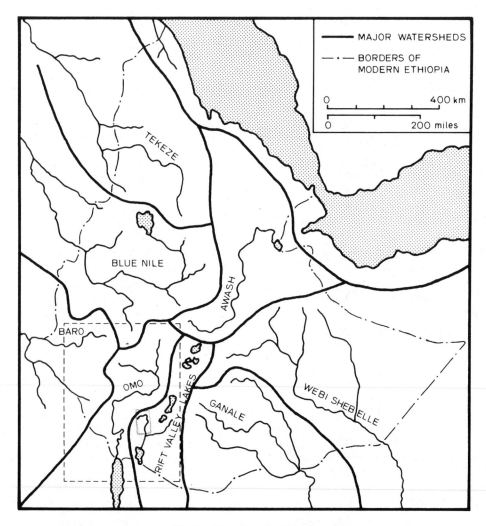

Map 2. Watersheds in Ethiopia

With the advent of written (Semitic) records in the north about 2,500 years ago, Ethiopian history becomes less conjectural. Since then, two major movements have affected the history of Greater Ethiopia. First was the intermittent southward expansion of Semitic political power and languages until the fifteenth century, when nearly all of the Ethiopian highlands came under Semitic control. Second was the remarkable conquests of the Cushitic Oromo pastoralists in the sixteenth century, who spread from their homeland in the south to the northeast and northwest, driving a wedge between the Semitic speaking north and the Omotic speaking southwest. Map 3 shows the present distribution of linguistic stocks in Ethiopia—the outcome of these two vast movements, as well as many other minor ones.

These two expansions had different motives and different consequences. The first involved the political evolution of empires that were supported since the fourth century A.D. by a semiliterate Orthodox Christian clergy, and later animated by the Solomonic myth—the belief that its kings descended uninterruptedly from Solomon and the Queen of Sheba. The economic motives of its expansion into the south were to widen its sphere of neighboring tributary peoples and, most of all, to gain access to the valuable trade goods found in the south and southwest—gold, animal hides, ivory, and slaves.

Trade, in fact, appears to have been the life blood of the northern empires. To simplify a complex set of interacting forces, the following tentative summary might be made for the first millennium and for half of the second: Whenever the Red Sea became a major commercial route in world trade, northern Ethiopian empires tended to prosper and to extend their power farther and farther south to the sources of supply for many of the most valuable trade goods. In turn, whether the Red Sea became a dominant East-West trade link was related to the shifting boundary between Mediterranean and Middle Eastern empires. Egypt—at the terminus of the Red Sea route—was the pivot of the entire system as far as Ethiopia was concerned. With Egypt free or dominated by Mediterranean powers, the Red Sea tended to become a busy thoroughfare of trade. But with Egypt under the power of Middle Eastern empires, the latter were often able to shift a major portion of the trade up the Persian Gulf through their own territories and through their own capital cities.[1]

The high watermark of early Semitic expansion occurred in the fifteenth century. By that time, the northern Christian empire had expanded southward down the Blue Nile-Awash watershed and had defeated a similar move of Muslim Cushitic states inland along the Awash-Webi Shebelle divide. The southern limits of Christian power at the time are difficult to demarcate, but from the evidence of churches founded in the southwest (Haberland 1965: 246), the border of firmly incorporated territories must have passed very close to (if not included) Maale. In essence, the whole ecological zone of the highlands

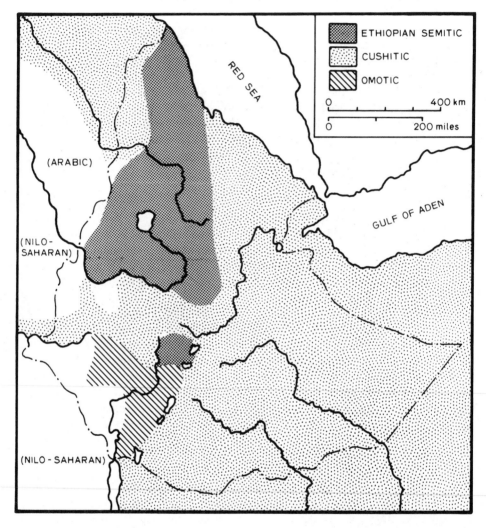

Map 3. Afro-Asiatic linguistic stocks in Ethiopia

comprising Semitic, Cushitic, and Omotic speaking peoples was politically unified in the fifteenth century for the first time in its history.

The sixteenth century was one of great international flux. In 1499 the Portuguese circumnavigated Africa and shortly thereafter began a determined campaign to take the Indian Ocean trade from the Red Sea to the Cape route. For the first half of the century, they managed to cut back Red Sea trade drastically, and a severe, if temporary, blow was dealt to the prosperity of Red Sea basin countries (Hodgson 1974: 21). Also in the second quarter of the sixteenth century, the Muslim Cushitic states that had been consistently defeated in the previous century rose up under a charismatic leader, Mohammed Gran, and conquered three-fourths of the Christian territory. However, with no firm economic base (the Gulf of Aden trade which drew on the Awash-Webi Shebelle route was "greatly diminished" at this time according to Abir 1975: 550), the invasion collapsed when Gran was killed.

It was in these troubled times that Cushitic Oromo began streaming out of their homeland in southern Ethiopia, and their expansion was the second major movement of peoples and languages that contributes to the linguistic map of modern Ethiopia (Map 3). As in many other East African pastoral and semipastoral societies, the dominant institution in Oromo society was a complicated set of age classes. Every eight years, each age class graduated to the next level, and in order to make their transition, young warriors had to carry out raids against a community that their elders had not previously fought. It was this ritual war every eight years combined with a growth in population and a progressive incorporation of neighboring peoples that led to the "pulsating frontier of Oromo dominions in the sixteenth century" (Legesse 1973: 8).

With international trade routes in the highlands disrupted, with the life blood of the north draining slowly away, it was as if the Oromo swept into the void and invaded the arteries of the northern Ethiopian economy. Attaining the strategic heart of the country, the Oromo spread along the old Muslim trade routes, the Awash-Webi Shebelle divide; north along the major Christian-held trade route, the Awash-Blue Nile divide; and west to the rich Omotic areas along the Blue Nile-Omo divide (Lewis 1966). Even after the Red Sea trade revived in the latter half of the sixteenth century (Braudel 1972: 543-570) and the caravan trade in the highlands expanded in the seventeenth century (Abir 1975: 550-551), the momentum of Oromo conquests carried them on. By the third quarter of the seventeenth century, they had driven a wedge between the Semitic north and the Omotic southwest wide enough to prevent regular communication and the payment of tribute (Abir 1975: 562).

Since the Oromo were politically decentralized with power divided among several cross-cutting groups, their expansion was not as coordinated as that of Semitic speaking groups. They did not seek tribute nor control of trade routes, nor did they attempt to convert those they conquered to their own religion.

"[Oromo] style was not to stay and rule but, initially at least, to hit and run: attack the enemy by surprise and carry off the most booty in the shortest time. When population pressures, the increasing distance of raids, and other considerations prompted the Galla [Oromo] to stay and settle, they were more inclined to adopt the culture of their new neighbors than to spread their own" (Levine 1973: 80).

By the eighteenth century, northern Ethiopia, like most of the Middle East (Hodgson 1974: 152), was exhausted. The lucrative Mediterranean-Indian Ocean trade had been finally and decisively drawn from the Red Sea to the European-dominated routes around the Cape. The north, cut off by the Oromo from tribute and trade with the Omotic southwest, gradually disintegrated into a collection of more or less autonomous kingdoms, only very weakly united. By the end of the eighteenth century, the river systems of the north had become boundaries: between the coast and the Tekeze River lay Tigrean territory; the land between the Tekeze and the northern Blue Nile constituted Amhara; Gojjam was encircled by the great bend of the Blue Nile; and Shoa stretched from the Blue Nile to the Awash. Ethiopian chroniclers called this period the "Era of the Judges," an analogy, after the Old Testament, to the Hebrews before their kings.[2]

How from this low point of economic decline and political devolution the Semitic speaking peoples managed to reunite, to expand their borders past the limits of the highlands to include a lowland buffer zone, and—alone among African peoples—to defeat their would-be colonial masters on the battlefield is a remarkable story with many complex facets (Gabre-Sellassie 1975; Levine 1974; Marcus 1975; Rubenson 1976). Not the least of these is the wider context of international wealth and power. In the nineteenth century as before, Ethiopia's secret history was the history of Egypt. Under innovating and (with Western capital) modernizing monarchs, Egypt saw a rise in commercial prosperity and political power that probably put her ahead of any other Islamic land at the time (Hodgson 1974: 240). The Egyptian economy was centralized, political control extended to the Sudan and Arabia, and large-scale development projects like the Suez Canal (completed in 1869) were undertaken. Ethiopia could not help feeling the impact: "Within a decade of Muhammad Ali's invasion of Arabia the economy of most of the Red Sea basin had begun to revive . . ." (Abir 1968: 4).

The southernmost kingdom, Shoa, was well placed to take advantage of the economic boom in the first half of the nineteenth century. To the north, it was protected from the predations of other Semitic speaking kingdoms by intervening settlements of Oromo, and to the immediate south lay the confluence of the principal north-south and east-west trade routes in the highlands. By 1830 Shoa had expanded south and had begun to regulate and tax the caravan trade. In an attempt to monopolize gold, ivory, and musk, the

Shoan king forbade any of his subjects to buy or sell those products. Foreign merchants coming from the coast were not allowed to travel past Shoan territory (Abir 1970: 124), and the Oromo and Omotic speaking traders who supplied Shoan markets apparently did not have the organizational capabilities to reach the coast. Shoa thus made itself into the major emporium of highland trade. Revenues from the trade financed military strength and political expansion through the purchase of guns and artillery.

By the end of the century, the economic and political edge that Shoa enjoyed allowed its emperor Menilek to reunite the Semitic speaking north under his own leadership in 1889, to defeat the Italians at the Battle of Adwa in 1896, and to ward off other surrounding colonial powers by expanding Ethiopian borders to their present limits, a process more or less complete by the end of the century. Once again the Omotic southwest was incorporated into an empire dominated by northerners and extending across the entire highlands. And once again the exploitation of trade from the southwest seems to have been the initial motive and later a part of the economic foundation of northern political strength and efflorescence. Although more historical research remains to be done (for hints, see Marcus 1975 and Markakis 1974), it may well prove to be true that the incorporation of the southwest and the resulting advantages for the north had just as much to do with the survival of Ethiopian independence as the other factors commonly emphasized—the forbidding mountainous territory of Ethiopia, the self-defeating competition of European powers for the area, or northern Ethiopia's sense of cultural identity and historical mission, preserved over the centuries in written documents. Before inquiring further into those sets of interrelationships, I want to interrupt this skeletal outline of Ethiopian history to focus more closely on the Omotic societies that existed in the southwest at the end of the nineteenth century, and, in particular, to examine the principal features of Maale economics and politics at that time.

Maale and Other Omotic Societies in the Nineteenth Century

Had I begun this historical sketch with the nineteenth century, as would have seemed prudent given the lack of sources specifically for Maale history in any earlier period, I doubtless would have entitled this section "The Traditional Political Economy of Maale and the Southwest." The late 1890s, when Maale and the surrounding area was incorporated into the Imperial Ethiopian Empire, would have seemed a great turning point, a watershed between the time when Maale existed as a free, independent, traditional polity and the time when it was colonized, dominated, and therefore changed by northern Ethiopia. As I have pointed out, it is exactly this tack that many anthropologists have taken in analyzing "primitive" economics and politics. Such a strategy, however, arguably distorts the study of the Maale past as well as the analysis of the present. As I have tried to show, Maale and the Omotic southwest had been colonized by northern Ethiopia once before and, more than that, had been affected by a "world economy," through indirect and fluctuating links, for almost 2,000 years. The theoretically crucial question (one I do more to pose than to answer) is not, therefore, the usual anthropological inquiry about how incorporation into a modernizing, Westernizing Ethiopia affected traditional Maale, but rather how—almost from the beginning as it were—the role of Maale and other Omotic societies in the whole political economy of Greater Ethiopia affected their internal structure.

From this perspective, a striking feature of southwestern societies as we survey them at the end of the nineteenth century is the prevalence and pattern of "kingship."[3] Omotic societies, to use Edmund Leach's phrase (1954), shared a common ritual language. From Kefa on the west to Wolayta on the east to Banna and Hamar on the south, the prosperity of peoples, the fertility of their lands, and the multiplication of their cattle and goats were said to depend on the vitalizing presence of divine kings. Some of these kings, such as those of Kefa and Wolayta, were powerful rulers who held sway over large territories. Others like those of Dorze were mainly ritual figures who sometimes held less political power than notables or "big men" (Sperber 1975; Halperin and Olmstead 1976). Maale kings, somewhere in the middle of this continuum, were certainly more powerful than those in Dorze while lacking the centralized state apparatus that Kefa or Wolayta kings enjoyed.

Over the preceding centuries Omotic kingdoms must have risen and fallen, and the power of kings waxed and waned. At the end of the nineteenth century, when the flux was frozen by another conquest, the effect of the configuration of trade routes on political centralization was evident: At the two great gateways into the Omotic southwest, at the Baro-Omo watershed and at the Omo Rift Valley Lakes watershed, were situated the two largest and most powerful kingdoms—Kefa and Wolayta (see Map 4). Past a buffer zone of tributaries and relatively decentralized peoples, there was a second tier of less powerful but still centralized societies such as Gofa and Maale. Mordechai Abir (1970) notes that each of these polities tried to prevent merchants from the north and the east from going beyond its territory into the south, and many of the kings declared gold, ivory, and the skins of large game animals royal monopolies and taboo for commoners to sell. In this way, Omotic kings attempted to control both production of these goods within their own territories and trade coming from farther south. The total catchment area, while expanding and contracting, probably extended at most times past the southwestern highlands into the surrounding lowlands.

Maale kings ruled as a part of this wider network of Omotic kingdoms.[4] Of all Maale institutions, kingship was the most culturally elaborated. A veritable halo of mythical charters and dramatic rituals set off the king from the

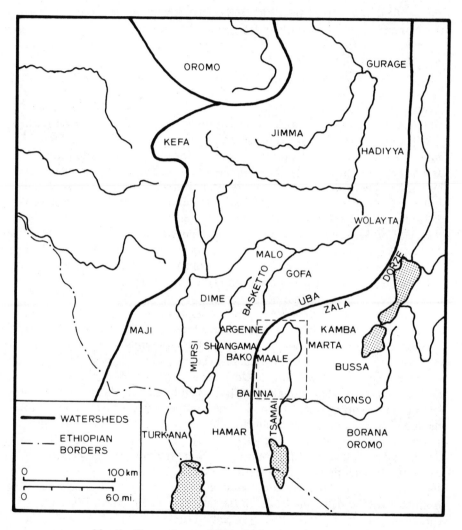

Map 4. The southwest of Ethiopia showing selected peoples

more mundane aspects of everyday life. It is with these ideas that I want to begin a description of Maale political economy. How the Maale—or at least the dominant strata of Maale—saw kingship will provide an introduction to the ways in which ideas were translated into social action, to what economic and political powers the Maale king and chiefs actually wielded, and finally to the manner in which particular features of Maale economic and political organization were related to the overarching patterns in the historical development of Greater Ethiopia.

To summarize, three major notions express the Maale conception of kingship: first, what I will call the doctrine of the original life-giving king; second, the concept of the unbroken but perilous transmission of his vital force; and third, the idea of politics as the orderly union of hierarchical status groups.

The first notion, hardly unusual among African kingdoms, is a kind of colonial myth of the origin of culture. Indeed, one is tempted to read the myth as a depiction of the actual colonization of Maale and the surrounding region by northerners in the fifteenth century. In any case, as Maale elders tell the story, the first men to live in Maale came up out of the earth in a stream bed called Kunkula. Grasping hold of the tough long grass that grew in the ravine, the chief of Makana (or rather the man who would become the chief of Makana, for Maale do not make this or other similar distinctions in their telling of the story) and a man named Are pulled themselves out of the earth. When others behind them were about to come out, Are pushed the dirt back and stamped it down so that no one else could get out.

The chief of Makana and Are built houses in Maale, but since they did not know about fire, they had to bake their bread in the sun on the rocks. Finally one day four strangers, brothers, along with their company, arrived from a country to the east, Bussa, and they camped below the chief's house. They spent the night, and the next morning the eldest brother, the king of Bako, got out his fire drill and attempted to make fire. But when he twirled the fire stick, taro instead of fire sprang forth. Then the others in the company said, "You go to the high country! You were meant for there." So he left for Bako. The next eldest brother, the king of Shangama, then tried his hand at the fire drill, and like his elder brother, he failed. When he twirled the fire stick, ensete (the so-calld false banana plant) sprang forth. They all said, "Ah! Your country is the same as his. You also go to the high country, Shangama!" The next eldest brother, the king of Banna, took up the task and he too failed. When a cow sprang forth from the fire drill, he was sent off to Banna. At last, Maaleka, the youngest brother, took the fire drill and he, after all of the others had failed, produced fire.

Not having seen fire before, the chief of Makana and Are were amazed. "What's that red thing down there? Let's go and see." The chief and Are went down to the camp where Maaleka and many of his followers were gathered around the fire. Standing a little way off, the chief called out to the children around the fire, "Please give me that flickering thing. Give me the flicker." Maaleka answered, "Why don't you come and take it?" Afraid, the chief ran and hid behind a tree. Maaleka called out, "My chief!" Responding, the chief called back, "My king!" Then Maaleka said, "Come here!" But again the chief was afraid and refused. Are had to go out and get some of the fire, and the two returned back up the hill to the chief's house.

That night they made a fire and cooked their food for the first time. The food was so good that the next morning the chief and Are became afraid that someone would steal the fire while they were away at work. So the chief hid the coals in the roof of his house under the thatch. When he and Are were on their way up to their fields at a place called Dergala, the house below began to smoke and smoke. The fire ate up the house and burned all the way from Lailo to Kaiso, the borders of Maale territory to the east and the west. Maaleka said, "The land that the fire burned will be mine." Assenting, the chief replied, "Let me go around the borders of your land to establish your rule." Maaleka agreed. That, the Maale say, is how the chief of Makana became the most important of all the chiefs in Maale. All of the other chiefs were installed afterwards. And because the chief of Makana was afraid and hid when he took the fire, it has been taboo ever since for the king and the chief to look at each other. Also according to the Maale, this was the beginning of their moiety system. The autochthonous people, Are and the chief of Makana, became the *raggi* moiety while the king and his followers (including the other twelve of the thirteen Maale chiefs) became the *karazi* moiety. Ideally, from then onward, *raggi* married *karazi* and *karazi* married *raggi*.[5]

As the elders tell the story even today, it is almost as if the original fire had made all of Maale into Maaleka's field, and henceforth Maale's production and prosperity would depend on Maaleka's cultivation. (Firing, of course, is one of the first steps in making a swidden field in Maale, and it establishes the boundaries of one's plot.) Every year before the time for burning new fields, each of the thirteen chiefs came to the king's compound in prescribed order with tribute and asked his permission to begin burning their fields. Having first burned his own field, the king gave his blessing. Then the chiefs fired their fields followed by the subchiefs followed by the common people. This ritual ordering of Maale horticulture was reenacted again at the time of planting. First the king planted and prayed for rain, then the chiefs, then the subchiefs, then the common people. The fertility and prosperity of the land in all of its aspects— the ripening of the crops, the fecundity of men and women, and the reproduction of cattle and goats—were said to flow from the energizing and seminal presence of the king.

With so much dependent on the king's powers, succession was perhaps more than usually problematic. What I have called the unbroken but perilous transmission of Maaleka's fertilizing force was expressed and enacted in a Wagnerian cycle of installation rituals that lasted over the whole lifetime of the king. When an old king died, his death was not publicly acknowledged until one of his sons had been chosen as successor. The old king's body was dried and preserved, and his ritual functions were taken over by a nonroyal stand-in for the duration of the interregnum, which could last for years. The first stages of the installation cycle focused on, as Eike Haberland (1965) has called them, rituals of epiphany, or rituals designed to confirm the charisma of the new king. On the day that the dead king's body was finally buried, a queen bee (which the Maale call "king" bee) from a hive brought from Bussa was place on the big toe of the son who was to succeed. If indeed he was the king, the bee climbed up the son's leg of its own accord, the Maale maintained, to his chest, to his forehead, where it danced about in circles and then flew off back to Bussa.

Later rituals, still part of the cycle which made the successor into king, focused on magnifying and enlarging royal potency and power, with mock cattle raids against neighboring peoples and with the ritual slaying of enemies and taking their genitals as trophies. A king never finally became king, however, until after he had died, his son had succeeded, and (in the middle of his son's installation cycle) those vital parts of his body not buried—fingernails, toenails, teeth, tongue, and genitals—were mixed with the similar remains of all past kings in a special quiver located in Maale's *sanctum sanctorum*. Then he had "met his fathers." Then he had actually become king, and the line which began with Maaleka was extended yet another generation in a perfect chain of interconnecting father-son links.

With the life-giving, superior force of Maaleka preserved through his descendants, politics in the present was looked upon as the harmonious and fertile union of unequals. Best expressive of this idea was the layout of the royal compound, what the Maale called the "lion house" *(zobi mari)*. From archeological remains of the lion house built in the early part of this century and from informants' reports, I was able to reconstruct, as shown in Figure 1, the royal compound as it probably existed in the nineteenth century.[6]

The compound in its entirety was incomparably large and grand by Maale standards, and the lion house, its roof rising to about 35 feet, could be seen from great distances. With two stories, the house was built around a cedar center post, the uncut top of which extended through the roof as a spire ten or fifteen feet in the air. The whole compound was overwhelmingly a male preserve (the main exception being the king's mother who had her own house to one side of the lion house), and it was taboo for a woman of childbearing years even to enter. Grinding in the compound was done by male transvestites *(ashtime)* or by elderly women past menopause. To use a biological metaphor, the royal compound was the male nucleus of the Maale polity, dominating the surrounding female medium.

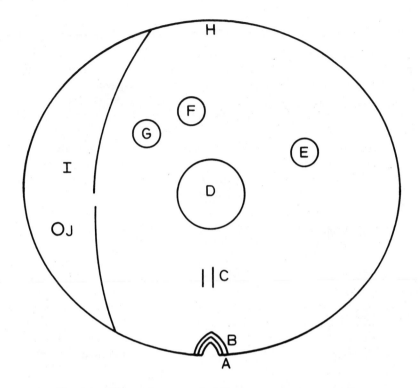

Figure 1. The royal compound of Maale

A — The place outside the compound where the chief of Makana sat when he visited the king (the chief could not enter nor could he be allowed to see the king)

B — *doddi* or "union," the main gate through which all Maale men entered

C — *ko'bo basso,* the second gate through which only men of the *karazi* moiety went

D — *zobi mari* or "lion house," the ritual center of Maale where the king prayed

E — the queen-mother's house where she and her guests feasted

F — the *merto* or "song" house where *karazi* men feasted

G — the *raggi* house where men of that moiety feasted

H — *pulto karro* or "small gate" through which *məni* potters and tanners and women past menopause entered

I — cattle corral of the king

J — *ts'osi,* literally "god," a low house in which was suspended the quiver containing the remains of all the past kings of Maale

If the privilege of entering the royal compound generally separated men from women, the way men entered also reflected an order of precedence. Maale men, for instance, entered the compound through the main gate or "union" *(doddi),* which consisted of three cedar posts on each side which met overhead in a pointed, Gothic arch. Specialist pariah groups like potters and tanners, in contrast, entered by way of the back gate or the "small gate" *(pulto karro).* For Maale who came in through the main gate, a second gate, *ko'bo basso,* composed of four posts on each side, parted entrants according to their moiety membership. Only men of the king's moiety, *karazi,* passed through the second gate and entered the lion house. Men of the *raggi* moiety walked around the second gate, and instead of going into the lion house (taboo for them), entered a smaller house of their own to one side of the lion house. Finally, inside of the lion house which only *karazi* men could enter, the king sat on a kind of rude throne *(terk'inso)* when he prayed, while all the other men sat on the floor.

Behind this configuration of houses, gates, and fences lay a particular conception of politics as at once the hierarchical separation and the harmonious joining together of social orders. The name for the main gate, "union," seems to express the idea well. It was the union, almost the sexual union, of the king with his people, *karazi* with *raggi,* Maale with specialist castes, and men with women, that produced political tranquility and economic abundance. Equality between the elements of these dualities was an alien philosophy; such an arrangement, according to the dominant Maale way of thinking, could lead only to chaos and anarchy. These same ideas were echoed almost a century later when the Maale kingship was abolished by the revolutionary government in 1975. The conservative faction of elders who opposed the change asked rhetorically, "How can we live without a king? Bees have a king. Termites have a king. Cattle follow a leader. How can we survive without a king? We will kill each other off."

The three notions discussed above formed the dominant framework in which politics and especially kingship were conceived, talked about, argued over; they constituted the outlines of what might be called Maale political culture. Given the structure of the ideology of power, how was it translated into social action? In practice, what were the powers of the king and the chiefs and on what economic base did they rest? And finally, how did Maale economics and politics relate to the wider Ethiopian economy?

The political hierarchy in Maale was composed of three levels: at the lowest rung were the subchiefs *(gatta),* the number of whom varied from zero to four in each of the chiefdoms in Maale; next there were chiefs *(goda),* each of whom presided over one of the thirteen chiefdoms; and last there was the king *(kati)* who lived in Bola chiefdom (see Map 5). At the heart of the kingdom, politics was dominatd by three officeholders—the king, the chief of Makana, and the chief of Bola. Of all the chiefs in Maale, the latter two lived closest to

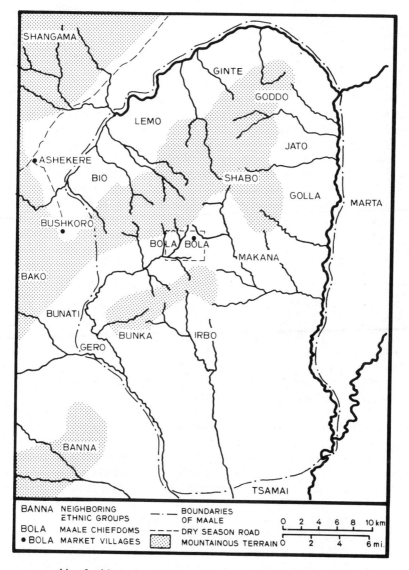

SHANGAMA

GINTE

GODDO

LEMO

JATO

●ASHEKERE

BIO

SHABO

GOLLA

MARTA

BUSHKORO●

BOLA ●BOLA

MAKANA

BAKO

BUNATI

BUNKA

IRBO

GERO

BANNA

TSAMAI

BANNA NEIGHBORING
       ETHNIC GROUPS
BOLA   MAALE CHIEFDOMS
●BOLA MARKET VILLAGES

—·— BOUNDARIES
      OF MAALE
——— DRY SEASON ROAD
      MOUNTAINOUS TERRAIN

0 2 4 6 8 10 km
0   2   4   6 mi.

Map 5.   Maale, its chiefdoms, and surrounding ethnic groups

the king and were the most powerful. They, along with Bola elders, determined succession to the kingship, and they inherited their offices while all the other chiefs (theoretically, at least) were appointed by the king.

The coalitions and cleavages in the triangle formed by the king, the chief of Makana, and the chief of Bola shaped the dynamics of Maale politics. Two of the three were apparently often in alliance against the third. If the king grew especially strong, the two chiefs were likely to unite against him (cf. Caplow 1968), and their opposition could vary from passive measures like delaying prescribed rituals in the king's installation cycle to razing the king's lion house. Similarly, if one of the chiefs grew especially powerful and rich, he invited a coalition of the king and the other chief against him.

In the uneasy equilibrium of power in this political triangle, the king, if not a despot, was usually dominant. Besides the greater ideological and (as I will describe later) economic resources of the king, he also enjoyed certain political advantages. When, for instance, a successor to the kingship had been chosen, all of his siblings were exiled from Bola chiefdom and required to live elsewhere. His brothers and all other members of the royal lineage could not hold political office, and it was taboo for them even to enter the lion house, Maale's ritual and political center.

Protected in this way from the division of his power with members of the royal lineage, the king in addition had at his disposal a very small "police force." Men of the pariah group of potters and tanners, *mani*, were renowned as hunters, and those living in Bola were the king's personal servants. In war, *mani* led the attack, and in times of peace, the king, albeit with the agreement of the *gojo* (alter ego to the king whose participation was required in all royal rituals), could order the *mani* to execute offenders and miscreants.

During interregnums, the triangular order at the heart of Maale politics broke down. With two instead of three dominant sides, it was a more complicated task to engineer a consensus. And since the power of the chiefs of Makana and Bola often waxed strong while the king was dead (but said to reign), they sometimes had little incentive to install a successor. Consequently, interregnums often lasted for long periods of time, sometimes up to three or four years. As the Maale tell the story, disasters invariably intervened—crops failed or enemies raided Maale or epidemics struck—and elders from over the land called for a new king.

The eleven chiefs located in more peripheral areas had much less influence on royal politics. Conversely, however, they seemed to have had more autonomy in their own districts. An elder in an outlying chiefdom explained that since the king did not leave the lion house in former times and since few of them went to Bola, his people did not know much about the king. Only a few of the wealthy and influential elders from the area kept contact with Bola and were known to the king. The local chief, in contrast, was much more involved in and conversant with the affairs of his people and, within his own boundaries, was likely to become a miniature king.

Theoretically, each of the eleven outlying chiefs served at the pleasure of the king and could be replaced at any time. In fact, there was a strong tendency for the chiefship to be passed from father to son. And as a chiefly line became entrenched, it was difficult for the king to make a new appointment. Elders could recount only four times in the nineteenth century or before when Maale kings had appointed new chiefs, and in two of these cases, the king had had to relent, and the chiefship reverted back to the original line. Typical of these latter instances is the story told to me by the chief of Bio in 1975:

> Our forefather was a great hunter. He killed buffaloes. He killed leopards. He killed everything. He went hunting so often that he was never at home when the king sent for him. Messengers told the king, "When we go and look for him, he's always out hunting." The king became angry and ordered the *mani* to beat and kill our forefather. The land was completely destroyed then. Indeed, hadn't our first forefather come with the first king from Bussa? Crops didn't sprout. The rains didn't come. First one and then another man was made chief but to no avail. Finally the subchief of Bio went to the king, prostrated himself and said, "You have your wife. You have your mother. I have nothing. I am alone. I have no chief. I have no husband. I am a wife without a husband." The king asked, "Is there anyone of his line left?" "Yes, there's a child. I will bring him to you." Then the subchief brought the child to the lion house and when the child extended his hands to the sky to pray, the rain came down in sheets. Since then we have been chiefs here. We can't be removed. All of the other chiefs can be replaced but we cannot be removed.

Characteristic of the pattern in what Southall (1956) called "segmentary states," Maale chiefs, especially those away from the center of the kingdom, apparently often claimed powers essentially similar to those of the king, only on a smaller scale. Maale kings, however, were apparently strong enough to keep peripheral chiefs in line, and the logical endpoint of the segmentary tendency—a peripheral chief breaking away and establishing an independent kingdom—did not, so far as I could determine, ever occur during the last century or so.

Within the chiefdoms, subchiefs were appointed by their respective chiefs. Here again the office tended to be passed down from father to son, although subchiefs, who enjoyed less political power and less ideological support, were apparently easier to replace than chiefs. The number of subchiefs that a chief appointed was loosely related to the size of his chiefdom. Gero, for instance, a very small district, had no subchiefs. Both Bola and Bio had one subchief, while Irbo, a large chiefdom, had four. Of all the subchiefs, the one in Bola who oversaw work on the king's fields had the highest status and he, like the chiefs of Bola and Makana, inherited his office and could not legitimately be replaced by another line.

From subchiefs to chiefs to king, the Maale political hierarchy formed an unstable and wobbly pyramid. The position of each block, or each officeholder, depended on the pushes and pulls of those about him, and even the king at the apex had rather limited resources with which to enforce unpopular decisions. The rich and elaborate ideological forms surrounding kingship, rather than reflecting the despotic power of the king, seemed almost designed to conceal his weaknesses. When adjudicating disputes, for instance, the king's was not the last court of appeal. In the exceptional cases in which the king could not use his position and influence to effect a settlement, the affair could be taken to the chief of Makana. Also, apparently, the king sometimes could not prevent blood feuds from establishing their own version of local justice. If the murderer managed to flee to the royal compound and to pass through the second gate, he came under the protection of the king who was then in a good position to settle the case and ritually to reconcile the two warring families by washing their hands together. Otherwise, the murderer or one of his close kinsmen was likely to be killed in revenge.

Supporting (and in turn supported by) this delicately balanced hierarchy of political power was an array of economic privileges and perogatives. The king and the chiefs all enjoyed labor tribute, *haile,* and none of them cultivated their own fields. To call people from various parts of the kingdom to come and work, the king first sent messengers to the chiefs, the chiefs informed their subchiefs, and on the appointed day the subchiefs, blowing antelope horns, summoned their people to Bola to work on the king's field. There were three large areas in Bola that kings cultivated (the name of one of the fields was *warshabashe,* "too much for a multitude"), and the grain from these fields allowed the king to entertain his guests in the lion house with openhanded generosity. A famous king named Sago had, at least according to the Maale today, 28 granaries. "In our forefathers' day, they were always eating and drinking beer in the lion house."

Labor tribute also supported the chiefs, but in their case, of course, only people within the borders of their own chiefdoms were required to work. Again, subchiefs organized the work, and produce from the fields made chiefs' houses into lesser centers of plenitude and generosity. The chief of Irbo described how in the early twentieth century people worked on his fields and how afterwards he blessed them: "I would say then, 'Because you all have called me father, may God from the heavens make you fat.' Then the rains would come; the bees would make honey; cows would calve; goats would kid; and women would bear children. We didn't go to funerals morning and night the way we do now."

Besides labor tribute, tribute in kind also upheld the Maale system of political stratification. For all of the sacrifices that he made, the king sent messengers to the chiefs, who informed their subchiefs, who in turn decided whose cattle or goats should be sent to Bola. (The power of subchiefs to decide exactly whose cattle would be taken must have been a strong sanction for their authority in other local matters and in organizing labor tribute.) After the king had passed a certain point in the cycle of his installation, he could legitimately send for goats and cattle not meant for sacrifices but for his own use and that of his guests at the lion house. Honey in particular was a royal perogative, and only the king and a few others whom he permitted (most notably the chiefs of Makana and Bola) could brew honey wine.

Exactly how much tribute in kind and in labor chiefs and the king received is extremely difficult to estimate. There were, it seems, limits past which chiefs and kings could not go without endangering their positions. Maale elders to whom I talked emphasized, glorified, and probably exaggerated the wealth of past kings, but they also seemed to realize (though none ever stated the proposition in exactly this way—indeed, the ideology of kingship was almost "thick" enough to cover up the fact) that the kings' wealth came from their own hands. Elders said, for example, that it was a great misfortune for the land if the king had many children. If members of the royal lineage became numerous, they would be strong enough to order everyone around, and no one would have time for his own work. That is why, they said, the chiefs of Makana and Bola cast a spell over the king's wife, sterilizing her, after she had borne two sons or so. Similarly, Arregude, king in the early part of the twentieth century, was opposed by his people when he decided to build his lion house on the site of Sago's former lion house. Since Sago had been one of the most powerful kings in Maale history, the people were afraid that Arregude (who, in fact, was gaining newfound power by that time from his role in the northern system of indirect rule in the south) would become similarly powerful and oppressive. When Arregude was gone on one of his trips to the provincial capital, his people uprooted the center post and pushed over the partially built lion house.

Both labor tribute and tribute in cattle and honey played an important role in Maale political economy, but neither had the internal significance nor the external connections that tribute from hunting had. And neither cultivation nor raising animals was as culturally elaborated nor so bound up with personal prestige as was hunting. The killer of any large and dangerous wild animal— elephants, leopards, buffalo, or an enemy man—was accorded a special status. The songs, *merto,* that Maale men sang recounting their adventures and detailing their deeds were taken up mainly with hunting stories. Men who made an important kill while hunting together had special forms of address. And finally at the funerals of successful hunters, special songs were sung commemorating their courage.

When anyone killed a buffalo or leopard or elephant, he was required to present the skins or the ivory to the king, unless he happened to belong to the lineages of one of a few important men, like the chiefs of Makana and Bola, in which case the chiefs in question appropriated the skins or ivory. First the killer took a trophy from the animal—a tail or a leg or in the case of the enemy man, his genitals—to his minimal lineage head who ritually made the kill again, apparently drawing some of the original killer's power and charisma to himself. The same was repeated by the killer's subchief, then by his chief, and finally by the king, who took possession of the animal hide or ivory. Only the king and, as exceptions, the chiefs of Makana and Bola along with a few others, could sell these items, and in exchange they obtained iron, finely crafted spear heads, beads, perhaps cattle, a very few slaves, and (toward the end of the nineteenth century) guns from foreign traders who visited Maale.

Several Ethiopianists have drawn attention to the cult of the hunter in the southwest, indeed in all of Greater Ethiopia (Levine 1974: 53). What has gone unanalyzed, however, is the relationship between hunting with all of its ideological elaborations and long-distance trade. In the case of Maale, it is almost as if the prestige and status that was accorded to successful hunters otherwise compensated them for what they lost to the king—the most valuable goods in demand by foreign traders. With a near monopoly over leopard skins, buffalo hides, and ivory, Maale kings were important nodes in the regional trading network of the southwest. Foreign goods were funnelled into Maale through the kings, and kings retained some goods for their treasury and for their own use and no doubt redistributed others to faithful chiefs and loyal retainers. Proceeds from the trade thus strengthened the king's political position and helped to maintain the supporting pyramid of chiefs and subchiefs.

The Formation of Modern Ethiopia

At the end of the nineteenth century, the southwest was once again incorporated into the northern empire. From the 1870s onward, kingdom after kingdom submitted and paid tribute to the Shoan ruler Menilek or was conquered and pillaged. In the former case, native kings often retained their positions and became intermediaries between their peoples and the newly established administration in the southwest; in the latter case, kings and chiefs were killed or exiled and replaced by northern governors.

In 1881, Jimma, for example, chose not to oppose the northern army sent against it and agreed to pay tribute. And when in 1897 the king of Jimma, a Muslim named Abba Jifar, helped the north to conquer his traditional enemy, Kefa, he insured himself a special place in the expanding Ethiopian empire. Until Abba Jifar's death in 1932, Jimma remained an independent enclave, tributary to the Ethiopian emperor. Situated advantageously on the trade routes to the southwest and with the other powerful states in the southwest ravaged by northern conquest, Jimma became one of the richest trading centers in all of Ethiopia. Colonies of Muslim traders from Jimma spread out over the whole southwestern region, and as early as 1904 Jimma paid in tribute "approximately 350,000 talers [Maria Theresa dollars] in cash, about 150 kilos of gold, 10 to 20 richly caparisoned horses, 100 to 120 muleloads of wooden furniture, and a special gift of gold plates and silver cups for the emperor" (Marcus 1975: 191).

Kefa, in contrast, resisted and was devastated. After three bloody campaigns which lasted nine months and which dispersed and killed large numbers of Kefa, northern armies (reportedly with 20,000 guns to Kefa's 300) finally captured the Kefa king. The king demanded to be taken to the Ethiopian emperor in chains of gold and is said to have told the latter, "You think yourself a great king, but your claim bears no comparison to mine. Your crown was placed on your head by the hands of men. Mine came down to me straight from Heaven on high" (Perham 1969: 318). The divine mandate of the Kefa king did not, however, protect his countrymen from the ensuing rule of northern soldiers, expropriation of their land, and in some cases enslavement. Early twentieth-century travelers invariably commented on the number of abandoned houses and fields in Kefa. By 1936 an observer cited by Perham (1969: 321) estimated that the population of Kefa had declined by 75 percent since the northern conquest; while such a figure seems certainly an exaggeration, it indicates the extent of disruption and decline.

Besides expanding into the south, Menilek also reunited the north. After assuming the title, "king of kings," he began to centralize the government and to bring the provincial nobility, who had dominated the country in the preceding eighteenth and early nineteenth centuries, firmly under his rule. Menilek established postal and telegraph services to the provinces, chartered a national bank, and contracted for the building of a railroad from Addis Ababa to the coast. The decade from 1896, when Menilek defeated the Italians at the Battle of Adwa, to 1906, when he was taken seriously ill, saw the zenith of Menilek's power and the final expansion of Ethiopia to its present borders (Marcus 1975: 174-213).

Menilek's administration of the southwest relied on a network of military garrisons perched on the highest mountain tops and manned by northern soldiers. From these settlements, soldiers went forth to keep a minimal degree of social order and to collect tribute. As northern rule became more firmly established, garrison towns often moved down the mountain side to more convenient locations. Fortifications were discontinued and gradually periodic markets grew up. In 1975 nearly all of the administrative centers in the southwest were the lineal descendants of Menilek's garrison towns.

During the first years of the administration, the northern governors stationed at garrisons had to rely on indirect rule through local kings and chiefs. Kings in the southwest who peacefully submitted were recognized as authorities, *balabbats,* and were held accountable for collecting tribute and for settling local disputes. Among peoples who resisted conquest, the highest ranks of the indigenous political hierarchy were eliminated but lower chiefs were recognized and retained in the new administrative system.

In return for their services, local kings and chiefs were given economic privileges (a portion of the tribute they collected) and political power (backed by northern soldiers) greater in some cases than they had enjoyed before. Many of the southern *balabbats* began to adopt the more prestigious dress and manners of their conquerors, to speak rudimentary Amharic, and to take Christian names.

> The *balabbats* proved themselves indispensable as intermediaries between the northern governors and the southern masses. In return, they were accorded status and privileges and gradually emerged as a distinct group associated with the northern ruling group and emulating its dominant characteristics. . . . Ethiopian rule in the south reinforced the pattern of stratification where it existed, and introduced it where it did not (Markakis 1974: 107-08).

As northern government penetrated to the countryside, governors still collected tribute through *balabbats,* but much of their own support and that of soldiers under them now came from temporary *maderia* fiefs in the surrounding areas that gave their holders the right to appropriate goods and services from the people *(gabbar)* living on those fiefs. The higher the official, the larger the fief and the greater the number of *gabbar* he controlled. The lowliest soldiers depended on at least two *gabbar,* while provincial governors lived off the services of hundreds. Each *gabbar* was required to turn over grain and cash to his master as well as to provide services like grinding, cutting firewood, caring for animals, and building houses. All of these goods and services *gabbar* had to render for as long as they lived on the fief; only their freedom to move away acted as a brake on the exactions of officials, for a fief without tenants was useless. According to Markakis (1974: 116), " . . . there was no mass displacement of cultivators, nor any sudden appearance of a landless class. The primary economic effect was a depression in the level of living for the peasantry. . . . "

The imposition of tribute payments in cash by the northern administration went hand in hand with the trading diaspora of Muslims from Jimma and with the growing network of periodic markets. At least in Maale during the initial years after the conquest, northern soldiers demanded tribute in spent bullet casings—a direct reminder of the basis of northern rule. After a few years, coins were substituted for spent bullets, but of course the only access of *gabbar* to either was through trade with merchants from Jimma. In order to obtain cash, *gabbar* had to sell goats, honey or cattle; and most of their cash then went to their masters in the form of tribute. Still vivid in the memory of many southerners are scenes of governors and lesser officials leaving for Addis

Ababa after their stays in office with mules loaded with boxes of money. This whole movement of resources depended on the symbiotic relationship between Christian administrators and Muslim traders, the first creating the initial demand for cash, the second providing the supply.

With proceeds from the developing trade in the southwest indirectly under Ethiopian control (in the form of tributes from Jimma, the major trading center) and with lucrative new governorships to bestow and to take away, Menilek was able to expand his power dramatically. One final aspect of northern policy in the southwest added yet another fund of resources to Menilek's control. Besides giving temporary *maderia* fiefs to governors and soldiers in lieu of salary, the emperor gave *gult* fiefs (lifetime tenure) and *rest gult* fiefs (permanent tenure), along with the customary rights over *gabbār*, to his faithful retainers and successful soldiers. From the point of view of the emperor, such grants fulfilled a number of functions: with men personally indebted to him settled in the southern provinces, Menilek held an independent check over the actions of governors who were far removed from the capital; such grants were an important resource for rewarding followers and retaining political support; and finally, appointments to these fiefs sometimes served as a form of genteel exile for those whom the emperor wished away from the center of Ethiopian politics.

The centralization of government that Menilek effected did not last. After a long illness, Menilek died in 1913. A combination of circumstances—the lack of a living son to succeed and the reluctance of the nobility to support any strong successor—led to a devolution of power. After the abortive reign of one of Menilek's daughter's sons, Yasu, a rough division of power was instituted at the center of Ethiopian politics in 1916, designed apparently to guarantee the independence of the nobility. Menilek's daughter, Zauditu, became empress and Tafari Makonen (later known as Haile Selassie) was appointed regent: "... provincialism reemerged in full force in Ethiopia, with powerful *rāses* [provincial nobles] ruling the provinces like autocrats, paying little heed to the government in Addis Ababa which was immobilized by the profound mutual suspicion between its top leaders" (Markakis 1974: 199). It was not until the late 1920s that Tafari began to gain the upper hand, and in 1930, his rivals eliminated, he declared himself emperor, "king of kings," taking the throne name of Haile Selassie. Five years later by the time of the Italian invasion, Haile Selassie had only begun to recentralize the government and to reverse the flow of power from the provinces back to Addis Ababa.

The period from 1906 to 1935 was therefore a reasonably consistent phase in Ethiopian historical development: central authority was weak and provincial governors strong, especially those in the newly conquered territories where there were no local countervailing powers. As power flowed to the peripheries of the Ethiopian system, people followed, and provincial governors in the southwest attracted large followings of northern immigrants out to seek their fortunes. Each new governor, particularly those in the early part of the period, brought large retinues from their home bases in the north. These followers, who collectively became known as *naft'añña* or gunmen, entered service in the provincial armies, were appointed to lower-level administrative positions, and became clergy in the newly established Orthodox churches in the southwest.

The most successful of these northerners bought land and stayed on in the southwest even after their original patrons had been posted elsewhere. So-called "unoccupied lands" (in actuality, grazing and hunting lands) were expropriated by the Ethiopian state after the conquest and it was these lands that northerners bought (*k'alad,* or measured land), often at minimal prices. The government encouraged such sales since they increased tax revenues and brought the southwest more securely within the empire.

All of the settlers who occupied positions with the administration were assigned *gabbār* from the surrounding peoples. With the increasing number of administrative personnel, the *gabbār* system expanded to encompass more and more southwesterners. And with the increased military presence in the area, *gabbār* could be more closely controlled. It was during this period that the rule of northerners in the southwest grew most exploitative. In some cases, land was simply seized; in some areas, *gabbār*, for want of tribute, were forced to sell their children into slavery. And in place after place, *gabbār* rose up against their masters, especially when northern troops had to be removed to Addis Ababa.

> Through the use of political power [by the northerners], landholding rights were converted from temporary to permanent form; inaccurate measurement enlarged private landholdings; fraud, intimidation, and force were employed to deprive the southern *gabbārs* of their ill-defined rights: and frequently, outright seizure converted sizeable areas of land into the private property of powerful officials (Markakis 1974: 117).

Resources from the conquered territories that had up until 1906 aided Menilek in building modern Ethiopia now flowed into the hands of provincial governors and northern soldier-settlers. Gradually a class system overlaid with religious and ethnic differences developed in the southwest with politically privileged, northern Christian landlords versus pagan or Muslim southern peasants. As might be expected, religion, ethnicity, and class were not perfectly correlated. There were poor landless Christian northerners as well as powerful landowning southerners, mainly chiefs and kings. These, however, were the exceptions that proved the rule, for poor Christians usually married native women and to some extent began to assimilate to southern ways, while southern kings and chiefs generally adopted Christian culture.

The Italian occupation (1935-1941) temporarily and drastically changed the political economy of the southwest. The *gabbār* system which had upheld the political position of northerners was quickly abolished; northerners, at least in some areas, were forcibly relocated to special villages; and the Italians cultivated the support of southern peasants by reducing their tributes and by building mosques in Muslim areas. When, therefore, Haile Selassie was restored to power in 1941 by the British, he returned to a changed country. Many of the soldier-settlers in the south had been killed in the war, and the anti-northern feelings of the southern peasants had been fanned and given a political shape. In the north, many of the nobility had also died or had been disgraced by collaboration with the Italians.

All of these changes, as it happened, aided Haile Selassie in recentralizing the government under his strong rule and, to some extent, modernizing it. In the south, the growth of the landlord class who appropriated tribute but held no tax obligations to the state was siphoning off funds that otherwise could have gone to the central government. And the northern nobility of course had long been enemies of centralized rule in Ethiopia. For the next 33 years, from 1941 to 1974, Haile Selassie pursued a deft and delicately balanced policy of restoring and supporting (in basic respects) the old stratification systems in the north and south and, at the same time, undermining them when they interfaced with his own power and that of the central government.

In the south this policy was accomplished by the slow and complicated revision of land law. First of all, temporary fiefs for government officials were abolished in 1941 and instead of goods and services from *gabbār*, salaries from the treasury in Addis Ababa supported provincial administrators. Former *gabbār* in turn were required to give their taxes directly to the government. Land held in other tenures by northerners, including measured lands, were restored to them after the Italians, and landlords continued to enjoy a privileged position in relation to the state. It was not until 1967 that landlords' total incomes from rents were declared taxable under the provisions of the graduated income tax law. By then, according to Markakis (1974: 129), the agricultural sector of the Ethiopian economy (that landlords dominated) produced 65 percent of the gross domestic product, employed 87 percent of the population, but contributed only 7 percent of state revenues.

With regard to the northern nobility, the emperor began to weaken their power (already moderated by the Italian occupation) by supporting and promoting a new group of younger men to government positions. Educated and often from poor families, these men became an important counterbalance to the old power of the nobility. And because the new educated elite had no source of power except through their relationship to the emperor, Haile Selassie was able to take on more and more of the powers of an autocrat and to extend his influence more completely through the whole Ethiopian polity. According to Clapham (1969: 68), the proportion of nobles in the central government dropped from 53 percent in 1948 to 13 percent in 1966.

To recruit this new elite, Haile Selassie took a personal interest in developing the Ethiopian educational system and, for a time, served as his own Minister of Education. The number of schools rapidly increased from 1941 when the first secondary school was founded in Addis Ababa. Since most government schools were established in the larger cities and towns of the north, missionaries (generally excluded from the north by the opposition of the Orthodox church) were allowed to set up schools and churches in the south. As the mission schools began to teach and evangelize in Amharic (as they were required to do), small groups of southern Protestants gradually grew up. Although only a pale imitation of the educated elite who entered service in the central government, mission-educated Protestants performed a similar counterbalancing function *vis-à-vis* the southern landlord class. For the first time in the south, indigenous groups developed from humble origins with an orientation toward the national state, a knowledge of Amharic, and a determination to better their economic standing. And as such they eventually became a threat to the old landlord class composed of northerners and southern *balabbats*.

The post-Italian period of Haile Selassie's ascendancy came to a dramatic close in 1974 when the emperor was deposed by a military government. Private ownership of all land was abolished; many of the most influential nobility and the most powerful of the educated elite were executed; and Ethiopian foreign policy turned from a reliance on the U.S.A. to a closer relationship with socialist countries, in particular the U.S.S.R. In short, 1974 was the end of an era in Ethiopia and, as I will show below, in Maale.

Maale in the Context of Modern Ethiopia

In the three periods described above—strong central rule under Menilek, the ensuing devolution of power during the 1920s and '30s, followed by strong central rule again by Haile Selassie—the power of provincial governors in the south waxed and waned inversely as the power of Ethiopian emperors fell and rose. From the point of view of local Maale history, the oscillation can be most simply indicated by the average time governors of Bako province (which included Maale) spent in office. During the first period, Bako governors spent an average of four years in office; in the second period, almost six years; and in the third, less than three years. Strong Ethiopian emperors classically used the technique of quickly reappointing officials *(shum shir)* to prevent their building up local power bases, so that the shortest terms of office naturally occurred during the phases of strongest central authority.

The Maale remembrance of these periods is also quite different. Almost all elders could recount the succession of Bako governors during the middle phase (their ascendancy). Indeed, the Maale tended to use the idiom of divine kingship when they recalled the rule of the governor who had stayed longest in Bako, *dajāzmāch* Merid Habte Mariam. After describing the lavishness of Merid's feasts, one Maale elder said, "He was from a true royal line. In those days, cattle grew so old that a kind of insect built nests in the holes of their horns. Merid was a real king." In contrast, almost no one could name the complete list of governors during the first or third periods. While the elders' lack of knowledge of the earlier period may be the natural result of loss of historical memory, their ignorance of the recent governors of Bako reflects the changed nature of the governorship: with little prospect of staying long, officials spent less effort in penetrating local politics; their economic support now came from Addis Ababa not from local *gabbār*; they were simply less powerful than the kingly figures like *dajāzmāch* Merid.

The changing balance of power between the emperor and the provincial governors formed the wider political field in which the Maale king and the chiefs functioned in the twentieth century. Simply stated, my basic hypothesis is that the power of the Maale political elite tended to rise as that of their immediate superior, the provincial governor, fell. The political strength of governors depended, in turn, on the degree of central control the Ethiopian emperor could exert. This set of interdependencies is illustrated in Figure 2.[7]

Ethiopian Emperor	Ethiopian Emperor	*Ethiopian Emperor*
Provincial Governor	*Provincial Governor*	Provincial Governor
Maale Political Elite	Maale Political Elite	*Maale Political Elite*
1894-1911	1911-1936	1941-1975

Figure 2.   The ebb and flow of strength in the political hierarchy over Maale in the twentieth century (Note: The relatively powerful positions are indicated by italics.)

Of course the scheme in this diagram is oversimplified. Maale political history during the twentieth century was always the outcome of a complex interaction of various factors, both internal and external. If a weak Bako governor left a vacuum in local Maale politics, that was a necessary but not a sufficient cause of the rise in power of the Maale king and chiefs. Their rise to power, as the following discussion shows, always depended on local policies and personalities, local economic and political structures.

In 1894, Maale submitted peacefully to the army of *rās* Wolde Georgis that had just demolished Wolayta and was continuing southwestward establishing forts near Dorze, in Kamba, and in Gofa. The Maale who had recently lost considerable territory in a war with their neighbors, the Bako, invited the intervention of the northerners. The chief of Makana sent two messengers to Gofa to guide northern gunmen to Maale. The army came, and as one elderly Orthodox priest in Maale recalled, "There were so many young men with spears and guns they were like locusts." Accompanied by Maale, the Ethiopian army pushed the Bako out of Maale territory (except for one chiefdom which the Maale ceded to Bako), a peace was decreed, and a fortified garrison was built on a strategic mountaintop in Bako. The fort in Bako became the provincial capital of the surrounding territory, Maale included. A subsidiary and smaller settlement, surrounded by trenches, was established in the Maale highlands at Goddo and there the governor of the subprovince of Maale was stationed along with his soldiers.

For the first few years the rule of these fortified settlements of soldiers was limited but strong enough, apparently, to protect themselves. In about 1896 the Bako, after having given tribute for two years, rebelled. The king of Bako is reported to have said, "Why should a man give tribute? I'll give my spear as tribute. Oxen and honey I won't give." But spears could provide no match for guns, and the king was killed, beheaded, and his necklace—the insignia of royal office—confiscated.

By 1900 the colonization effort began in earnest when Menilek, then at his height of power, appointed trusted relatives to the governorships of Bako and Gofa (the province bordering Bako to the north). Both governors established churches in the garrison towns of their provinces, and both encouraged the formation of periodic markets. By 1905 European travellers who found their way through the southwest reported market towns in Bako, Uba, Gofa, and Maale (Maurette 1905: 450). All of these towns, as they moved from the mountaintops to lower-lying plains (except for the original market in Maale) continued to be major marketing centers in 1974. Finally, both governors brought retinues of soldier-settlers from their home bases in Shoa. Because they were among the first arrivals in the area, these immigrants and their children became dominant in local affairs. Until the revolution in 1974, the wealthiest and most influential northerners living in Maale were the descendants of this first wave of northern settlers.

The northern presence in Bako and in Maale was still small enough and provincial governors were changed often enough that relatively greater reliance had to be placed upon a policy of indirect rule through the Maale king and chiefs. As I mentioned before, it was the chief of Makana who took the initiative in guiding the northern army to Maale. Arregude, the Maale king who succeeded to power in about 1903, had by that time acquired a gun, and he accompanied and assisted northern soldiers on several campaigns to subjugate peoples to the south of Bako. After he became king, Arregude was held responsible for collecting tribute. If he could not give ivory, then Arregude was required to give children as slaves. The Maale of course hated the enslavement of their children; Arregude's role in it, even under the coercion of imprisonment, must have threatened to undermine his political position in Maale. In a daring and successful journey in about 1906, Arregude traveled to the north all the way to Menilek's court to protest the taking of Maale children. According to the story Maale elders still tell, Menilek asked Arregude what he would give in tribute instead of slaves. Arregude replied that he would give ivory, honey, cattle, and goats. Menilek assented and Arregude took a letter from the emperor to the governor of Bako instructing the latter not to take slaves from Maale. Although a few slaves continued to be taken from time to time, their number was slight compared to those from neighboring countries like Bako and Shangama where cattle, for instance, were in far fewer numbers.

Arregude's newfound power as intermediary between Maale and the northern administration invited the local opposition of the Makana and Bola chiefs. Arregude, in what was perhaps a piece of bravado, chose to build his lion house on the site of the house of Maale's most famous and powerful king, Sago. Fearing that Arregude would thereby become as powerful (and exploitative) as Sago had been, the chiefs and elders united and in a plain warning that I have already mentioned, they uprooted the centerpost of the partially built lion house during one of Arregude's absences from Maale. Arregude retaliated by refusing to live in Bola, the traditional residence of Maale kings, any longer. During the next few years, according to the elders, a near famine hit Maale and did not end until the house had been rebuilt and Arregude installed in Bola. God, as he often appears to be, was evidently on the side of the politically dominant.

By about 1911 the governor of Bako was becoming more and more powerful as his rule spread farther into the surrounding countryside and as central authority in Ethiopia decayed. That year, *dajāzmāch* Merid (who was to stay in office for the next nineteen years) took up the governorship of the province. One of his first moves in respect to Maale was to establish a second settlement of soldiers at Bunka south of Goddo, the subprovincial governor's residence (see Map 5). The Bunka site was unfortified and was situated in the valley lying in the heart of Maale territory. The change in type of site signaled the growing penetration of northern power. With a police force stationed in the center of Maale with about six officers, each of whom had six or seven ordinary soldiers serving beneath him, Merid had a great deal of control over Maale affairs. The Bunka soldiers, while the personal retainers of Merid (*karami,* literally "servants"), were under the nominal authority of the subprovincial governor who lived four hours away at Goddo.

At about the same time that Merid was appointed governor, three *gult* fiefs were carved out of Maale territory, corresponding to the three western chiefdoms of Bio, Lemo, and Ginte. The northern fief holders who took up residence there, each of whom kept a retinue of from ten to twenty northern soldiers, oversaw public order in their areas, settled local disputes, and completely replaced the local Maale chiefs, who never recovered their influence and prestige. Holders of *gult* fiefs were not answerable to the subprovincial governor of Maale; instead they were under the formal authority of the provincial governor in Bako. Since both of the latter, however, were personal appointees of the emperor, *gult* holders' political influence in practice sometimes approached that of provincial governors.

The resulting hierarchy of administrative officials over Maale was then unstable at best and held room for considerable maneuver. Fief holders, for instance, could use their personal relationship to the emperor to go over the head of the provincial governor, their nominal superior; Bunka soldiers through their personal ties to the governor of Bako likely did the same in regard to the subprovincial governor of Maale. The room for maneuver evidently widened still further during the period of weak central authority in Ethiopia. In Maale, a rough version of frontier justice held sway: northerners sometimes seized Maale land, converted temporary tenures into permanent ones, and sold indigent *gabbār* into slavery.

From the provincial governor on down, all of these officials, along with their retinues of ordinary soldiers, were supported by the services of Maale *gabbār*. The Maale inhabitants of the chiefdoms of Bio, Lemo, and Ginte all became the *gabbār* of the fief holders of those districts. The subprovincial governor of Maale was given rights over the inhabitants of Gollo chiefdom, while Bunka soldiers took *gabbār* in Irbo and Bunka. Makana residents came under the control of one of Merid's sons, while those in Gero came under the control of the wife of another of Merid's sons—a daughter of Haile Selassie. Maale living in Jato, Goddo, and Shabo (the area closest to the residence of the subprovincial governor) were divided among Merid's retainers who lived in Bako. Finally, most of Bola was left to the Maale king (now designated *bālābbāt,*) who was given the right to appropriate goods and services just as the other masters of *gabbār* were.

One Maale elder who was about five years old when his father became a *gabbār* to one of the soldiers in Bunka recalled the system in the following way:

An Amhara [northerner] took a *gabbār* first of all by getting *dajāzmāch* Merid's permission. Then he scouted out possible Maale families, asking people who lived in what house and writing down people's names. By bribing the Maale man's neighbors, the Amhara sneaked up on the man at night, captured him, and took him to Bunka where he remained a prisoner until Maale they already knew and trusted—a chief or another *gabbār*—stepped forward as the man's guarantor. Then he was permitted to go free and then he began his work as a *gabbār*. Any time an Amhara met a Maale on a path, he would ask, 'Whose *gabbār* are you?' If the Maale said nothing, the Amhara would beat him; if he named his master, the Amhara said 'All right,' and let him pass.

According to the same informant, the load on *gabbār* was a heavy one. For a week at a time, the *gabbār* lived in his master's house, cut firewood, brought water, farmed his master's fields, and cared for his mule. He had to cook his own food and to sleep outside his master's house on straw. At the end of the week, another *gabbār* arrived and the first left—carrying a sack of grain that his wife would grind and that he would return when he came for the next week of service. In addition, he had to pay four dollars (Maria Theresa dollars) a year for his master's "salary" *(demoz)*, a large gourd of honey worth approximately three dollars twice a year on holidays, and five dollars whenever his master went on a long journey. Not surprisingly, many Maale chose to move away rather than endure such exactions. And they were able to do so because Maale, situated at the edge of the high plateau where it sloped down to the drier pastoral lands, was apparently at the southern limit of the *gabbār* system. Many Maale, including chiefs, simply moved to Tsemai, which was to the south and across the provincial boundary. Northern rule there was less firmly established and tribute was exacted by periodic forays to seize cattle rather than to impress *gabbār* into service.

Maale who stayed in their ancestral homes and who became *gabbār* had to have cash, and with the need for cash went increased trade and the settlement of Muslim traders from Jimma in Maale. The fief holder of Bio, *fitāwrāri* Turunih, encouraged settlement of traders by taxing them lightly and protecting them from other northerners. By about 1915 a village of Muslims had established itself on his fief in Bio and, according to one of my Muslim informants who moved there in about 1925, the village had grown to about fifty-six households by that time: "Those were good days. We grew fat then. A huge gourd of honey could be bought for three dollars. What did the Maale know about prices? We really ate in those days." A smaller settlement of traders from Jimma who specialized in ivory grew up later in Samworo near the residence of the provincial governor in Goddo. All of these traders bought products in Maale and other peripheral areas and sold them in the marketing centers then growing up in the southwest or to more distant higher-level centers like Jimma and Addis Ababa.

As the commercial and political hold of the empire over Maale tightened, the old role of Maale kings and chiefs as intermediaries became more and more anachronistic. At the same time, more and more Maale *gabbār* were needed to support the increasing numbers of northern soldiers in Maale. At first, *gabbār* were not taken from the immediate vicinities of most chiefs and the king, the families living in those areas being left to perform the services on which the Maale elite traditionally depended. As the demand for *gabbār* grew, however, the governor of Bako in the early 1930s decreed that all Maale—even those previously serving the king and the chiefs—should become *gabbār*.

The Maale elite reacted in various ways: Arregude, the king or *bālābbāt* as he was then designated, had recently died, and since a successor had not been installed, the office was at a low ebb in any case. The chief of Bunka simply left Maale and went to live in Tsemai. The chief of Irbo, enraged when one of the Bunka soldiers claimed his neighbors as *gabbār*, attempted to shoot the man. The bullet grazed the soldier's arm, maiming him, and killed his servant sitting nearby.

It was the double effect of the progressive undermining of the power of the Maale elite along with the increasing exploitation of ordinary *gabbār* that seems to account for the Maale reaction to the Italian occupation in 1936. In many ways Italian rule was not easy. The Maale recount, for instance, forced labor to build the road from Gofa to Bako and taxes taken in cattle, grain, and honey. Despite all that, Maale still remember the Italians as liberators, and in telling their history many of them made comments like, "When the Italians came, we became people again," "We got back our lives."

Had the Italians stayed longer, perhaps the Maale would have retained less positive memories. In any case, the Italian interlude from 1936 to 1941 ended one phase in Maale history and prepared the way for the next. Many of the northerners living in Maale died when the subprovincial governor of Maale led the Bunka soldiers to the battle front. As I pointed out earlier, Haile Selassie took advantage of the losses and disarray caused by the war to institute reforms and to recentralize the government.

Among the first reforms that Haile Selassie promulgated was the abolition of the *gabbār* system. Henceforth, administrative officials would be supported by salaries from Addis Ababa, and the old role of soldier-settlers was given to a new semiprofessionalized police force. Both governors and policemen now circulated from post to post, usually staying in one place only a few years at most.

It would seem that these changes, by separating the northerners remaining in Maale from their former place in the state apparatus, would have ended their economic and political superiority over Maale peasants. Such was not the case, however, for most of the northerners above the rank of ordinary soldier had bought measured land in Maale, which they retained after the occupation. The entire lowland plain which surrounded the mountainous heart of Maale territory (see Map 5) had been declared government land and had been sold to northern settlers often at low prices from about 1911 onwards. In some cases, simply paying the land tax was enough to institute a claim to a plot of land. When, for instance, the subprovincial governor of Maale sent soldiers to the southern plain to guard Maale against northern hunters from the adjacent province, he claimed the land as his own, began paying taxes on it and taking rents. As it turned out, these low-lying lands were perhaps the most valuable in Maale from the point of view of collecting rents from tenants. The production of all of the most valuable Maale products—cattle, goats, and honey—depended on the grazing areas and flowering thorn trees found in the lowland plains. Few Maale lived there, but most grazed their cattle and tended beehives there. Therefore, the number of "tenants" who could be tapped for rent was comparatively great, and northerners who could sustain any kind of claim to these lands had a lucrative source of income.

Sustaining land claims nearly always meant bringing, and defending one's self in, court cases in Bako, then the subprovincial capital. The boundaries of plots were poorly defined at best, and because of its lack of resources, the provincial administration had little independent check on the extent of plots located far from the capital. There was then considerable latitude for manipulating land claims, and wealthy and powerful landowners were often able to expand their holdings, sometimes by less than legitimate means, including bribing officials and witnesses. Landowners who lived too far away from the administrative centers to play the political game often found their plots progressively whittled away. Whereas before the occupation the personal supervision of *gabbār* focused settlers' attention locally on Maale, afterwards, the pull of land cases prompted many to build second houses in Bako, an to spend large portions of the year there currying the favor of officials who came and went every year or two, and keeping abreast of the latest cliques and coalitions. In addition, the town was the site of the modern educational and medical services that Haile Selassie's government was developing. Rents from Maale could be collected in a two- or three-month stay in the countryside.

With settlers living most of the year outside Maale and with their old function of keeping order taken over by a police station of only three or four men, indirect rule through Maale chiefs and the king once again became a useful policy of local government. By the early 1940s, the royal family had adapted to its revived role in the administration remarkably efficiently. One of Arregude's sons, Yebirka, had become king in about 1936. He carried out the traditional roles of the king as sacrificer and bringer of rains, while his younger brother Hilla assumed all of the duties relating to government work. It was as if Yebirka became *kati* while Hilla played the role of *bālābbāt*.

The chiefs and the king collected government taxes from the Maale through the first decade of the post-Italian period. In the highland center of the country, there were no northern landlords left. The three grants of *gult* fiefs made by Menilek in Bio, Lemo, and Ginte, had all expired when their owners died. The money that *gabbār* formerly gave to soldier-settlers, or at least a major portion of it, now went to the government through the chiefs and the king. And it was partly from these revenues, apparently, that the government paid out salaries to officials and policemen.

In 1951 tax collection was regularized by dividing the ownership of the highlands into plots of *gabbār rest* assigned to individual Maale. The king, or rather his brother, Hilla, along with a representative of the government, took a major role in setting up boundaries and assigning ownership. The final division of land reflected a rather complex interaction of Maale and government expectations and understandings of who should get land. Traditionally the Maale land tenure system had assigned plots *(dini)* to individuals, and the owners of the largest numbers of plots tended to be "big men," often wealthy heads of large and ramified lineages. When Hilla met with the chiefs and elders of each area in Maale to decide who should get land, it was generally the chiefs and big men who were given precedence. From the government point of view, land was being assigned to former *gabbār* who now would give their taxes directly to the government instead of to soldiers and officials stationed in Maale. The two views more or less coincided in practice, for in creating the *gabbār* system northern settlers had naturally tended to chose the wealthiest Maale as *gabbār*.

While the *gabbār* system, in its last years of operation, worked to undermine the Maale political elite, the post-Italian land division had the opposite effect: the Maale stratification system was strengthened. The king and chiefs (who, of course, were never *gabbār*) now controlled comparatively large plots of land, and the king and some of the more powerful chiefs required (even until 1975) the traditional forms of labor tribute from tenants as well as rents. The rest of the new Maale landlords—big men and notables like subchiefs— lacked the sanction of custom in requiring labor tribute, but nonetheless the authority to collect taxes from tenants added to their local status and influence.

With their positions reinforced, the king and the chiefs began more and more to take on the character of northern landlords. Most grew visibly wealthier, and a few, most notably the chief of Bunka, became very adept at dealing with the provincial courts and influencing local officials. The Bunka chief, for instance, threatened to sue the richest northern landlord in Maale, Abebe, for false land claims in his district. (Abebe was the son of the former subprovincial governor of Maale who had claimed land in the southern lowlands without ever paying for it.) Rather than expose the weakness of his title to the land, Abebe agreed to share half of the proceeds from tenants' rent with the chief. The two then worked together to extract high rents from the many Maale who grazed cattle on their land, the chief using his traditional status and influence in Maale and the northerner his connections with local officials. The area in question contained the only dry season watering hole for the entire plain to the south of Maale so that almost all Maale with cattle there were subject to payments. According to informants, the amount of rent that the chief and his northern partner took varied: for Maale on good terms with the two, the yearly amount (in the early 1970s) could be as low as thirty or forty Ethiopian dollars (the price of a young ox). For tenants who had somehow alienated the two landlords, the amount could reach over one hundred

Ethiopian dollars. Rents were, therefore, not only a rich source of income but a keen instrument of political control.

The structural transformations that dominated this period are perhaps best analyzed in relation to one event which, more than any other, dominated recent Maale politics. Yebirka and his brother Hilla were deposed from power in 1963. The story—Maale's social drama par excellence—illustrates both the complexities, the apparently accidental details, and what I take to be the bedrock economic and political realities of recent times.

The Recent Maale Past

To pick up the threads of the story, I begin with the last years of Arregude's reign, in the early 1930's. Arregude had four wives and ten children who lived to have children of their own. His first son (by his first wife), a handsome, forceful, and at times violent man named Girpe, was expected to inherit the kingship. In about 1933, however, he was accused (falsely, it seems) of murdering a northern settler. He was finally imprisoned in Addis Ababa and, apparently, killed during the Italian invasion. How and why Girpe met this end is a complicated and revealing bit of history in its own right; for my purposes here, let me simply note his disappearance and presumed death.

After Girpe was taken to prison in Addis Ababa, Arregude, according to the Maale, died of grief for his son. And when the Italians arrived in the southwest in 1936, they found no king in Maale. Pressed to name a successor, the traditional kingmakers, the Bola elders (who had suffered under Girpe's oppression) and the chiefs of Bola and Markana (who probably hoped that goodnatured Yebirka would sit lightly on the throne) chose Arregude's first son by his second wife—Yebirka. Meanwhile, Girpe had left four wives and many young sons in Maale.

If Yebirka had personally taken on the role of *bālābbāt,* perhaps the chiefs' expectation of a weak rule would have been born out. As it happened, Yebirka delegated those political duties to his younger brother Hilla. And Hilla proved to be as powerful a figure as his brother Girpe. To illustrate Hilla's character, a man who had served him told me the following story:

> One day while I was going to Cenca [the provincial capital at that time] with Hilla, we almost met our end. God must have helped us. We had a mule loaded with money, taxes that we were transporting to Cenca. We came up to someone's house, and the mule was just about to die. Hilla ordered me to turn the mule into the yard. (Whoever lived there had a small garden in the yard.) The wife came out of the house and started yelling for help. Her husband, a big man, came running along with the neighbors and cried, "By the law, stop! By the law, stop!" By that time Hilla had already taken over the house and laid down. When the husband began chasing the mule out of the garden, Hilla shot out of the house and pulled his gun. We all ran for cover, and the man asked, "Is he crazy?" I said, "He's the king of Maale. Haven't you ever heard of Hilla, king of Maale?" "Oh, my God," he said, "I'm going to get myself killed for this

little garden?" And he went up to Hilla, flattened himself on the ground and said, "Oh, king, I've erred. I've erred." Hilla said, "If I burned your house down now, what could you do in Cenca?" The man gave us a big pot of beer and a sheep to slaughter. We spent the night there, and in the morning he gave me five dollars and the boy who was leading the mule two dollars. That was Hilla for you—turning his mule into people's crops. A person can be powerful in his own country, but to do something like that in another country . . . Only now that Hilla is dead do people think he was an ordinary person.

With Hilla gathering power into his own hands, conflicts began to develop—as they were wont to do under strong kings—between the kingship (both Hilla and Yebirka) and the chiefs of Makana and Bola. According to Yebirka, who was still alive at the time of my fieldwork, friction developed between Hilla and the chiefs because Hilla monopolized the government of Maale; he heard all the court cases and therefore enjoyed all the gifts and bribes that this political office entailed. The chiefs were jealous. "My brother was a little crooked," Yebirka admitted, "But at least he didn't send cases outside Maale to Bako [where, he implied, there was still more crookedness]."

Only accidently related to the developing structural tensions at the center of Maale politics was another incident that widened still further the rift between the royal family and the chiefs. As it turned out, the real murderer of the man Girpe had been imprisoned for killing was the brother of the Bola chief. After Yebirka had become king, the Bola chief asked his mother's brother, the chief of Makana, to intercede with Yebirka and to reconcile the two families by washing their hands together—the customary ritual of conciliation for the families of a murderer and a murder victim. (In effect, the Bola chief's brother had caused the death of Girpe, Yebirka's brother.) Yebirka adamantly refused the Makana chief's mediation and tried to exile the Bola chief's brother. The dispute rankled and was unsettled even in 1975. "The chiefs have destroyed Maale," Yebirka said; "They're liars and thieves."

Yebirka and Hilla probably would have weathered these disagreements and dissensions without much difficulty, but the combination of the deepening cleavage between the royal family and the chiefs of Makana and Bola along with another that developed between Hilla and the northern landlords in Maale proved fatal in the end. Hilla began his political career during the Italian occupation when the Maale were being encouraged to unite against northerners (and, therefore, not against the Italians). From those years, Hilla seems to have developed a heightened sensitivity to the exploitations of northern landlords, for after 1951 when some of the owners of measured lands in the lowlands began to make claims extending farther and farther toward the mountains and into plots held by Maale, Hilla took the lead in opposing them. He argued court cases, appealed decisions, even went to Addis Ababa, and often he won. Perhaps Hilla opposed the northern landlords because he saw them as a threat to his own power (as they were), or perhaps he had other reasons. In any case, he came into direct and unyielding confrontation with Abebe, a northerner who had apparently tried to ally himself with Hilla by marrying the latter's daughter. Abebe was the son of the subprovincial governor of Maale before the Italians, and the landlord with whom the chief of Bunka had developed such an accomodating relationship.

The factions opposing Yebirka and Hilla, after the latter had been in office for about twenty-five years, finally went to court in order to despose them and to install Girpe's eldest son, Bailo, then in his late thirties. The chiefs of Bola and Makana both went to the Bako court and testified that Yebirka was not the first-born son of Arregude and that a mistake had been made: Yebirka was not the true king, for people were not prospering, cattle were dying, and the bees did not make honey. The chief of Bunka joined in the accusation and, combining court savvy with the idiom of Maale divine kingship, wrote the judge a list of Maale who had died during Yebirka's reign (augmented, some said, by fictitious names made up from Maale words for tree species).

The main mover behind the court accusation, however, was Abebe, the northern landlord. When I talked to him in 1975, he said, not boastingly, just matter-of-factly, "What do I have to hide? I was the one who deposed Yebirka. His brother, Hilla, kept testifying against me in court, trying to take away land that belonged to my father. I asked him to stop. I didn't want to quarrel. But he wouldn't stop." Abebe guided the case through the courts and made the requisite gifts and bribes to judges and officials. As the case moved slowly to a close, Bailo, the pretender, in a politically adroit move, went to the provincial tax collection office and pointed out that Hilla had divided Maale lands into plots three or four times too large. The government was being cheated. In 1962, then, Bailo along with a government representative redivided Maale lands. Many of Bailo's supporters were rewarded with plots and, at the same time, the government officials increased their tax rolls.

The resulting coalition of chiefs, northern landlords, and government officials in Bako was simply overwhelming. Yebirka's only supporters were the elders in Bola (who, along with the chiefs of Bola and Makana, traditionally chose the successor to the kingship) and many of the outlying common people. I asked an elderly man in the south of Maale how they felt when Yebirka was deposed and he said, "We just cried. All of our children had been born during Yebirka's time. We had built up our herds during this time. We just cried." But Bola elders and commoners elsewhere had almost no access or influence in the courts of Bako, and Yebirka was finally deposed in about 1963.

Policemen took Yebirka and the master of royal rituals, the *gojo*, to the sacred forest called Dufa. They ordered the *gojo* to break Yebirka's necklace. The old man said, "Ah! How can I do that? We have never taken the king's necklace before his eyes were darkened." A policeman kicked the *gojo* toward Yebirka, and finally he broke the necklace. Yebirka told me, "My neck was sore for months afterwards."

The events that led up to Bailo's accession in about 1963, although finally the result of many complex and heterogenous causes, nevertheless lay bare, I think, the major structural transformations in Maale political economy that dominated the post-Italian period: the Maale political elite were no longer really kings and chiefs but Ethiopian landlords. Differences in power no longer rested so much on the ideology of divine kingship, customary forms of labor tribute, and control over valuable trade goods as upon assimilation to northern culture, the ability to use and to influence the Ethiopian state apparatus, and, above all, the ownership of land—an institution backed and regulated by the power of the Ethiopian state.

All of these changes that Bailo's accession heralded proceeded at an accelerated pace after 1963. In Jinka (the new subprovincial capital after it had been moved down the mountainside from Bako), Bailo bought a house and spent much of his time there in the courts and with officials. He, along with the chiefs of Gero and Bunka, enrolled his sons in school in Jinka. And he scandalized Maale elders by removing his necklace when he went to Jinka. In Maale, the necklace was the most sacred insignia of kingship; in town, it merely identified Bailo as pagan and provincial. Henceforth, he would live as an "Amhara" he proclaimed; he would not observe old Maale taboos.

In Bola, the traditional residence of kings, he built the first tin-roofed house in Maale, and nearby on his own land he established a weekly market and encouraged traders to settle in Bola. Christians (the descendants of early twentieth-century soldiers in Maale too poor to claim and keep land, along with a small group of southwesterners assimilating to northern culture) and Muslims (descendants of the pre-Italian settlements in Maale at Bio and Goddo) built houses around the marketplace. Bailo began to rely on these settlers, some of whom knew how to write, as his representatives in collecting rents and settling minor court cases. Previously, the Bola elders had played this role as the king's intermediary with the surrounding populace. Now they were disqualified on two grounds—politically, because they had supported Bailo's opponent, Yebirka, and technically, because they neither knew Amharic nor the procedures of northern government.

Finally Bailo, the chief of Bunka, and to a lesser extent many of the other chiefs, began to use the courts to expand their holdings of land in the classic manner of politically powerful Ethiopian landlords. During Yebirka's time, the Bunka chief held only two plots of land. By 1975, he had increased the number to seven. Two of these were given to him (for his political support, presumably) by Bailo in the redivision of Maale land in 1962. Two more, the chief claimed when the Maale owning them died without heirs. On slim evidence, apparently, he convinced the court that his father had owned the two plots of land according to the Maale system of *dini* tenure and that the dead men actually had been his father's tenants. Finally, one additional plot of measured land the chief bought from a northerner. Whether informants exaggerated the purchase price I am not certain, but they reported that the chief paid 3,000 Ethiopian dollars for the last plot.

While the Maale elite was assimilating economically, politically, and culturally to the role of Ethiopian landlords, 1962—the same year that Bailo redivided land in Maale—saw the beginning of another development which was to provide Maale peasants with an organizational focus for political opposition. Four native Wolayta missionaries trained by the Sudan Interior Mission, a fundamentalist Protestant mission supported mainly by North Americans, settled in Maale along with their families. They taught Amharic, which many Maale were eager to learn, and they evangelized. Besides preaching belief in Christ, the missionaries taught hard work, honesty, bettering one's lot, and a certain contempt for traditional ways. Backed by occasional visits from American missionaries in Bako who, the Maale realized, lived at an economic standard higher than any northerner in the area, the prestige of these newcomers was high, and many Maale began to convert to Protestantism.

Inevitably Maale Protestants came into conflict with Bailo and many of the chiefs who, after all, claimed their own special relationship to God. The political focus of Protestant activity, however, quickly went past religious matters to comprehend the economic and political issues related to land ownership. In several of the land cases that developed between Protestants and encroaching landlords, the Protestants were able to win. The network of co-believers that stretched over the entire province of Gamu-Gofa, the resulting ease of traveling to appeal cases to the provincial capital, the ability to use Amharic, and finally in a few cases the direct intervention of American missionaries in court cases—all of these factors contributed to the success of Protestants and helped to galvanize their opposition to rich landlords in Maale. Protestants became a rising economic segment of Maale society, able to hold their own in the court system; many of the new converts began producing more and more for the new markets in Maale, while others entered into part-time trading. Increasingly, Protestants became an economic threat to the Maale *balābbāt* and chiefs, as well as to rich northern landlords.

Suddenly in the summer of 1970, Bailo died. His early death, which opponents naturally tended to see as a sign that he had not been meant to hold his office, reopened the issue of succession. Yebirka was still alive. Bailo's eldest son, an educated young man of about twenty, was also a strong contender. From the point of view of the government, there was no question of who should be *balābbāt*: Bailo's son was called back from school and given authority over Maale, and for the next five years the young man continued the strong rule that his father had begun. The Maale, however, could not agree upon who should be *kati*. For the entire five years, the Bola elders and the chiefs of Makana and

Bola were deadlocked. The Bola elders tacitly supported Yebirka, but afraid of alienating a future king, they did not openly oppose Bailo's son. The Makana chief was a strong supporter of the son. The Bola chief, finally, had taken offence at the young man's strong rule and refused to back either candidate. During the entire time, Bailo was said still to reign as *kati,* and his body lay in a special house in the sacred forest of Dufa. The question of the succession which had previously seemed so important quickly became irrelevant as the revolution reached Maale in 1975: the kingship was abolished. Private ownership of land was ended. And rural cooperative societies were organized to take over local governmental functions.

To summarize then, there were three major political segments in Maale politics at the beginning of my fieldwork in 1974: (1) traditionalists—most notably the Bola elders—who tended to support Yebirka's claim to the kingship, who had little orientation toward or expertise in government affairs, and who chafed under the exploitations of northern landlords but viewed the similar exactions of the Maale king and chiefs as legitimate, (2) rich landlords—northerners, many of the Maale chiefs, and the Maale king—most of whom were adept at dealing with government courts and most of whom supported Bailo and his son for the Maale kingship rather than Yebirka, and (3) Maale Protestants who were opposed to the existence of kingship, whether occupied by Yebirka or Bailo's son, and opposed to the encroachments of rich landlords, whether by northerners or by the Maale elite.

Plate 2.   Bola on Market Day

3

Domestic Groups and Work

To continue the progression made so far from Ethiopia to the southwest to Maale, I want to narrow my field of vision a step further now to focus on one locality—Bola. As long as the Maale can remember, the political center of Maale has been Bola. Bola is the name of both a chiefdom and, more specifically, a hamlet. It was Bola hamlet located in the highlands at the approximate midpoint of Maale territory that was the traditional residence of Maale kings. Whenever outlying Maale went to Bola, they always said they "went up" *(odene)*. Often, of course, their journey did involve a climb, but they meant more by the phrase—Bola was the highest point in the Maale political hierarchy.

In 1975 Bola still served as the political center of Maale; the Maale *bālābbāt* continued to live and to hold court there. About twelve years before, the *bālābbāt* had established a weekly market in Bola and encouraged immigrant traders to settle around the new marketplace. Soon Bola market was linked onto the far end of a string of periodic markets that stretched all the way to Jinka, the subprovincial capital (see Map 5). Traveling merchants who sold ready-made clothes, flashlights, aspirin, and razor blades and who bought honey, butter, and skins left Jinka every Sunday, arrived in Bola, the end of the line, on Tuesday, and returned to Jinka every Saturday. In Jinka, wholesale merchants brought their wares from Addis Ababa by plane and truck, and it was to Addis Ababa that planes and trucks carried away coffee and skins. As a part of this regional and national network of markets, Bola increasingly became an economic as well as a political center in Maale.

Because of its placement within the network of towns in southwestern Ethiopia, Bola was the natural endpoint of my first journey into Maale in May 1974. From Addis Ababa, I carried a letter of authorization to the next lower level in the Ethiopian administration, the Governor of Gamu-Gofa Province. From his office, I took a letter to the Governor of Hamar-Bako Subprovince in Jinka. Finally from Jinka, I followed the route of merchants to Bola with an official letter to the Maale *bālābbāt*. For the first four months of fieldwork, I lived in the compound of the *bālābbāt*.

Gradually as I explored neighboring settlements, I chose Bola and two nearby satellite hamlets—Dofo and Kaiyo—for intensive study. Map 6 shows that these three Maale settlements were spread out, straggling collections of households. Dofo and Bola were both relatively large hamlets and Kaiyo, only three households, was sandwiched in-between. Dofo and Kaiyo were inhabited only by Maale, while half of the Bola hamlet was inhabited by *məni,* (low caste potters and tanners), the other half by Maale. Situated in the middle of Bola hamlet and contrasting to it in its tight, agglomerated settlement pattern, the market village was inhabited by non-Maale traders.

This whole area including Maale, immigrant traders, and *məni,* 63 households in all, was a fairly self-contained social unit, at least in terms of everyday life. It was separated from hamlets to the east by a steep escarpment that led down to the drier and hotter Woito plain. To the north, a large sacred forest tabooed for farming separated my study area from its nearest neighboring hamlet, Kuile, about 40 minutes away. And to the south, it was a 30 minute walk through fields, fallow and grazing land to the nearest hamlet, Dajo. Only to the west was there a close neighboring hamlet, Golla, with which Dofo and Kaiyo (and to some extent Bola people) had everyday social contact.

My choice of this locale for intensive study and not another was largely fortuitous. As I said, Bola was the natural endpoint of my initial journey into Maale. Having arrived, I chose to study the community nearest at hand. That Bola and its environs was, in fact, a strategic choice became clear only later. Certainly it was not an average or typical community from which I could generalize about *the* Maale pattern of production. In fact, Bola was unique: it was the major point at which Maale articulated with wider Ethiopia; it was the economic center where Maale and non-Maale met in the weekly market; and it was the political seat of the king, who was both *kati* of the Maale and *bālabbāt* in the Ethiopian administrative hierarchy.

An intensive study of Bola and its surrounding could, I gradually realized, provide a concrete example of how production was organized in one community and, at the same time, show how that community related to the encompassing economic and political structures of Maale, the southwestern region, and Ethiopia. That, at least, is one of the major themes—in Clifford Geertz's words, "to discover what contributions parochial understandings can make to comprehensive ones"—that I attempt to present and elaborate in following chapters.

To understand the organization of production in the locale of Bola requires, beforehand, a brief examination of the swidden cycle and the annual horticultural cycle. There are two types of fields cultivated in Bola, *le* and *silo,* which are related to the two rainy seasons, the heavy rains of March-June and the lighter rains of September-October. The first kind of field, *le* ("yearly"), is the more important. Usually chosen from bottom lands with heavy soils, *le*

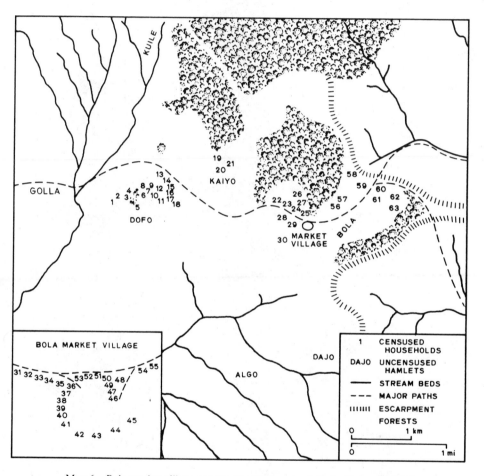

KUILE

GOLLA

KAIYO

19 21
20

13
14
8 9 12 15
4 6 10 16
1 2 3 7 11 17 18
5

DOFO

26
22 27
23 24
28 25
29
30 MARKET
VILLAGE

58
59 60
57 61 62
56 63

BOLA

BOLA MARKET VILLAGE

31 32 33 34 35 36 53 52 51 50 48 54 55
49
37 47
38 46
39
40
41 45
42 43 44

DAJO

ALGO

1	CENSUSED HOUSEHOLDS
DAJO	UNCENSUSED HAMLETS
——	STREAM BEDS
− − −	MAJOR PATHS
ⅢⅢⅢ	ESCARPMENT FORESTS

0   1 km
0   1 mi

Map 6. Bola market village and the Maale hamlets of Dofo, Kaiyo, and Bola

Plate 3. A Newly Burned *Le* Field

fields are planted mostly in sorghum and maize each March for three or four consecutive years. Then they are left in fallow for about twenty years. The second kind of field, *silo,* offers a number of contrasts; *silo* fields are usually cleared on hill-sides or on other places with light covering vegetation and with light soils. Also, *silo* fields are planted first in September, usually with *t'eff* (a very small Ethiopian grain), and then only once again during the following March, usually with finger millet. Though I do not have detailed information on the period of *silo* fallow, it appears to be shorter than for *le* fields.

The various tasks for these two kinds of fields combine to produce the annual horticultural cycle shown in Figure 3. Broadly, there are two seasons whose contrast dominates the ecological and social rhythm of the year. From mid-November to the first of March, there is hardly any rain. Deciduous trees begin to shed their leaves, the landscape grows paler and drier, and midday temperatures rise to about 90° F. Since granaries are usually well stocked at this time and since there is relatively little work to be done, the dry season is the social high point of the year. Adults are often preoccupied with sponsoring rituals with their accompanying beer drinks or attending marriage feasts or just visiting. At night, children and young people gather to dance and to play flutes.

The merriment and relative leisure of the dry season come to an abrupt end with the arrival of the rains. After the first showers that begin to settle dusty paths, the rainy season begins in earnest in early March. In 1975 during both March and April, Bola vicinity received about eight inches of rain. With the rains, cooler weather arrives, maximum temperatures fall to about 80° F, and the landscape slowly turns from gold to green. The cultivation, planting, and weeding of *le* fields which has to be accomplished from the first of March to the first of June is the most intense time of work in Bola. During that time, a visitor will not find Maale in their homes, much less at ritual congregations or at night dances. During weeding time, especially, it seems that almost everyone is in the fields.

These are the two extremes of the year. As Figure 3 shows, the intervening period has its own tasks, but these are not as demanding as those of the heavy rainy season nor as leisurely as those of the dry season. In early June, there is a brief respite after *le* fields have been weeded and before *silo* fields have to be cleared. July and August are relatively cool and dry months, and by September, the beginning of the light rains, *silo* fields have to be ready for planting. It is within these yearly rhythms, these time constraints and sequences, that horticultural production in Bola is socially organized and carried out.

Since Maale households working alone carried out about half of all their horticultural labor, household organization seems the appropriate place to begin a study of production in Dofo, Kaiyo, and Bola.[1] In this chapter then, I will consider the major social, economic, and political forces that shaped

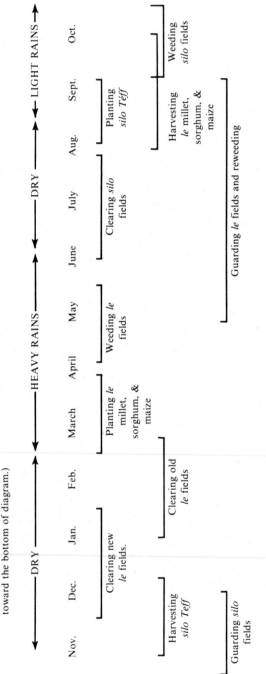

Figure 3. The annual horticultural cycle in Bola (Note: Tasks which are relatively less time-consuming or less intensive are listed progressively toward the bottom of diagram.)

households as units of production and that affected household labor supply. Marriage and the constitution of new households, inheritance and the developmental cycle, and descent groups and their pattern of segmentation— all of these influenced the labor supplies of households, and each is considered in succeeding sections of this chapter, first for Maale inhabitants of Bola vicinity, then for immigrant market villagers, and finally for low-cast *mani*.

Maale Household Organization

Marriage was the fundamental social relationship on which Maale households were constituted. Without a wife, a young man could not found his own household; he had to remain a member of his father's house under the formal authority of the latter. Marriage was the first step in the process by which young men began to control their own labor (and that of wives and children) and to assume more independence and political influence.

A boy could not court or marry a girl of his own clan *(tooki)*. In addition, each Maale clan was linked to one or more other clans, helpers in ritual matters *(geta)*, that were also prohibited. A young man could marry into his mother's clan provided that no recognized bond of kinship linked his bride with his mother. Given these prohibitions, a young man usually had to marry outside his own hamlet, and in a different direction from that his father married in. Even so, young men generally married girls from hamlets not far from their own.

Most marriages grew out of the Maale system of courtship, *lali gocane,* "pulling out a girl." (The phrase comes from the fact that young men courted at night after adults had retired, by stealthily pulling their girlfriends out of their parents' houses by the hand.) But courting and marrying were never simply the choices of the young people involved. Marriages linked families as well as individuals, and the families of the boy and girl exerted influence, sometimes in decisive ways, over whom their children married. While mothers often used persuasion (one girl, for instance, told me that she had stopped courting a young man because her mother had forbade it), fathers and brothers sometimes used physical force to prevent a girl from marrying someone they disliked. When one of the daughters of the Bola chief married a man of whom the chief disapproved, the girl's brothers beat her and forced her to return home. And to prevent her from going back to the man, the chief "gave" the girl to a man of his own choosing who lived far away, a rather wealthy man.

A young man's family was much less likely to disapprove of his choice, for as wife-takers, they were structured inferiors to the girl's family. From their point of view, simply to marry finally outweighed other considerations. After all, any wife, whoever she might be, would work in their house and fields (at least for the first year or so), and would bear grandchildren. When I asked what qualities a wife should have, Maale said that, before everything else, she should be a hard worker.

A young man's family was more likely to intervene in another way—to help him use force to marry a girl against her will. Instead of, as the Maale say, "preparing by pulling out," *goci gigene,* a young man with his kinsmen sometimes took a girl "by force," *miri ekene.* These marriages, when the girl was not retrieved by her kin, were less likely to endure. In Bola, young men who married by force often enlisted the help of the *bālābbāt.* One particularly unhappy case that occurred during my fieldwork illustrates the local politics of marrying and how girls' fathers and the Maale *bālābbāt* sometimes became involved in these issues.

In November of 1975, Duno, a young man from Dofo, was courting a girl named Kababo who lived close to the market in Bola. They decided to marry and, as the Maale put it, "broke the day." Somehow Kababo's father heard about her plans (whether from the girl's mother or from someone else, I do not know). He became extremely angry and, as others told the story, tied up his daughter, beat her, and forbade her to see Duno again. The beating apparently only made Kababo more determined than ever, and secretly she saw Duno. Again, her father heard about it. This time, in desperation, he sent Kababo to live with his sister in a hamlet four hours away. Duno followed her there, and when she went alone to carry water to her aunt's house, Duno met her and the two of them went into hiding. As the Maale say, *iyata kaize gelene,* "they went into the forest." Kababo's father and his kinsmen combed the countryside looking for the couple, going even to Marta, the country to the east of Maale. One day I happened to meet Duno's mother and, not expecting an answer, I asked her where Duno was. She smiled and said, "Duno will show up when Tinke [the *bālābbāt*] gets back home . . . He and Kababo won't be found until then." Duno, more than any other of the young men in Dofo and Bola, had served Tinke by accompanying him on his trips, carrying his gun, and looking after his mule. Duno's mother expected Tinke to come to her son's help.

While the couple were in hiding, Duno's father went to Kababo's father to try to persuade him to accept the marriage. A mild and almost timid man in any situation, Duno's father pleaded with the girl's father to drop his opposition. The latter refused—refused even to speak one word in reply. When Duno's father told me about his attempt later, he said that Kababo's father just wanted a marriage gift, that he was acting this way to force them to give much money. Other people (reliable informants), however, told me that Kababo's father was convinced that Duno's family were sorcerers. (The Maale say that when someone marries a sorcerer, his or her children will die one after another until the innocent partner gives in and is initiated as a sorcerer also. Then the children will live, all of them growing up to be sorcerers.) Whether for this reason or some other, Kababo's father was adamantly opposed to his daughter's marriage to Duno.

Had Kababo's family been more powerful than Duno's (like the Bola chief who prevented his daughter from marrying whom she liked), they probably would have been successful in prohibiting the marriage. As it was, the two families were about equal in local status and influence, and Duno was able to tip the scale in his favor by enlisting the support of the *balābbāt*, whom he had served repeatedly in the past. When Tinke, the *balābbāt*, returned home, just as Duno's mother had foretold, the young couple came out of hiding and took up residence in the compound of the *balābbāt*. They lived there until passions had died down somewhat and then moved in with Duno's family in Dofo.

Duno's successful marriage to Kababo was finally the result of a complex set of local political factors. The principal economic consequence of the outcome, I would stress, was the potential foundation of a new household and a new labor unit. By marrying, Duno set in motion his exit from his father's household and, simultaneously, his assumption of a measure of control over the fruits of his and Kababo's labor. Kababo's status, in turn, changed from that of "daughter" to "wife." While still a dependent in a male-headed household, she had perhaps more voice *vis-à-vis* her new husband than previously with her father.

Besides threading their way through local politics as Duno did, Maale young men faced other obstacles in marrying. The most burdensome of these was the presentation of gifts and the sponsorship of a feast for their bride's relatives. Gifts were given, in different instances, to a variable range of the bride's kin but mostly to her female relatives. When asked who should receive gifts, Maale almost always replied, "the bride's mother and her *misho*" (*misho* is a term that covers several generations of relatives: elder sister, father's sister, father's father's sister...) And in practice, whoever else received gifts, the bride's mother, her elder sisters, and father's sisters were always included. By way of explanation, the Maale said that it was these women who had cared for and raised the bride, who had had their clothes spoiled when the girl, as a baby, had urinated on them. To this core of women who always received gifts, the bride's father's brother's wives were sometimes added. And much less frequently, mother's sisters were also included.

For the bride's father to accept a wedding gift was once taboo *(ketse)* according to some Maale men. They contrasted themselves with Bako men, their neighbors to the west, who demanded a number of cattle in bridewealth when their daughters married. (Maale used the word, *wa'dissi*, for the Bako custom of bridewealth.) With an unmistakable air of superiority, Maale men said, "We don't sell our daughters." Even so, in about half of the marriages in Dofo, Kaiyo, and Bola, the bride's father had received a gift (which, however, was never described as *wa'dissi*); and occasionally the bride's father's brothers were also included. During the past twenty years, a few men—especially rich men, chiefs and their brothers, the *balābbāt* and his brothers—had begun to

Plate 4. A Marriageable Maale Girl Pouring Water

demand large gifts. Such gifts, as much as one hundred Ethiopian dollars, were patterned after the custom of northern landlords living in Maale and called *c'ilosh* in Maale (from Amharic, *c'ilosh*), never *wa'dissi*.

The case of Wege, a young man who married in about 1963, serves as a concrete illustration of the range of bride's relatives who received marriage gifts:

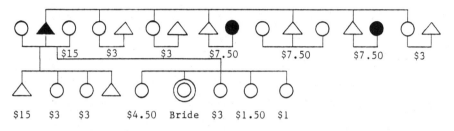

In total, Wege gave $77.50 in cash (Ethiopian dollars) to his wife's relatives. By the standards of other young men's marriages, the amount of Wege's gifts was high and reflected, in part, the fact that his wife had so many close relatives. Table 1 shows the marriage gifts of all young men residing in Dofo, Kaiyo, and Bola who had married between 1960 and 1975. The average amount of total gifts that these young men gave to their wives' relatives was $55.

Besides gifts, there was also the expense of the wedding feast. Since most young men had few resources of their own, they had to depend on help from kinsmen and neighbors for all of these outlays. By the age of about twenty (the approximate age at marriage for most males), young men often had their "own" fields, sometimes with separate granaries. But most of the produce of unmarried young men's fields went toward feeding their natal families, and if a portion was sold or traded, their fathers could ask for part or even all of the receipts. There was no wage labor in Maale nor any enterprise nearby that drew migrant laborers, so that this source of cash did not exist for young men. Trading was about the only way a young man could make money; through buying honey or butter in the Bola market and selling it for a profit in Boshkoro or Ashekere markets (see Map 5), a young man could accumulate a nest egg, but this rarely amounted to more than about fifteen or twenty dollars by the time of marriage.

For the rest, a young man depended first of all on his father or, if his father were dead, on his eldest brother. Typically, the father's help amounted to about fifty or sixty dollars. Several times during my fieldwork, fathers of prospective bridegrooms sold or traded an ox or a sterile cow in preparation for the marriage. Second, a young man's older brothers, sister's husbands, father's brothers, and father's brother's sons often helped with lesser amounts of cash varying from about three to fourteen dollars each. Third, the young man's maternal relatives (who, of course, usually lived in another hamlet) and his

Table 1.   Marriage Gifts Given by Maale Men in Dofo, Kaiyo, and Bola
to the Relatives of Previously Unmarried Girls

Estimated Years of Marriage	Gifts to: Father	Gifts to: Mother and Others	Total
1960	90[a]	70	160
1960	50[b]	15	65
1962	0	30	30
1962	0	15	15[c]
1962	0	10.50	10.50[c]
1962	7.50	16.50	24
1963	15	62.50	77.50
1964	5	38	43
1964	0	52.50	52.50
1964	0	75	75
1965	0	39	39
1965	12.50	42	54.50
1966	10.50	11[d]	21.50
1967	0	82	82
1967	45[a]	5	50
1969	50[b]	18	68
1970	10	27	37
1975	0	59	59

a. These were daughters of the chief of Makana's brother, a very influential man.

b. Both of these girls were orphans. Gifts were given to the male household head who raised them.

c. In both of these cases, gifts were given only to the bride's mother so that the totals were unusually low. It is possible that the women had been married before and did not report it in interviews.

d. In this case, the mother of the bride refused to accept a gift because, as she said, she "liked the groom."

unrelated neighbors contributed in small amounts varying from fifty cents to about three dollars each.

The case of Kolo, a young man in Dofo who married in 1975, illustrates the total costs of marrying and the range of kin and others on whom a young man depended for help. To prepare for the wedding feast, Kolo's father bought six dollars of butter from the market and traded a young ox for a very large gourd of honey worth approximately $60. Not counting the grain that he expended for bread and for thirteen gourds of beer, Kolo's father's outlay was about $66.

In making the cash gifts to his wife's relatives, $57 in all, Kolo obtained help from six of his close kin (elder brothers, sisters' husbands, and father's brothers) totaling $32. Four maternal kin and twenty-four unrelated neighbors in Dofo, Kaiyo, and Bola hamlets together contributed $25. None of the costs of the marriage, as far as I know, were met by money that belonged unambiguously to Kolo alone. The total cost, $123, was borne by others.

Kolo's case was not atypical. In general, a young man depended on a rather large group of neighbors and distant kin to help with small contributions. He depended on a much smaller group of close kin (above all on his father or eldest brother) for larger contributions.

Young men's need for assistance in meeting the costs of marrying contributed to the unequal relationship between elders and juniors in Maale. Many of the kinsmen and neighbors who were in a position to contribute to a young man's marriage fund were elders; and, of course, the principal contributor was the young man's own father. To be able to tap those sources of support, a prospective bridegroom could not afford to alienate his elders. Within bounds, fathers were able to defer the marriages of their sons (and therefore postpone the departure of their son's labor from their own households). Of course, a father could not properly delay too long or refuse to help his son without good reason; such a father would have met with strong disapproval in Maale. On the other side of the relationship, if he traded long enough, an obstinate son could perhaps have accumulated by himself the funds needed to marry (although I know of no such case), or he could have married a divorcee (for whom marriage gifts would not have to be given). Within those limits, elders did influence the timing of their son's marriages and the consequent founding of new units of production.

During the past five decades, the dependence of young men on their elders for help in marrying appears to have increased. Elders maintained that the practice of presenting cash gifts to bride's relatives began in about 1920. Before, wedding feasts and perhaps a gift of cloth to the bride's mother were the only drain on resources. In about 1920, the king's proud and headstrong eldest son, Girpe, married and, for the first time, presented cash gifts to his wife's female relatives. From that time onward, brides' relatives had begun to expect and to demand more and more such gifts. In the first marriages of Maale men and women living in Dofo, Kaiyo, and Bola that took place from 1920 to 1940, the average value of gifts equaled $9; from 1940 to 1960, the average rose to $40; and, as I have pointed out, from 1960 to 1975, the average rose still further to $55. This increase in marriage gifts reflected the cumulative absorption and integration of Maale into the money economy of Ethiopia, and one consequence of that process was the growing economic dependence of young men for assistance in marrying.

As I have pointed out, marriage was the potential first step in the founding of new households. Not all sons, however, established new households following their marriages. Eldest sons (who, as we shall see, inherited most of their fathers' property) were expected to continue to live and to cultivate with their parents—as the Maale said, "to feed their mother and father." Younger sons, after they had married (and usually only after their first child had been born), moved out of their fathers' households and established independent households nearby with their own fields and granaries. These arrangements produced a characteristic pattern of household development. As Table 2 shows, over the developmental cycle, the extent of domestic labor supply (the number of adults) varied rather widely in relation to consumption requirements (those of adults plus children). A household's stage of development was, therefore, an important index for how it entered into the production process.[2]

Households in the first stage of Table 2, typically those of younger sons who had recently married, had small adult labor forces but also small consumption requirements since few children had yet been born. With few children, the bond of marriage on which the household depended was most brittle. Half jokingly, one elder commented, "Young wives are a man's enemy in Maale. If you give them too much, they will run off with another man. But a woman who has borne many children is a man's relative. She can be trusted."

Households in the second stage of development comprised those of younger sons who had simply grown older and those of eldest sons whose father (and sometimes mother) had died. The typical household in this category had the same number of adult workers as those in the first stage but significantly more children to feed. Therefore, the supply of household labor relative to consumption needs was considerably lower. With several children born, the marriages of couples in this second group had more or less stabilized as they moved into middle-age.

The final stage of development was that of elders presiding over extended households composed of their wives, unmarried daughters and younger sons, married eldest son, and the latter's wife and children. In that culminating phase, there were a great many adult workers in relation to the number of mouths that had to be fed. Relative labor supply was at a peak. Besides being an economic climax, the third stage of development—the so-called "stem" family household—was a cultural ideal as well. The elders who headed such households and their wives became known not by their own names but by the more respectful phrases, "father of X," or "mother of X," X being the name of their eldest child (whether son or daughter). As I said, the eldest son lived with his parents in order to "feed" them as they grew older and weaker. Even after his parents died, the eldest son continued to "feed" his parents at yearly first fruits rituals. And when the eldest son died, his eldest son would continue the line and the ritual feeding. It was as if every eldest son's household was permanently extended to include the line of past ancestors.

In European peasant societies such as that of eighteenth-century Austria analyzed by Berkner (1972), the development of stem families was directly

Table 2. Composition of Maale Households by Age of Head, Dofo, Kaiyo, and Bola, 1975

Households Headed by Persons Less than 30 Years Old		Households Headed by Persons From 30 to 45 Years Old		Households Headed by Persons Older than 45	
Adults	Children	Adults	Children	Adults	Children
2	2	1[a]	0	1[a]	0
2	2	1[a]	2	2[a]	0
4	2	2	3	2[a]	0
		2	4	2	2
		2	4	3	5
		2	4	4	1
		2	5	5	4
		2	5	6	3
		2	5	6	4
		2	5	6	5
		3	2	7	3
		3	5		
		4	4		
Median 2	2	**Median** 2	4	**Median** 4	3

a. Households headed by women.

related to a system of inheritance in which only one son inherited his father's land while other children received money or valuables. In Maale, the way households fit into the larger political economy was entirely different, but the pattern of inheritance does seem to have conditioned the domestic cycle that I have just described. There were several ways in which property could be divided in Maale, but in all of them, the eldest son—who continued to live subordinate to his father even after his younger brothers had their own households—received, by far, the largest share.

Occasionally, some Maale elders, before they died, distributed their property themselves. In that case, the eldest son was always given his father's house and granaries as well as the majority of cattle. Iroka, an elderly man with two sons who lived in Kaiyo, provides an example. Before he died in 1974, he had given four of his five mature cows to his eldest son (who slaughtered two of them at his father's funeral) and only one to his younger son.

At other times, old men chose to divide their property only on their death bed. An elder's spoken "will" *(ilkəmi)* became binding upon the eldest son, who then divided the property according to his father's wishes. In Argile, a community south of Bola where cattle were relatively more numerous, an elder gave his will while I was visiting there. A few days later, the old man died leaving four sons. To one, the youngest (about eighteen years old), he left nothing. Two other younger brothers received three and six cattle respectively. By contrast, the eldest was left with his father's house and granaries and twelve cattle, of which two were killed at the funeral.

Finally, a few men made no disposition of their property at all before they died, and their eldest son divided the family estate. In that case, I asked one of my Dofo informants, how many cattle an elder brother would give to the younger if the herd totalled about fifty. An eldest son himself, he replied that if the two were on good terms, the older brother might give his younger brother three or four. When I asked if he would not give more, the old man replied, "Oh no, if the two of them had argued, then the younger brother might get only one cow."

The fact that eldest brothers stood to inherit the bulk of their fathers' property did much, I believe, to keep them in their fathers' households. Evidently, the position of eldest son was a difficult and ambiguous one. While he was clearly higher in status than his younger brothers, an eldest son enjoyed considerably less independence while his father was alive. Within extended households, fathers still directed the activities (including labor) of the whole unit. The chief difficulty with the extended household, according to the Maale, was that the eldest son's wife might not get along with her mother-in-law. If quarrels between the two women got out of hand, the eldest son might have to move his conjugal group out of his father's household temporarily.

In Dofo, there was one case in which just this had happened. Several Dofo men and women told me how the eldest son's wife and his mother had argued from morning to night, day after day. Finally, they said, the young man had to move out of his father's household. That was in 1965, and ten years later during my fieldwork, he still lived apart from his father. When all of the father's younger sons had married and established their own households, the eldest son and his wife (mellowed by then it was hoped) would move back into the father's household.

As the Maale (especially the men) saw it, women were to blame for occasionally breaking up the ideal stem family household. There is some merit in this stereotypical view. As an outsider in a patrilineal virilocal system, a young bride was virtually thrown into conflict with her mother-in-law. The mother-in-law supervised the new daughter-in-law's work, directed her to draw water, to grind, and to cook. Thrust into this new environment, many young wives of eldest sons probably did wish for their own households. Out from under the thumb of their mothers-in-law, young wives could run their own households.

But of course the same was true of eldest sons. In separate households, they would have much greater independence; moreover, there were few aspects of the production system that tied eldest sons (or other sons for that matter) to their fathers' households—land was available to be cultivated and new conjugal units, at least in their early stages of development, had adequate labor supplies of their own.

The key to the system was that eldest sons, if they alienated their fathers, stood to lose their lion's share of inheritance. Because their fathers had recently helped them to marry and in the future would decide how many cattle they would inherit, eldest sons were under the economic power of their fathers to considerable degree. The moral emphasis on the relationship between fathers and sons tended to suppress open conflict, but the weight of moral injunctions fell more lightly on young wives. And in the first few years of marriage when divorces were most frequent, young wives perhaps paid less attention to their husbands' inheritance prospects than they would later.

In this context, an unruly wife may actually have been convenient for an eldest son. Once outside his father's household (because of his wife, not because of his own immoral behavior) an eldest son enjoyed both a measure of independence and long-term inheritance prospects. This outlet was closed when all of his younger brothers had married and had founded their own households. Then, on pain of giving up his majority share of the inheritance, the eldest son had to take his place in the ancestral homestead "to feed his mother and father."

While conflicts such as these caused deviations from the developmental cycle described above, in aggregate the pattern of Table 2 is clear: Maale elders' households in Dofo, Kaiyo, and Bola tended to be labor-rich while middle-aged mens' were labor-poor. Neither relatively rich nor poor, young mens' households stood in the middle of the labor continuum.

So far, I have simplified somewhat the relationship between Maale brothers. Even after a younger brother had established his own household and come into his inheritance at the death of his father, he still continued under the authority of his eldest brother in certain respects. A set of brothers formed a minimal lineage segment, and the eldest brother served as the head or "first" *(toidi)*. Only *toidi* could act as ritual intermediaries between members of the minimal lineage and their ancestors. When for instance, a cow that belonged to any of the brothers had a calf, no one could drink the new milk until the *toidi* had ritually offered the milk to the ancestors. The same held for new crops. No one could begin to eat new grain until his *toidi* had fed the ancestors. The dependence of younger brothers in these matters continued until the minimal descent group formally segmented, and each brother became a *toidi* of a new minimal descent group. With each new minimal descent group went the founding of a new line that would, it was hoped, be perpetuated through succeeding generations by eldest son after eldest son.

The status and ritual preeminence that *toidi* enjoyed had important economic consequences. Some *toidi,* for instance, used their positions to increase their cattle herds at the expense of younger brothers. Many of my Protestant informants told me that some *toidi* actually declared that the ritual offering of new milk had not been done properly and that consequently the cow had become unusable *(iitene)* for a younger brother. The *toidi* then would appropriate the cow for his own use. This, for the Maale Protestants, was one of the most galling injustices of the Maale social system. One old Protestant man, a younger brother who had inherited very little but who had worked hard and gradually built up his herd by trading grain for cattle, told me how his *toidi* had taken several of his cattle. This conflict between *toidi* and junior minimal lineage mates provided the impetus for many younger brothers in Maale to convert to Protestantism. As Protestants, younger sons escaped the ritual authority of their eldest brothers.

While Protestants may have exaggerated the deviousness and ritual abuse of *toidi,* non-Protestant Maale did not deny the exploitation implicit in the traditional arrangement. When asked, younger brothers tended to smile resignedly and say something to the effect, "that's the way things are." Indeed, traditional Maale appeared to recognize that the relationship between elder and junior brothers was a persistent source of conflict, for many of the mythical stories about the origin of present-day lineages involved some mention of a fight between an eldest son and his younger brothers.

Minimal lineage heads or *toidi* held power over younger brothers until the descent group segmented, and segmentation occurred through a ritual of expulsion, *kessane* (literally, "making go out"). All of the property (cattle, goats, spears, knives, cloth) of the minimal descent group was placed in the cattle corral of the *toidi,* the burial site of lineage ancestors for most Maale clans, and the *toidi* ritually divided the lineage property. According to informants (themselves *toidi*), *toidi* could divide lineage property as they pleased. "If there has been any quarreling between a younger brother and his *toidi,* the *toidi* can take all of the junior's cattle and give him only a stick of wood."

This second division of property, therefore, apparently functioned much as the first one. The power of eldest brothers (like that of fathers) was enforced and upheld by their role in determining the final division of minimal lineage property. In practice, however, the power of eldest brothers to divide lineage property this second time was considerably more circumscribed than that of fathers. First of all, a *toidi* could not take away a cow that had been willed to a younger brother by his father. Second, a *toidi* could not take a cow that had been given to a junior kinsman by an unrelated *belli* friend (*belli* are bond friends, one of whom has given the other a cow in return for goats, honey, or cash; well over half of the cattle of Dofo, Kaiyo, and Bola Maale men were given to their owners by *belli*.) As a result of these proscriptions, many of their younger brothers' cattle were beyond the legitimate grasp of *toidi*.

Exactly when the minimal lineage segmented was a negotiated matter. Apparently some *toidi* were loath to agree to division; at the same time, Maale said that it was unfortunate if a younger brother died before founding his own line. In fact, custom varied from clan to clan. Most Maale minimal lineages divided as sibling sets reached elderhood, but among others it was the custom to wait until after the eldest brother had died. Then the eldest brother's eldest son (who became *toidi* of his father's younger brothers) carried out the ritual of expulsion, and the descent group formally segmented. Each of the original younger brothers—now in their old age—became *toidi* of a new minimal descent group, consisting of their children.

After the ritual of expulsion had divided an old minimal lineage into several new minimal lineage segments, each new segment and its *toidi* was economically and ritually independent in crucial respects: each new *toidi* controlled his own cattle and made his own sacrifices to ancestors. Still the unity of related minimal lineages that continued to live close to one another, what I will call simply the "lineage," was recognized and maintained. Men from related minimal lineages looked on each other as close kin and would, for instance, help a young man from their group with moderately large amounts of money when he married. In general, a household with many lineage mates in the vicinity was in a stronger economic and political position than one without.

Within the lineage (what has also been called a "conical" clan), there was a hierarchy of status associated with how close each member was to the primary line of eldest sons of eldest sons. Every member was either senior or junior to every other member. The pattern of lineage seniority was preserved in Maale memory in at least two ways. One involved the Maale kinship terminology for lineage mates, which is illustrated below:

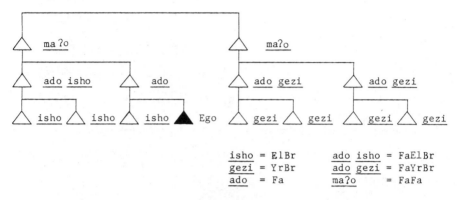

isho = ElBr	ado isho = FaElBr
gezi = YrBr	ado gezi = FaYrBr
ado = Fa	ma?o = FaFa

The other way in which the hierarchy of lineage status was expressed was through the prescribed order in which minimal lineage heads yearly offered first fruits to their ancestors. In making the offering, each *toidi* had to wait until his *toidi* (the head of the next most inclusive lineage segment) had completed the ritual. Therefore, the main lineage head—the eldest son of the eldest son, etc.—made the first offering, and he was followed then by successively more junior heads. A lineage from Dofo and Bola offers a concrete illustration:

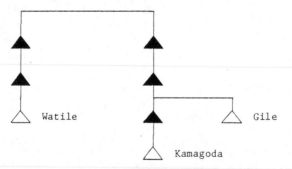

In making his offering to the ancestors, Gile had to wait until Kamogoda had completed the ritual, and Kamogoda had to wait in turn until Watile, the main lineage head, had made his offering. No one could eat new crops until his *toidi* had made the required offering to the ancestors.

In the long run, whether or not a lineage managed to stay intact and ramify seems to have depended mainly upon the wealth of *toidi*. In all of the cases of large, coresident lineages for which I have data, the main *toidi* were rich and influential men, either chiefs or "big men" who owned many cattle and who, after the early 1950s, possessed *rest* land. The wealth of *toidi* affected lineage size in at least two ways. First, rich men tended to marry more wives and to have more children. One rich and influential chief in 1975 had eight wives and thirty living children. Second, younger sons of wealthy fathers, even though they inherited little of their fathers' wealth, still had access to help and to political influence through their eldest brothers. Apparently, moving to another area was less attractive for them than for younger sons of less wealthy fathers.

In Dofo, Kaiyo, and Bola the level of wealth was relatively constant. There were no big men who outshone all others, and lineages were small, comprising no more than three minimal segments. Consistent with all of these facts, outmigration was fairly common: four of the seven lineages had members (mostly younger brothers) living in other communities. The principal explanation for this homogeneity in wealth is, I think, the history of direct domination of local economics and politics by the king. After the Italian period, the king had come to own all of the land surrounding Dofo, Kaiyo, and Bola. Within that local system, the king's clout was apparently sufficient to prevent the rise of any elders to the status of big men, and consequently lineages did not ramify into large groups.

The foregoing description of lineage structure and ancestor worship is only a sketch; my purpose is not to analyze those topics in themselves but to illustrate briefly the principal ties that linked households into more inclusive social units. Maale households were not so many "potatoes in a sack." A household with many descent mates living nearby occupied a position in the local political economy different from that of neighboring households without agnates. How, for example, this difference shows in cooperative labor arrangements will become clear in Chapter 4.

Market Village Household Organization

Located in the middle of the Maale hamlet of Bola, the market village, also called Bola, was established in about 1964. Since it had been so recently established and was inhabited mainly by non-Maale Muslim and Orthodox Christian traders (25 households in all), my first impression was that the market village could be ignored in a study of Maale production.

As my research proceeded, however, it became clear that Bola traders, while not exclusively dependent on horticulture like the Maale, had increasingly taken up cultivation during the past few years. In 1975, most traders planted substantial fields, though still smaller ones than Maale, and many had entered into traditional Maale cooperative work arrangements, oftentimes with Maale households. Eventually I saw that the market village and the Maale hamlets surrounding it were constituent parts of a single social system. And in the end I realized that certain aspects of "Maale" production could be understood only with reference to the market village.

These issues will be taken up and analyzed in the following chapter. Here I want to lay the groundwork for that discussion by describing household organization among market villagers. In many instances it will be useful to proceed by presenting contrasts to the Maale pattern discussed above. Perhaps the most striking contrast was household size: the average in the market village was 2.7 people, while that in the surrounding Maale communities was 6.8. Most of this difference resulted from the fact that there were far fewer children in market households—an average of 0.8 compared to 3.7 for Maale. A second contrast was the higher percentage of households in the market village headed by women, 26 percent, as against 14 percent for the surrounding Maale. Some of the reasons for these differences will become clear in the following description of how market village households formed, developed, and reproduced.

Young men from Bola market looked for wives, not among the neighboring Maale, but mainly in other market towns nearby and in the Muslim settlements in northwest Maale. These were the places, after all, to which they were drawn by trading. When they married, young men presented marriage gifts called *c'ilosh* (in Amharic) to the girl's family. Ordinarily gifts were given to three people: to the bride herself (unheard of among the Maale), and to the bride's mother and father. Only the bride's nuclear family received gifts; more distant relatives, as among the Maale, were not included. Gifts usually totaled about forty Ethiopian dollars and appear not to have changed much in magnitude over the past fifty years (see Table 3). Considering the fact that the groom did not have to sponsor an expensive wedding feast, the costs of marrying were lower for market villagers than for Maale.

In making these outlays, young men from the market tapped kinsmen for support, but the range of groom's relatives who helped with the payments (like the range of bride's relatives who received gifts) was limited. First of all, young men depended upon themselves and their own profits from trading. By the time of their first marriages, most young men had been involved in trade for many years, first by helping their fathers and then gradually on their own. Second, young men called on their fathers and brothers for help. More distant relatives were not involved. Since young traders were less dependent in marrying than young Maale and dependent on fewer of their elders, marriage arrangements appear to have had considerably less effect in establishing inequalities among traders than among Maale.

At the time of marriage, young men from trading families established their own households. Eldest sons did not remain in their fathers' households. As might be expected, eldest sons were not favored in inheritance. Brothers, as far

Table 3. Marriage Gifts to Previously Unmarried Brides and Their
Parents in the Marriages of Men and Women Living
in Bola Market Village

Estimated Year of Marriage	Total Amount in Ethiopian Dollars Given to Bride and Her Parents
1926	0[a]
1926	48 (calf + $30)
1944	32 (cloth + dress + $12)
1945	0[a]
1948	40
1948	50
1950	0[b]
1953	0[b]
1954	0[b]
1956	70
1958	50
1962	100[c]
1963	30
1964	45
1968	30
1969	30
1969	20
1970	30
1970	25
1970	40
1973	30
1974	15
1975	50

a. These women may have been married before and not reported it in my census.

b. All of these women were Maale. The absence of marriage gifts may reflect the weakness of social ties between Maale and immigrant traders, even in the context of marriages between the two.

c. This woman married a government soldier whose income made him considerably richer than most other men represented above.

as I could tell, inherited equally. Not only did sons not remain in their fathers' households, they tended to live in separate villages. From the personal histories of the men residing in Bola market, it appears that few had lived for long in their fathers' villages. Sons tended to separate from fathers, and brothers from brothers. And marriage, of course, separated women from their families. Apparently, the exigencies of trade pulled relatives apart. The resulting pattern of dispersal seems to have had a positive value in trading since in their travels about the region, traders could call on relatives for help, information, and hospitality.

Despite centrifugal forces, families or parts of families managed to congregate and recongregate in the same villages. In Bola in 1975 three elderly women lived in independent households close to sons or daughters; and one elderly man lived with his son and son's wife. There were also a number of sibling sets in Bola. Of the 39 adults in Bola for whom I have information, 30 had living siblings. Of these, ten had siblings who lived in Bola. It is noteworthy that these ten cases involved three sets of sisters, one brother-sister set, and only one brother-brother set. The predominance of coresident sisters (a mirror image of the Maale residence pattern where brothers tend to live close to one another) may have been related to the functional value that living apart had for brothers who traded.

But how did sisters, who presumably tended to marry in various directions, manage to congregate with other sisters and brothers? The answer—at least a major part of it—is that divorce was relatively frequent. On divorce, a woman often went to live with a brother or sister. By distilling spirits, a woman could support herself fairly easily (much more easily than a single Maale woman could support herself through cultivation). Enjoying the attentions and gifts of lovers, a divorced woman could choose to remain single for a time. (As I pointed out above, the percentage of households headed by women in the market village of Bola was higher than that among the Maale.) Eventually she was likely to remarry within her new village, thus continuing to live close to her sibling.

The history of one family living in Bola in 1975 illustrates how sisters were separated by marriage and reunited by divorce. The family history began with the father and mother, both Orthodox Christians born in Gofa. They married in Gofa and in about 1944 they moved to Bako, the capital of the subprovince that included Maale at that time. Their move may have been a response to the revival of commerce in the middle 1940s after the Italians were expelled from Ethiopia and after peace had been re-established in the southwest.

The couple had three daughters—Balainesh, Asnaigetch, and Workinesh. In about 1956, the first daughter married an Orthodox Christian man in Debre Tsehai, a market town similar to Bako located not far to the north of it in Argenne. About four years later the second daughter married an Orthodox Christian who lived in Bunati, a strip of very rich land sandwiched between the territories of Maale and Bako. Marriages were beginning to disperse the family, but in about 1962 the first sister divorced her husband (in Debre Tsehai) and went to live with her second sister in Bunati. After several months, she remarried there and the two sisters were reunited. It was not long, however, before the whole family was dispersed again for in 1963 the second sister's marriage broke up, and she left Bunati and remarried in Boshkoro, a newly established police and market town in Maale, about three hours away from Bunati. And in 1964, the third daughter changed her religion and married a Muslim who lived in Samworo (in Goddo chiefdom) in northwest Maale. At that time, the three sisters were scattered among the three most important trading centers of western Maale—Bunati, Boshkoro, and Samworo. Perhaps their father's trading from Bako through Maale may have had some influence on the placement of these women. However that may have been, his influence was not felt for long.

In about 1965, the first daughter divorced her husband in Bunati and left to live independently in Jinka, the newly established town near Bako that had just been made subprovincial capital. (With governmental functions transferred to Jinka, Bako gradually declined to a rather inconsequential weekly market.) In Boshkoro the second daughter divorced and remarried, this time (1966) a Muslim trader. Her old name, Asnaigetch, became Alima. Bola market had been established several years previously and in about 1967 the Muslim trader took the second daughter to live in Bola. Getting older, influenced perhaps by Bako's decline, and attracted by a lower cost of living in Bola, the father and mother moved from Bako to Bola in 1968 and built a home near their second daughter. Within a year, the father died. Not long afterward, the first daughter, who had been living independently in Jinka, came to Bola and married an Orthodox Christian butcher there.

The upshot as of 1975 was that the widowed mother, her first daughter (and Christian husband), and her second daughter (and Muslim husband) all lived in Bola village in 1975. The third and youngest daughter, Workinesh, continued to live in Samworo (also with a Muslim husband), about four hours to the northwest.

These three sisters, all in their thirties in 1975, had experienced a total of four divorces. This figure was fairly representative of market women generally. The histories of 26 adult market women of all ages yielded an average of 1.4 divorces per woman. This was almost four times the divorce rate of Maale women in the three hamlets closest to the market village. There, 32 women of all ages had an average of only .34 divorces per woman.

Of course this apparent difference might reflect nothing more than an age structure that was older for the market women than for their Maale counterparts. In fact, however, market women were on the average younger than their Maale counterparts. The market village itself had been founded in only 1964, and since then, it had attracted mostly younger inhabitants. The proportion of nubile women over 40 years of age was only 27 percent in the market village as against 41 percent among the surrounding Maale. Thus the difference in divorce rate for market women and for Maale may have been more than that indicated by the figures above.

Among the Maale, even if a young woman divorced her first husband, she would then very likely settle into her next husband's household as children were born. Toward middle age, she became closely tied to her husband and his kin both directly and through her children. As an old woman (addressed then not by her own name but as "mother of..." the name of her first child) she held a ,respected position in her hamlet and among her husband's kin. This

Plate 5.   A Prosperous Market Woman Spinning Cotton

progressive attachment to one point in geographic and social space was not characteristic of market women. Freer, less tied down to husbands, more able to support themselves, market women were considerably more mobile, as the story of the three sisters illustrates.

One of the major functions that tied Maale women to their husbands—bearing children—did not operate as strongly among the market women, for they bore significantly fewer children. Of the twenty-seven women in Bola market village who had been married at least once, seven were apparently sterile. All over thirty years of age, none had ever conceived. Four of these were Maale or women from surrounding ethnic groups who probably came to the market village at least in part *because* they were sterile. Unable to fit into the traditional cycle described above, unable to become a "mother," these women found their way to Bola. There they could marry traveling traders who often had wives with children elsewhere, and they could support themselves by distilling spirits.

Three of the seven sterile women were raised in trading families. And it seems quite probable that their sterility was related to an apparently higher incidence of venereal disease in towns and market villages (cf. Olmstead [1975] for a similar pattern in the Gamu highlands, about sixty miles northeast of Maale). Market women who lived independently sometimes saw many lovers and probably had a relatively greater chance of contracting venereal disease. Even market women who were married were probably exposed by their husbands, back from trading trips.

Not only were sterile women relatively numerous in the market village (there were none in the three Maale hamlets I studied) but general measures of fertility were consistently lower. For Maale women past childbearing age (roughly 45 or older), the average number of live births (n = 9) was 9.3. The corresponding figure for market women (n = 5) was 6.0. For women between 28 and 33 years old, the average number of live births for Maale women (n = 12) was 5.2. The corresponding figure for market women (n = 6) was 2.0. Although these various indices are based on very small numbers of cases, they add up to a pattern: market women in Bola bore fewer children than Maale women hiving in the surrounding hamlets. Bearing fewer children, they were less strongly tied to husbands, freer to divorce, and more mobile. All of these differences reflected the fact that marriage among the Bola market villagers did not serve the same economic functions as among Maale cultivators. To the extent that villagers pursued trading, they did not depend on marriage as a crucial means of beginning and expanding their enterprises.

Aspects of the marriage system described above gave the developmental cycle of market households a very different shape. By contrast with the Maale pattern of gradual build-up followed by hiving off of younger sons, market households showed little variation over stages of development. Marriages were ended and begun anew. Fewer children were born. And children were more apt to live apart from their parents. Sometimes they were sent away to school— school being the gateway to greater success and integration into national Ethiopian life. In other cases, children were sent to live with influential or elderly relatives. In general, children, even older children, appear to have been less of an asset in the household economy of traders than among Maale horticulturists.

Table 4 (an analogue of Table 2) shows the relatively constant composition of market households throughout the developmental cycle. By middle age, a few couples had developed fairly stable marriages and had produced three or four children, but these were exceptional. Most households in the middle stage of development had no more children than households in the first stage. As Table 4 shows, the median number of children in households at both stages was one. Household size and composition tended to be relatively constant until the third stage of development. Households whose head was 45 years or older comprised various combinations of kin: Widows lived with unmarried sons or daughters, otherwise they lived alone. Widowers, as long as they were healthy, remarried and lived with their wives. As a result, extended households of married sons living together with parents almost never formed. Elders did not control large pools of labor and, in fact, there was little variation in the labor supplies of households over the whole developmental cycle.

Instead of stage of development, an altogether different set of factors seemed to have conditioned household size and composition in the market village. With few exceptions, Maale households in the three hamlets close to Bola market were fairly uniform with respect to wealth. Each household owned about the same number of cattle (the principal source of wealth) as every other household. In the market village, by contrast, it was fairly obvious that households were differentiated by wealth.

Exact information on market villagers' wealth was, however, difficult to collect. Some refused to answer my questions, while others underreported the number of cattle they owned (cattle were usually the main source of wealth, although some traders had considerable funds tied up in honey or sacks of salt). For households that kept their cattle in Bola, of course, I was able simply to count for myself. And over the course of my fieldwork, various other observations—level of buying and selling in the market, expenditure on clothes, and general style of living—when taken together gave a fairly accurate picture of economic stratification.

The category of poorest households in the market was, in any case, clear. None owned cattle or other animals like donkeys nor did any have appreciable trading capital (that is, less than approximately fifteen Ethiopian dollars). Almost all were headed by young men under thirty years of age or by single women. Women in this category, especially single women with their own

Table 4. Composition of Households by Age of Head, Bola Market Village, 1975

Households Headed by Persons Under 30 Years Old		Households Headed by Persons 30 to 45 Years Old		Households Headed by Persons Over 45 Years Old	
Adults	Children	Adults	Children	Adults	Children
2[a]	0	1[a]	0	1[a]	0
2	1	1[a]	2	1[a]	0
2	1	2	0	1[a]	0
2	1	2	0	2[a]	0
2	2	2	0	2	0
3	0	2	1	3	0
		2	2	3	1
		2	2		
		3	0		
		3[b]	4		
		3[b]	4		
Median 2	1	Median 2	1	Median 2	0

a. Households headed by women.

b. Male household heads with two wives.

Plate 6.　　The Weaver of Bola Market Village

households, were engaged in distilling liquor. The young men cultivated small fields and, to the extent they could, entered trade in small amounts of butter and honey. One man was a weaver.

Middle-level households, all of which were headed by men, were neither as poor as the previous strata nor as rich as the one to be discussed below. All owned between one and three mature cattle, or possessed amounts of trade capital so that their wealth fell into that range of value. Men from these households were the most active traders in the village and since they were often away on trips, cultivation was a distinctly secondary occupation. Two were salt merchants, one a butcher, and one sold razor blades, aspirin, beads, and cheap soap in the market. The standard of living for these households impressed me as about the same as for average Maale; of course they had more access to the money economy, but they were also more dependent on it, since most had to buy a fair proportion of their food grain.

The boundary between the upper part of the middle-level villagers and rich households in Bola was the most difficult one to draw. When a number of criteria were considered, four male-headed households stood out as the richest in the market village. Two of the household heads kept large herds of cattle in the village, composed of about ten mature cows each. The remaining two had large investments in trade, probably more than one hundred Ethiopian dollars; when added to the value of their herds (they probably underreported the number of cattle that they owned), the total wealth of these last two was equivalent to at least four or five cattle. Although all four were engaged in trade (the two Muslims were more active than the two Orthodox Christian households), they were not away from Bola for long periods, and they all cultivated large fields. Wives in this group were generally the only women in the market village who brewed the relatively more expensive (and profitable) honey wine to sell.

Socially, these four richest households formed a distinctive group: Two were the only villagers to have multiple wives. All tended to wear more expensive clothing than their neighbors, and the only radios in the village were to be found in their houses. Finally, it should be noted that three of the four had, at one time or another, served as representatives of the *balabbat* in collecting taxes or settling local court cases.

Table 5 shows the variation in household composition with wealth in Bola village. While there was no relationship between age of head and household composition, Table 5 suggests that level of wealth may have been positively correlated with household size. It is noteworthy that the only two villagers with multiple wives were relatively rich men; furthermore, the only men with more than two children were rich men. It was these men, as I have already pointed out, who cultivated the largest fields in Bola (in addition to trading). The larger adult labor forces of their households contributed to their horticultural

Table 5. Household Composition and Size as Related to the Wealth of Head in Bola Market Village, 1975

Households Headed by Persons of Poor Means		Households Headed by Persons of Modest Means		Households Headed by Persons of Rich Means	
Adults	Children	Adults	Children	Adults	Children
1[a]	0	2	0	2	2
1[a]	0	2	0	3	0
1[a]	0	2	1	3[b]	4
1[a]	0	2	1	3[b]	4
1[a]	2	2	2		
2[a]	0	3	0	Median 3	3
2[a]	0	3	1		
2	0	Median 2	1		
2	1				
2	1				
2	2				
3	0				
Median 2	0				

a. Households headed by women.

b. Male household heads with two wives.

production which, in turn, was required to feed their larger numbers of children.

Given the lower fertility of market villagers (few sibling sets contained two or more brothers) and given their mobility (brothers were likely to live in separate villages), nothing analogous to coresident descent groups formed. Sometimes, as I have pointed out, sisters managed to live in the same village, and less frequently, sisters and brothers lived in the same village. In general, the kinship ties that served to bind households among the Maale into more inclusive social units were far fewer in the market village.

Religious affiliation was perhaps the only social principle that gathered market households into groups somewhat analogous to descent groups in Maale. Orthodox Christians (12 households) tended to live on the higher ground in the northern half of the village, while Muslims (13 households) tended to live in the southern lower half.[3] Ritual proscriptions emphasized the opposition between the two groups: Muslims ate only meat from an animal that had been killed by a Muslim, while Christians ate only that killed by a Christian.

In terms of social origins, the two groups were quite distinct. As noted earlier, almost all of the Muslims in Bola had originated in Jimma, to the northwest of Maale. Genealogies for Bola Muslims and their places of birth went back town by town to the northwest, almost always converging on Jimma. As Table 6 shows, most of the Muslim men and women over 45 in Bola had been born in Gofa (the major trading center between Jimma and Maale) of Jimma fathers and Gofa mothers. Many of the younger generation, people in their twenties, had been born in Maale (in a settlement called Samworo located about four hours northwest of Bola in Goddo chiefdom) of Jimma fathers and Gofa or Maale mothers. Some of the younger generation could speak only Maale and Amharic and had not learned Jimma.

Orthodox Christians in the market village were a far more heterogenous group. Although most Christians identified themselves with Amhara culture, as Table 7 shows, only four of the twenty Christian household heads and their spouses had actually been born in northern Ethiopia or had descended from northern soldiers who occupied the south. At the lowest rung of northerners living in the southwest, these were the people who had been unable to claim and keep southern lands and so had been forced into trading, a low-status occupation in Amhara culture. They lived a life common to other market villagers and to Maale. Some, however, retained the fierce pride of conquerors. One old Amhara woman, born in Shoa, her back straight as a ramrod, refused to answer any of my prying questions. She said simply, as if to answer everything, "I am an Amhara."

"Amharized" southerners, that is, persons of southern parentage who had adopted northern culture, composed by far the largest proportion of Orthodox

Table 6. Birthplaces of Bola Muslims and Their Parents, Illustrating the Trading Diaspora from Jimma

Estimated Age	Place of Birth	Place of Father's Birth	Place of Mother's Birth
67	Gofa	Jimma	Gofa
55	Wolayta	Tigrai	Jimma
50	Gofa	Jimma	Gofa
48	Gofa	Jimma	Gofa
47	Gofa	Jimma	Gofa
45	Maale	Jimma	Gofa
35	Gofa	Gofa	Gofa
32	Zala	Zala	Zala
30	Jimma	Jimma	Jimma
28	Kamba	Jimma	Kamba
25	Maale	Jimma	?
25	Gofa	Gofa	Malo
24	Maale	Jimma	Maale
22	Maale	?	Gofa
21	Maale	Jimma	Maale
20	Maale	Malo	Gofa

Table 7. Ethnic Origins of Orthodox Christian Household Heads and Their Wives in Bola Market Village

Ethnic Origin[a]	Number
Northern Ethiopia	4
Gofa	6
Bashketto	2
Maale	2
Bako	1
Gamu	1
Jimma	1
Malo	1
Marta	1
Zala	1

a. Usually place of birth, but if father was an immigrant, his place of birth.

Christians in Bola. Born in the south, they had adopted Amharic names, the Amharic language, and an Amharic lifestyle. Coming from outside Maale and separated from old kinsmen and neighbors, these people evidently had greater latitude to develop new ways of life, new economic strategies, and new cultural identities. Twelve out of the sixteen "Amharized" adults in Table 7 were women, and almost all of them had been converted when they married a Christian man. Sometimes divorced afterwards, they nevertheless continued to live as Orthodox Christians.

For the few men among this Amharized group, it was difficult to gather information on how they had been uprooted from old lives. I heard stories from the surrounding Maale (not unbiased sources) that one man in the market village had been driven out of his home community for thieving. Another, they said, had been an outlaw. One of the men, finally, had come to Bola to work as a weaver.

While Christians and Muslims did generally represent different social origins and while ritual proscriptions divided them, neither group was particularly solidary and the opposition between them was rather weak. Everyday social intercourse was free and easy. A few Muslim women had even married Christian men, and vice versa; such marriages always involved a change of religion for the woman. Their coreligionists in larger Ethiopian towns (where apparently religious affiliation was more politically salient) would probably have thought Bola Christians and Muslims lax at best.

Thus, neither religion nor kinship was particularly effective in binding market households together. Market households were relatively autonomous economic units, much truer to the image of so many "potatoes in a sack" than were Maale households. Quick to move in order to take advantage of new trading opportunities and possessed of little labor, market households appeared adapted to commerce and trading. Nonetheless, the richest and poorest traders in Bola are engaged in horticulture. The richest cultivated in order not to consume capital invested elsewhere; the poorest because they had no capital.

Household Organization of the *Mani*

To the uninitiated eye, *mani* households appeared little different from those of the Maale. The main structural features of the developmental cycle and of inheritance were broadly the same; the standard of living for *mani* was about the same; and *mani* owned about the same number of cattle as did surrounding Maale. Given these considerations and given the fact that there were only seven *mani* households in Bola, a separate discussion of their household organization might seem unnecessary.

Yet the people of Bola emphatically maintained that *mani* were not Maale. Though many of the *mani* spoke Maale as fluently as anyone and most followed Maale customs *(dambe)* as closely as anyone, *mani* were a different "kind" of people. Their women potted, and their men tanned. No Maale carried out those tasks. Traditionally, *mani* had not cultivated at all but had traded their wares and services for Maale grain. In about 1963, the *balābbāt* Bailo, who owned by then all of the land surrounding Dofo, Kaiyo, and Bola, permitted *mani* to cultivate their own fields. By 1975, some of the *mani* had begun to plant fields as large as those of Maale, but no Maale had begun to pot or to tan. Perhaps most importantly of all, the taboos on intermarriage were also still observed. To my knowledge, no *mani* had married a Maale.

Because of these aspects of low-caste life, the patterns of household organization that overtly resembled those of the Maale sometimes worked out rather differently in practice. Below, I will briefly sketch the most important of these contrasts between the *mani* in Bola and the surrounding Maale. Perhaps the most striking of these was the "international" character of the *mani*: most of the married *mani* women in Bola had grown up outside of Maale. How this as well as other contrasts conditioned the organization of *mani* households is the main topic of discussion below.

Potters and tanners lived in small pockets scattered over Maale and beyond, and it was to those communities rather than to the immediately surrounding Maale hamlets that *mani* men in Bola went courting. Marriage with the Maale was unthinkable, a violation of traditional taboos. With the immigrant traders living in the market village, intermarriage was quite rare; the only such marriage known to have occurred was that between a Muslim man and a *mani* woman. Overwhelmingly, *mani* married only other *mani*.

Since there were relatively few *mani* communities in Maale and since neighboring ones tended to be populated by closely related kin, a high proportion of *mani* had to go outside of Maale in order to find wives. Two-thirds of the *mani* males covered by my Bola census—not only respondents, but their fathers, and grandfathers—had married foreign-born wives. Most of these women came from *mani* communities in Bako, Argenne, and Uba, countries that border Maale on the west and north (see Map 4). Far fewer came from Marta to the east or Tsemai to the south. Of all of these, Tsemai was unusual in that it apparently lacked "caste" taboos, so that Maale *mani* sometimes married ordinary Tsemai women. Of the wives of *mani* living in Bola in 1975, the wives of their fathers, and the wives of their grandfathers, 18 percent had been born in Bola chiefdom, 17 percent in other chiefdoms in Maale, 22 percent in Uba, 17 percent in Argenne, 13 percent in Bako, 9 percent in Tsemai, and 4 percent in Marta.

The extent to which various enclave *mani* communities had adopted the marriage customs of the ethnic groups among whom they lived and the effect of

Plate 7.   A *Məni* Woman Shaping a New Pot

such differences on "international" marriage exchanges among *məni* are fascinating questions. Unfortunately, I do not have data on communities other than the one in Bola. In Bola, *məni* followed Maale marriage customs whether they married Maale-born or foreign-born women, except that both gift-giving and feasting took place in very much attenuated form. The amount of marriage gifts that Bola *məni* men gave their wives' relatives averaged only about $18 (the price of a large goat in 1975) and as Table 8 shows, gifts had not changed much in magnitude over the past 25 years. Also, since *məni* wedding feasts were less elaborate than among the Maale, the total costs of marrying were significantly lower.

Table 8.   Marriage Gifts Given by *Məni* in Bola to Their Wives' Relatives

Approximate Date of Marriage	Total Amount of Gifts in Ethiopian Dollars
1950	9
1952	15
1955	15
1959	19
1965	75
1966	13
1968	15
1969	15
1969	8
1970	25
1970	15
1971	12
1973	0

This deflation of marriage gifts to almost token status may have been related to the fact that most *məni* marriages involved partners from culturally distinct and spatially distant communities. Apparently, no *məni* community in any of the ethnic groups around Maale was large enough to marry only within their own numbers; they had to intermarry with foreign-born *məni*, and under conditions in which no one *məni* enclave was large and powerful enough to insist on their "own" customs, marriage gifts tended to assume the form of least common denominator—that is, no gifts or only token gifts (cf. Goody 1970). My data on *məni* marriages revealed only one notable exception to this rule: in about 1924, a *məni* man from Bola married a *məni* woman from Bako and apparently agreed to pay two cows in bridewealth *(wa'dissi)*. In 1974 when the wife died, the two cows still had not been presented to her relatives. The husband, an elder by then, maintained that he would give the cattle "later."

Since marriage gifts were low, and since marrying did not require the strong economic support of elder kinsmen and neighbors, young men among the *məni*, by comparison with their Maale counterparts, appeared more independent of their elders. This difference showed, I believe, in the day-to-day affairs of both communities.

Among the Maale it was clear that elders were the primary local leaders: Elders' compounds were the social gathering points at morning and night, before and after work. Elders molded public opinion, settled disputes, and generally oversaw local communal work patterns. Among the *məni*, on the other hand, the same roles tended to be filled by middle-aged men, and elders were much less tied into the everyday affairs of their community. Often elders were gone for months at a time on visits to relatives outside Maale. At home, they joined in their households' cultivation work but seemed to exert less supervision over their dependents. In general, *məni* elders appeared more adapted to their roles as fulltime potters and tanners than as cultivators.

If marriage gifts among the *məni* were lower than among the Maale, the frequency of divorce was also higher. The *məni* women who lived in Bola in 1975 averaged 1.6 times as many divorces as surrounding Maale women, and since the age distribution of the *məni* women was skewed toward lower ages, the actual frequency of divorce may have been almost twice as large as that of the Maale.

A higher frequency of divorce, in turn, was one factor (possibly among others) that contributed to the smaller size of *məni* households. Upon divorce, children under the age of seven or eight years usually went to live with their mothers. Also, elders who lived with married sons oftentimes did not remarry after divorces. Table 9 shows *məni* household size and composition over the developmental cycle. The Bola *məni* followed the same pattern as the Maale: Eldest sons who stood to inherit by far the largest portion of their fathers' wealth lived permanently in their parents' households, while younger sons established independent homes when they married. The resulting variation in labor supply of *məni* households followed the same broad pattern as among the Maale, although over a much smaller range. Table 8 shows that elders' households had slightly larger labor forces, while young and middle-aged mens' households had smaller labor forces.

Part of the labor force in all *məni* households was still devoted to nonhorticultural tasks. Women in households at all stages of development made clay pots for the weekly market in Bola, and about a third of the men continued to spend appreciable amounts of time on tanning, and cultivated only secondarily. The men who remained tanners were all from households in the first and second stages of development with relatively small labor forces.

Households in their various stages of development were set within descent groups just as among the Maale. The preeminent role of the *toidi* or head, the

Table 9. Composition of *Mani* Households by Age of Head, Bola, 1975

Households Headed by Persons Less Than 30		Households Headed by Persons Between 30 to 45		Households Headed by Persons Over 45	
Adults	**Children**	**Adults**	**Children**	**Adults**	**Children**
2	0	2	4	3	0
2	1	3[a]	5	3	3
		5[a]	4		
Mean 2	.5	Mean 3	4	Mean 3	1.5

a. Men with two wives.

worship of ancestors, and the process of descent group segmentation all characterized the *mani* no less than the Maale. How these social principles worked out in practice was, however, very different.

Instead of establishing satellite households near their fathers, younger brothers often moved to distant communities, sometimes even outside of Maale. In the sets of married living brothers that occurred in my census and in genealogies of Bola *mani*, four out of five younger brothers had moved away from their birthplace to distant communities. Sometimes, they chose to live near their mother's or wife's kin; other times, apparently they moved to communities that included no close kinsmen. In the past, it may have been that the lack of any access to land along with the pull of new opportunities for potters and tanners in other communities contributed to this pattern of mobility. In any case, large ramified coresident descent groups did not have a chance to form among the Bola *mani*.

While descent mates occupied less of a place in the immediate social field of *mani*, kindreds (those related to one through both men and women) occupied a more prominent place. In Maale hamlets, genealogies tended to expand along lines of descent and only a few marriages established links between descent groups. Women tended to have few relatives nearby. Among the *mani*, in contrast, genealogical connections crisscrossed into a complicated web, and women as well as men tended to have relatives living nearby. This web of kinship united all *mani* households in Bola into a single social group, the boundaries of which were emphasized by the taboos on intermarriage with the surrounding Maale.

Maale Households at Work

Constituted through marriage, shaped by the developmental cycle, and conditioned further by such factors as descent, wealth, and fertility, households were basic units of production in Dofo, Kaiyo, and Bola. As units of production, one of the critical features of households is what Alexander Chayanov ([1925] 1966) called the dependency ratio—the number of household consumers divided by the number of workers (C/W). The higher the dependency ratio, the lower the relative supply of household labor becomes; and the lower the supply of labor, the weaker the household enterprise.

Figures 4a, 4b, and 4c show respectively the dependency ratios of Maale, market village, and *mani* households headed by males over the developmental cycle. Female household heads (six out of the twenty-nine Maale cases; seven out of the twenty-five market village heads, and zero out of the seven *mani* heads) are omitted since they constituted a secondary pattern of their own. As previous sections have explained, Maale and *mani* women who headed their own households were typically elderly widows without sons. In contrast,

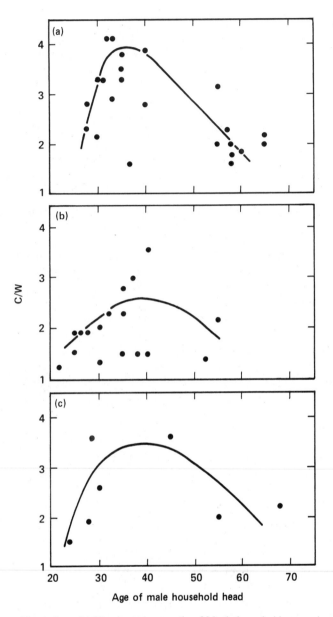

Figure 4. (a) The dependency ratio of Maale households versus
age of male household head.

(b) The dependency ratio of market village households
versus age of male household head.

(c) The dependency ratio of *mani* households versus
age of household head.

female-headed households in the market village were apparently more viable economic enterprises, and women with their own households tended to come from all age groups.

For the dominant pattern of male-headed households, the graphs of Figures 4a, 4b, and 4c illustrate the contrasting trajectories of typical Maale, market village, and *məni* households. Both Maale and *məni* households showed a marked rise in dependency ratio—i.e. a decline in relative labor supply—during the middle stages of development. With many children and few workers to support them, these middle-aged households were caught in a "demographic squeeze." For most market village households, by contrast, there was only a modest rise during the middle stage; the labor supply of market villagers was relatively constant over the whole developmental cycle.

How did Maale households in the middle stages of development manage to meet their subsistence requirements? According to Chayanov's theory of domestic production discussed in Chapter 1, workers in middle-aged households would have to work longer hours. Although I did not design field procedures specifically to "test" Chayanov's theory, I did nevertheless select nine sample households in different stages of development from the hamlet of Dofo and Bola for intensive study. Whereas Chayanov (also Sahlins in his modified version of Chayanov's theory) relied on field size as an indirect measure of labor time, I collected direct data: For one-week intervals spaced at three points in the horticultural cycle (weeding *le* fields, clearing *silo* fields, and harvesting *silo* fields, cf. Figure 3), I interviewed household members each night and made a record of their activities along with an estimate of the time spent on each.

These nine households were selected from a total of twenty-eight Maale households in Dofo, Kaiyo, and Bola. (None of the market village or *məni* households were chosen for this portion of the study since horticulture was not their only means of support.) In order to study households of widely different dependency ratios, I selected three households from each of three successive phases in the developmental cycle: (1) households headed by young men with two children or less, all under working age; (2) households headed by middle-aged men with three to seven children, all under working age, and (3) households headed by elders living with at least two adult working children. Of the nine households selected, three were located in Bola, while six were in Dofo. Five of the eight Maale descent groups in Dofo, Kaiyo, and Bola were represented.

The data afforded by this survey are relevant to Chayanov's theory, but to assess that relevance requires first a method of establishing units for measuring relative numbers of consumers and workers. How much, for example, does a seven-year-old child consume relative to an adult male? Or how much fieldwork does a young wife (with other duties such as child care and food preparation) carry out relative to her husband? These questions, in the present context, admit of only rough, approximate answers.

In the absence of an empirical survey of consumption levels in Maale households, I calculated consumption units by adapting the figures presented by Epstein (1967: 160) which were based on published nutrition studies. Adults, both male and female, fourteen years of age and above were assumed to require 1.0 consumption units, children aged seven to thirteen, 0.75 units, and children two to six, 0.5 units.

The problem of calculating labor units is more difficult. One possible solution is to derive relative labor units from empirical data on work time. Data from the nine sample households showed that males aged fourteen to fifty worked an average of 4.5 hours a day on fieldwork, while those over fifty worked an average of 2.6 hours a day. Unmarried girls of fourteen years of age and older worked an average of 2.2 hours a day, while married women worked only 1.5 hours a day in the fields. If, therefore, a young or middle-aged man is said to have contributed 1.0 units of field labor, an elder contributed 0.6 units, an unmarried girl 0.5 units, and a married women 0.3 units.

Utilizing the above figures on labor units, Figure 5a presents data on the variation of horticultural labor time with the dependency ratio of households. If Chayanov's rule held, there would be a positive slope in the graph of Figure 5a. That is, fieldwork time would increase as the dependency ratio increased; households with relatively fewer workers would tend to work longer hours. In fact, Figure 5a shows a slight negative slope. Households with relatively less labor appear to have worked shorter, not longer hours.

Before we can conclude that Figure 5a constitutes a possible exception to Chayanov's theory for the economy of Dofo, Kaiyo, and Bola, we have to examine the fact that household dependency ratios have not been specified independently of the other variable, labor time. The averages that were used to establish worker units came from the data on labor time. The only alternative to this impasse is to assume arbitrarily some distribution of labor units and see if the results differ from those above. (Chayanov's work was based on this more crude but more logically consistent alternative.) Figure 5b shows the same data as Figure 5a with calculations made on the assumption that all males and females above fourteen years of age contributed 1.0 units of labor and that children under fourteen contributed no labor.

Figure 5b shows an even more negative slope than Figure 5a. On either reading of the evidence, Chayanov's theory finds no support. Of course, nine households is a very small sample, and my sampling procedure was not random. Moreover, the variances in both Figures 5a and 5b are relatively large. Given these considerations, it is impossible to come to a firm conclusion. The data seem to support the idea that all households worked about the same number of hours—no matter the dependency ratio.

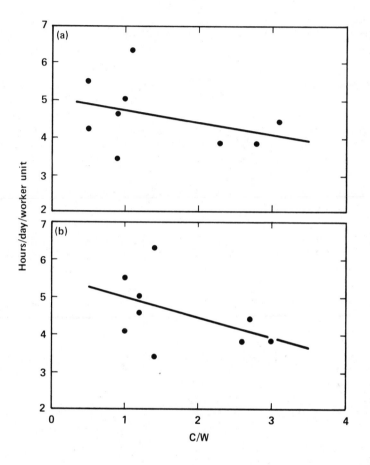

Figure 5.   The number of hours of field labor per day per worker unit versus the household dependency ratio:

(a) Worker units established empirically.

(b) Worker units arbitrarily assumed.

If Chayanov's theory does not appear to hold for the present case, its possible negation certainly poses an important question: How did Maale households in the middle stages of development with relatively greater subsistence needs meet those requirements if in fact they worked no longer than households with relatively modest needs?

There are a number of possibilities. Sahlins' theory of the domestic mode of production (1972) suggests one alternative: Certain households may have produced more than their consumption requirements, which allowed others to produce less. Various arrangements then channeled goods from the haves to the have-nots. A wealthy man may have, for instance, traded economic resources for prestige or power. Another man who had produced a "surplus" may have been impelled by moral ties to help less fortunate kinsmen. A household with many children and few workers might, therefore, have depended on kinsmen for help, rather than working longer hours as Chayanov's rule would predict.

As Sahlins' theory suggests, the Maale did have customary ways for a needy person to obtain *(zimane)* crops from a kinsman or neighbor. Wives apparently often asked their fathers or brothers for such help, and occasionally men begged a kinsman for help, usually a maternal kinsman who lived in a hamlet other than his own. My census of Maale households in Dofo, Kaiyo, and Bola for 1974 showed, in fact, that elders' households gave away more grain than they received. Five elders' households (all with low dependency ratios ≤ 2.0) gave away an average of 3.8 sacks of grain and received only 0.6 sacks. This, of course, is exactly what Sahlins' theory would predict. However, at the other extreme of the dependency ratio continuum, middle-aged households did not receive, according to their reports, more than they gave away. Five middle-aged households (all with high dependency ratios ≥ 3.3) gave away an average of 2.0 sacks and received only 0.4 sacks in return. In several cases, givers reported their gifts while takers did not, so that the actual number of sacks that middle-aged households received may have been higher than the numbers reported. But even assuming some underreporting, it seems unlikely that middle-aged households received a great deal more grain than they gave away. Sahlins' redistributive hypothesis, like Chayanov's theory, does not seem to hold for the present case.

One can imagine still other solutions to the paradox that higher dependency household did not work longer hours. Middle-aged households could have cut their consumption levels; such cuts could have gone only so far, however, before the reproduction of the next generation was endangered. Alternatively, consumption patterns could have operated so that members of needy households ate in others' households more often than the reverse. Apart from these possibilities which may have operated to some degree (I have no systematic data to support or to refute either hypothesis), the issue I want to

Plate 8.   The Blacksmith of Bola Vicinity

Plate 9.   A Maale Hunter South of Bola Where Game is More Plentiful

investigate here is a more fundamental one, more fundamental in regard to Chayanov's and Sahlins' theories: the assumption that theories of noncapitalist economies can be adequately developed in terms of domestic group structures taken by themselves, and, specifically, the assumption that households are self-contained labor units.

Chayanov believed that since wage labor is absent in noncapitalist economies, there is no other way that labor can be systematically transferred from one household to another. Sahlins (1968: 75) is aware that households are not self-contained labor units; nevertheless, he concludes that households are essentially independent economic units that dominate the economy of "tribal" economies. Households are, as it were, the atoms of noncapitalist economies:

> As far as the organization of production goes, the best word for it may be *anarchy*. The social economy is broken down into independent household existences, constituted to operate parallel to each other, and in an uncoordinated way. Beyond similarities stemming from common material goals, households are not inherently brought into relation by the productive process (Sahlins' emphasis, 1968: 76).

But in Dofo and Bola, nearly half of all horticultural work was carried out by communal work arrangements that bound households together in various ways and in various patterns. In the following chapter, I will argue that households were embedded and contained in a number of larger social units that worked together and shared labor. How these units related to one another turns out to be a political as well as an economic question, and I will argue that local Maale production can be understood only in relation to the productive activities of market villagers and *məni*. The Maale production process was no more (in fact possibly less) anarchic than a General Motors assembly line. What distinguishes Maale production from the latter is its peculiar and specific combination of forces and relations of production, its combination of technical and social means to produce the material foundation of society. To understand that combination requires not only an attention to local social units more inclusive than the household, but also to the currents of historical change in Maale. The following chapter places households within communal work groups and relates both to the historical transformations described in Chapter 2.

4

Work Groups and Power

Households in Bola vicinity carried out slightly less than half of all their horticultural labor in various kind of cooperative arrangements in which members of several households worked together. These work arrangements fall into two structural types which recur in a great many technologically simple economies in Africa and elsewhere (Abraham 1965; Ames 1959; Barth 1967; Bloch 1973; Charsley 1976; Gregson 1969; Gulliver 1971; Mayer 1951; O'Laughlin 1973; Seibel and Massing 1974; Uchendu 1970; Vincent 1971).

The first type of work group, called a "reciprocal work group" by Erasmus (1956) and Moore (1976), is composed of a group of households that work in rotation on each others' fields. Like a unilineal descent group, reciprocal work group membership is unambiguously defined, and each group is clearly bounded. And again like many descent systems, this kind of work group, especially if it contains more than a few households, tends to develop formal roles for leaders who direct the activities of the group and who help settle disputes between members. In short, the reciprocal work group is a corporate group. Note finally that reciprocity in this kind of group is strictly defined; since a schedule of rotation is followed, each household receives as much labor from others as it gives to them.

The second kind of work group is what Erasmus (1956) called a "festive work group" (although "festivity" is clearly not its most salient structural feature). Here, the sponsoring household brews beer or prepares food and, as the Maale say, "begs" neighbors to come and help them on the appointed day. After the work is done, the sponsoring household often retains an obligation, a loose and unenforced obligation, to send a worker at some future date to the festive work parties of the households who have worked for it. Over time, the people who work in festive work parties of any particular household may change. Each work party is recruited anew on each occasion and is not, therefore, a "group" in the strict sense at all. Each household apparently has its circle of festive work partners which overlaps then, more or less, with the work circles of neighboring households. Unlike the neatly bounded corporate work groups discussed above, the festive work party system produces a web of tangled relationships, not unlike the web of kinship. Note finally that exact reciprocity in labor given and received is not built into the system as in the first kind of work group; it remains to be seen to what degree giving and receiving labor is in fact balanced.

In Maale there were three varieties of communal work arrangements: *helma, mol?o,* and *dabo.* The first two are reciprocal work groups, while the third is a festive work party system. In this chapter, I take up each of these in turn and analyze its relation to the local organization of power.

The *Helma*

In Dofo, Kaiyo, and Bola, *helma* were small groups of workers, usually three or four, who worked in rotation as a group on each others' fields. Maale said that it was easier and more enjoyable to work in the company of others and that they got more done that way. Each day that *helma* assembled, they worked for about four hours, usually in the morning. Then the workers went home and in the afternoon followed their individual pursuits. Very occasionally the sponsor of a *helma,* the owner of the field on which the group was working, provided beer in which case work continued for a full day, about eight hours with time out for several rest stops.

Since horticultural tasks were to some extent apportioned on the basis of sex and age, *helma* groups were also usually differentiated along those lines. Adult men's *helma* were distinct from women's *helma,* and occasionally boys and girls (about fourteen to about eighteen years old) combined to form young people's *helma.* Men's *helma* were organized for all tasks in the horticultural cycle: clearing, cultivation, weeding, and harvesting. Women's *helma* formed only for weeding and harvesting, while young people's *helma* mostly weeded. Weeding made the greatest demand for labor and called out the full work force.

Being small groups, *helma* did not have official roles for leaders who directed and coordinated the group's activities. Scheduling work days and making sure everyone arrived on time were relatively easy matters for three or four people to accomplish among themselves. Without a differentiated structure of roles, *helma* work groups were relatively short lived. Usually they were organized for one horticultural task, and after that task had been finished, the group dissolved. Sometimes a group survived two tasks in the horticultural cycle (about three or four months) but almost never for longer periods.

While *helma* were organized and maintained mostly by the participants themselves, household heads of *helma* members (who are not themselves heads) offered encouragement and direction. Often a household head worked with the *helma* of his wife, son, or daughter when the group came to work on his fields. The head could direct that beer be prepared for the *helma* so that the group worked a full day rather than the customary half day. Very infrequently, an elder or his wife participated directly in a *helma*; in the three cases of this with which I became familiar, the older people were informal leaders of the *helma*, and the groups grew to six, seven, and eight members.

An elder's household in Dofo offers an example of how *helma* were organized and employed during the horticultural cycle. In 1974, Batunsa's household belonged to four different *helma*. Neither he nor his wife worked in *helma*, but three of their four children over the age of fourteen did participate. At the beginning of the year, Batunsa's household cleared new fields with other kinds of work parties (*dabo* and *mol?o*) and were not involved in *helma*. By the time of cultivation and planting, however, one of Batunsa's sons, about twenty, joined three other young men from households nearby in a *helma* that worked three times on each member's field. The weeding season arrived, and this *helma* continued to work, weeding each member's field twice before the group dissolved. Since the weeding season was a time of peak labor demand, Batunsa's daughter, about eighteen years old, joined another *helma* with two young married women, and the group worked twice on each of their fields. A younger son, about fifteen, joined yet another weeding *helma,* and his group, composed of six other young boys and girls, worked four times on each of their fields. Finally, at the end of the horticultural cycle, Batunsa's daughter joined a harvesting *helma* with four other young women, and the group worked once on each of their fields.

Maale were not the sole participants in *helma* work groups. Market villagers and *məni* also joined *helma*. Since Dofo, Kaiyo, and Bola constituted a relatively isolated local system, all groups—*məni* and market villagers as well as Maale—drew *helma* partners largely from within the system. Only five percent of their *helma* partners came from outside, and these exceptional cases were heavily concentrated in the nearest settlement, Golla. There a few Dofo people joined with Golla partners to work in *helma*.

With minor exceptions, therefore, the study area shown in Map 6 was bounded with respect to *helma* work groups and thus a proper unit for analysis. The most obvious feature of *helma* organization within the area was that no single network of *helma* ties covered the entire local system. Quite distinct boundaries were evident among the *helma* work groups in 1974 and 1975. First of all, people tended to work with neighbors from the same settlement. Dofo people worked mostly with other Dofo people, Kaiyo people with Kaiyo, and Bola people with Bola.

A simple spatial model, however, would obscure some of the most important features of *helma* work group organization. Sociological space, it turns out, was no simple reflection of propinquity. Some people systematically worked with neighbors more distant than nearby, so that group boundaries, although they tended to coincide with hamlet boundaries, did so only imperfectly.

For instance, the Maale inhabitants of Bola worked four times as often with more distant Dofo people than with their closer neighbors in Bola, the market villagers and the *məni*. So, despite the fact that Dofo and Bola Maale lived in separate hamlets, they appear to have belonged to a single *helma* pool. On the other hand, market villagers and *məni* lived next to one another in Bola and yet tended to work in separate *helma*.

As Figure 6 illustrates, four more or less distinct *helma* pools emerged. Each (except Kaiyo Maale) tended toward closure, although occasional *helma* ties did develop between units. Within each unit, individual *helma* formed and dissolved, each new *helma* often somewhat different in composition than the last. But the larger pools of possible *helma* partners remained constant, and each was in varying degrees independent of the groups about it. These four labor pools, in addition to being economic groups who cooperated in production, were also the smallest and most solidary social and political units at the local level. A web of ties of descent and sometimes affinity tended to link members of each group but only rarely bridged the gap between groups. In local politics, these units sometimes coalesced into larger political factions but the fundamental and apparently undifferentiable building blocks were these four groups. Below, I consider each in turn and its relation to *helma* organization: Dofo and Bola Maale, Bola market villagers, Bola *məni*, and Kaiyo Maale.

The eighteen households in Dofo and the eight Maale households in Bola were linked together by strong social ties. Dofo had been founded in about 1954 by several younger brothers from Bola. As a result, in 1975 three of the six lineage segments in Dofo recognized Bola men as their heads, or *toidi*. Besides ties of descent (the median household head in Dofo and Bola was related by descent to four other household heads out of twenty-six), several marriages had established affinal ties between descent groups in Dofo and Bola. In contrast, only one marriage had taken place between a Maale person in Dofo and Bola and one from any of the other three groups enumerated above—Kaiyo Maale, market villagers or *məni*. And no ties of descent, however remote, linked Dofo and Bola Maale to members of the other three groups.

While common ties of kinship appear to have played a role in setting off Dofo and Bola Maale as a discrete labor pool, they had much less effect on the composition of *helma* within that group. In 1974 and 1975, men in Dofo and Bola showed no greater propensity to work in *helma* with descent mates than with others. On the average, 28 percent of the *helma* partners of men in Dofo and Bola were their descent mates—a figure only slightly greater than the 24 percent that would be expected if they had worked randomly with others in that group. Women's *helma* were somewhat more affected, not by descent relationships among women themselves but by those among their husbands and fathers. Some 37 percent of Dofo and Bola women's *helma* partners came

from households headed by their husbands' or fathers' descent mates—
somewhat more than the 19 percent that would have resulted had women
worked randomly with each other. Finally, affinal ties between household
heads did not seem to have appreciably affected either men's or women's
helma. In sum, structures of kinship were related to the choice of people with
whom Dofo and Bola Maale did *not* work (that is, the boundaries between
labor pools), but kinship had little effect on exactly with whom people did
work.

Within the boundaries of the labor pool, almost all households
participated in at least one *helma* a year. In 1974, for example, only 10 percent
of the Maale households in Dofo and Bola belonged to no *helma* whatever.
While most households belonged to *helma*, the number in which they
participated was related to the size of the households' work forces and therefore
to the developmental cycle. The median Maale household in Dofo and Bola
among those headed by young and middle-aged men (i.e. households with
relatively few workers) belonged to two *helma* per year in 1974 and 1975. The
median household among those headed by elders belonged to three *helma*.

Since elders' households belonged to more *helma*, it would appear that the
network of *helma* ties clustered in knots around elders' households and that
elders might indirectly have influenced the operation of the whole system. Such
was not the case, at least for *helma* in 1974-75, for the simple reason that the
helma to which younger mens' households belonged tended to be larger (a
median of three other members) than those to which elders' households
belonged (a median of two other members). As a result, the total number of
other households to which any particular household was linked did not vary
with the stage of development: All households were linked through *helma* to
about six other households over the period of a year. Unaffected by the
developmental cycle and unaffected by structures of kinship, *helma* ties spread
evenly throughout the group, uniting it and setting it off as sociological distinct
from its surroundings.

That Dofo and Bola people worked in *helma* drawn almost entirely from
their own group, and that they developed few ties of kinship with neighboring
groups reflected the structure of political alignments at the local level. Led by
elders *(donza)*, Dofo and Bola represented what might be called the
"traditionalists." Historically, the elders from around Bola, the site of the king's
residence, had played an important role in Maale politics. They, along with the
chiefs of Bola and Makana, determined the line of royal succession. In
addition, Bola elders served as middlemen between the king and the
surrounding populace, collecting tribute (enjoying part of the largesse
themselves) and relaying messages and orders.

When the market village was established in Bola in about 1964, it was the
concrete result of a series of structural changes that were beginning to

undermine the position of the Bola and Dofo elders. Instead of tribute to a divine king who magically imparted fertility and life to the whole kingdom, taxes to landlords, whose positions were sanctioned by national Ethiopian land law, became the major economic device supporting and supported by political stratification. Instead of Bola elders as middlemen, literate traders began to collect taxes and to act as representatives of the king, by then more accurately called *bālābbāt*. Naturally, Bola and Dofo elders came into political opposition with the market villagers. Although a few Maale found mutual friends and allies among the traders, most tended to think of market villagers as conniving cheats. On the other side, traders often expressed an amused or exasperated condescension toward the "backward" Maale. Few ties developed between the two groups, and in most issues of local politics, the two ended up on opposite sides.

Since the market village was established only recently and since it was settled by a disparate group of Muslims and Orthodox Christians, social ties were weaker among Bola traders than among Dofo and Bola Maale. As pointed out earlier, the principal ties that linked market households were those between sisters and between elderly parents and their adult children. The typical household in Bola market village related to only one other household (out of 25) by parent-child or by sibling-sibling ties through either the household head or his wife. With the surrounding Maale and *məni*, there were even fewer ties: in the eleven years since the village had been founded, only two marriages with surrounding groups had taken place. One Muslim man had married a *məni* woman, previously twice divorced, and in 1975, a Christian weaver married a young widow from among the Bola Maale. These, however, were the exceptions to an overall pattern that established the market village as a separate and distinct social group.

The social boundaries that separated the market village from its surroundings were reflected in the composition of the *helma* work groups. Figure 6 shows that 85 percent of the *helma* partners of market villagers were other market villagers. As among the Maale, kinship did not influence who worked with whom. For instance, households related by sibling-sibling ties through either household heads or their wives did not work together in *helma* groups more than would have been randomly expected. Nor did religious affiliation affect *helma* organization; 60 percent of the *helma* partners of Muslims were other Muslims—about the same proportion of Muslims in the total working population of the market village.

The network of *helma* ties did not, however, spread evenly over the whole group. Market villagers organized *helma* only for predominantly male tasks, and women, who were mostly occupied with brewing and distilling, did not participate. Therefore, households of single women (a total of seven out of twenty-five in Bola market) were not included in the network of *helma* ties.

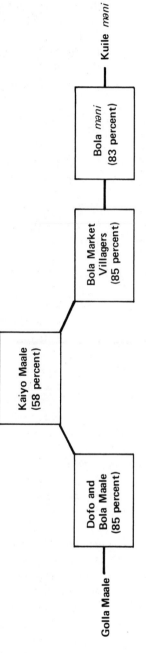

Figure 6. Dofo, Kaiyo, and Bola *helma* labor pools during 1974-75 (Note: The percentage in each block indicates the proportion of *helma* partners that came from within the boundaries of the block. Lines linking blocks indicate the presence of *helma* ties between blocks.)

Among households headed by men, approximately 40 percent did not participate in any *helma* during any given year; most of these came from the category of villagers of modest means who, as I have noted before, were primarily involved in trade and only secondarily in horticulture. In contrast, both wealthy and poor villagers spent more time on horticulture; the median household in each category belonged to one *helma* per year.

Within the village, the informal leaders were the small group of relatively wealthy men, most of whom had served as representatives of the *balābbāt* at various times since the village's founding. Speaking Amharic, acquainted with life in the larger towns of southern Ethiopia, and more knowledgeable (than the Maale, certainly) about the ways of the national system of courts and governmental administration, these leaders and many of the other market villagers viewed themselves as an outpost of national civilization. As Maale had become more closely integrated into the Ethiopian state, the political fortunes of the market villagers had risen while those of the Bola elders—their opposition—had fallen. Out of this social displacement, there developed a great deal of friction which dominated many of the local political issues in Bola vicinity.

Besides Dofo and Bola Maale and Bola market villagers, there was the Bola low-cast *məni* who also formed a relatively solidary *helma*-based group. Composed of only seven households, the Bola *məni* were a tightly knit social group. Ties of both descent and affinity linked households into a distinctive unit *vis-à-vis* the Maale and the market villagers. Since most of the women were involved in producing clay pots for the weekly market and since about a third of the men continued to devote a considerable amount of their time to tanning, *məni*, like traders, did not pursue horticulture full time. Women in the *məni* group hardly ever worked in *helma* groups, and *məni* men belonged to fewer *helma* than did Maale men. The median household among the *məni* belonged to only one *helma* per year in 1974 and 1975. As among the Maale and market villagers, descent mates and affines did not work together any more than would be expected if *məni* had chosen their *helma* partners randomly from within the group.

The social boundary between the *məni* and the Maale dated from the time when Maale was independent. Along with blacksmiths, *məni*—potters and tanners—were the only fulltime specialists in nineteenth-century Maale. Maale did not make pots or tan leather, and *məni* did not cultivate. Each depended on exchange with the other. To some extent, the traditional political cleavage between Maale and *məni* probably grew out of the opposition of economic interests. Maale said that *məni* were cunning and always trying to trick more grain out of them; *məni* said that Maale were always trying to pay them less than their work was worth.

Intermarriage between *məni* and Maale was unthinkable (at least from the point of view of the Maale), and a number of taboos traditionally circumscribed daily interactions: *məni* could not enter the fields of Maale, they could not eat from the same utensils as Maale, nor could they touch Maale cattle. Like sorcerers, *məni* were said to "eat" people, magically killing their victims in order to consume human flesh. In the wake of Maale deaths, *məni* sometimes apparently came under suspicion, and in a few cases Maale "drove away" *məni* and forced them to live in other communities. For protection, *məni* in Bola had depended upon the king and their relationship to him as special servants. In times past, they had served the king as "policemen," capturing and imprisoning miscreants, and when ordered, executing criminals. In times of war, *məni* had formed the front lines; they had attacked the enemy first.

After the northern conquest, the *məni* police function was increasingly taken over by the national administration, and trade goods, especially cloth, began to lessen the Maale need for *məni* tanning. By 1963 when Bailo became *bālābbāt*, he announced that henceforth he would follow "Amhara custom" in regard to the *məni*—they could enter his house and his fields. There was to be an end to ritual taboos; *məni* would cultivate their own fields. Traditionalists in Dofo and Bola resisted the king's leadership and continued to hold on to the old ways, but Kaiyo Maale (for reasons to be set out below) dropped the old customs, ate with *məni*, and sometimes cultivated with them. Social intercourse between the *məni* and Kaiyo Maale and between *məni* and market villagers was relatively easy, and it was with those two groups that *məni* usually allied themselves in local political matters. With Dofo and Bola Maale, however, the old cleavage tended to hold.

Finally, Kaiyo Maale was the last *helma*-based group. Kaiyo settlement was a very small, three-household hamlet located equidistant from Dofo and Bola. All three household heads belonged to the same descent group, and the men had no descent mates living in either Dofo or Bola, nor had any of them married women from Bola and Dofo. Among surrounding groups discussed above, Kaiyo was a fairly distinct social unit.

Kaiyo hamlet was not, however, a closed *helma* labor pool. While 58 percent of their *helma* partners came from within the group, 30 percent came from Dofo and Bola Maale households, and the remaining 12 percent came from the market village. In terms of *helma* partners, Kaiyo straddled the fence between Dofo and Bola Maale and the market village.

In local politics, Kaiyo also occupied an ambiguous position. On the one hand, Kaiyo people were Maale in social identity. Kaiyo elders, like those in Dofo, had been born and grew up in Bola. In the mid-1950s when Dofo was founded, one of the Kaiyo men, a younger brother, had moved from Bola to Dofo. By 1970, however, members of the descent group from both Dofo and Bola had gathered together in a new hamlet, Kaiyo. When I asked Dofo men why the younger brother had moved from Dofo to Kaiyo, they said that the man's wife had "a bad mouth," that she could not get along with neighbors. While the "bad mouthed wife" was a convenient interpretation (especially for Maale elders), it was perhaps not the most important part of the total explanation.

As it turned out, the head *(toidi)* of the descent group in Kaiyo was an early and strong supporter of the *bālābbāt*, Bailo, after the latter had been forcibly installed by the Ethiopian administration in about 1963. The other elders, still loyal to the former king, carried out their duties to Bailo but apparently remained rather cool. Describing the political situation at the time, one man said, "Dofo people just sat still." For whatever reason (I have no indication of what his motive might have been), the head of the Kaiyo descent group was an exception. He and Bailo became bond friends *(belli)* and Bailo built a second house in Kaiyo for his favorite wife.

All of this might have had little effect had not the new king, Bailo, died only seven years later in 1970. The question of the proper succession was painfully reopened. Would the old king, still living, be recalled to his "rightful" office? Or would Bailo's son be installed? According to the Ethiopian administration, there was no question. Bailo's son, an educated young man who spoke and wrote Amharic, was *bālābbāt*. Whether he would be ritually installed as Maale *kati*, however, was another matter that came up every year, and remained unresolved, until the kingship was abolished in 1975.

While most of the traditionalist elders in Dofo and Bola apparently leaned toward recalling the old king, Yebirka, the head of the Kaiyo descent group, already bond friend with Bailo, cemented his relationship to that line of the royal family by becoming a bond friend of Bailo's son (an unusual occurrence among other Maale, since the bond friendship between two men is said to continue over into the next generation, linking the two men's sons as well). It was this political split over the succession as well as old quarrels and disputes that defined the cleavage between Kaiyo and Dofo-Bola. Partially estranged from their Maale neighbors, Kaiyo people, who were few in number, needed new work partners. There were two groups at hand, market villagers and *məni*, both of whom were already at odds with the traditionalists in Dofo and Bola. Kaiyo elders dropped their observance of the old taboos against the *məni* (as the *bālābbāt*, Bailo, had taken the lead in doing) and began to work with both groups, while retaining a few work ties to particular households among Dofo and Bola Maale.

A number of factors—kinship, cultural identity, religious taboos, personal enmities, perhaps even the Dofo elders' version of the sharp-tongued wife—contributed to the definition of *helma* labor pools. The mutual reinforcement among these factors made *helma* pools the most solidary social and political groups at the local level. By themselves, however, *helma* pools did not provide the most comprehensive framework of or focus for local politics. As the following section will show, *helma* labor pools in Dofo, Kaiyo, and Bola combined and coalesced to form larger factions. To understand these factions requires an examination of *mol?o* work groups.

The *Mol?o*

Like a *helma*, a *mol?o* was a reciprocal work group in which members worked in rotation on each others' fields. In the phrase that anthropologists have used to describe many lineage systems, *mol?o* were "corporate groups." Members shared rights over the labor of the whole group; membership was clearly defined; and a set of officers directed the activities of the group. Being relatively large and long-lived corporate groups, *mol?o*, I will argue, provided the principal organizational framework for local politics in Dofo, Kaiyo and Bola.

If *mol?o* resembled *helma* in organizational form, it was partly for the reason that *mol?o* regularly evolved from successful *helma* groups. By the time a *helma* had grown from the customary three or four members to as many as six or seven, the work groups apparently had become too large to be coordinated by informal means. The overgrown *helma* became a *mol?o* when the group of founders chose leaders. Each *mol?o* had a king *(kati)*, a chief *(ziso)*, and a lowcast policeman *(mənzi)* as well as a queen-mother *(gesho)*. Each of these leaders in the *mol?o* hierarchy fulfilled different duties and contributed in different ways to the functioning of the whole group. Like Maale notions about the polity as a whole, the *mol?o*'s functioning was thought to depend on the harmonious union of hierarchically arranged statuses.

At the top of the hierarchy was the *mol?o* king. His essential function was to provide fair judgments in disputes among members. If two workers got into a quarrel while on the job, the *mol?o* king would try to settle the argument and smooth over the affair. In handling a case, the king had limited power with which to impose settlements. He could, for instance, fine members and make them provide a payment of beer for the whole group. Also, he could order physical punishment, blows to the shin, meted out to offenders. These measures were rarely used and depended, of course, on support for the king's judgment by the overwhelmingly majority of members. If someone continually offended the group (quarreled or arrived late or did not do his share of work), he was ostracized after several admonishments by the king.

The choice of a *mol?o* king was critical, according to informants. If he was a good king, the *mol?o* would last for decades; if not, then the group would quarrel and quarrel and the *mol?o* would probably break up after just a few years. A good king, according to the Maale, was a mild, good-natured man *(zosa asi)*, slow to anger, not given to arguments and fights. In the five *mol?o* in the vicinity of Bola for which I have relevant data, there was no tendency for the king (or other officers) to be wealthier than other *mol?o* members. Maale said that the *mol?o* king was "king of work." Beyond the work place, he did not necessarily have any special influence. On work days, "he was big, bigger than the [real] king's sons."

After the king, the next most important position was that of *mənzi* or policeman. The *mənzi* scheduled the days on which the *mol?o* worked. Although a prescribed cycle of rotation was more or less followed, a variety of circumstances interrupted its perfect unfolding, and the *mənzi* was responsible for maintaining a fair equilibrium of labor given and received: First of all, anyone who could not attend a particular *mol?o* could maintain his position by sending a substitute, usually another member of his household. (In this regard, large households, i.e. elders' households, had a definite advantage in keeping up with *mol?o* work.) If a worker did not attend a particular *mol?o*, then either he worked on the field in question at a later date or, when his own turn arrived, the fieldowner to whom he had not contributed labor would simply skip working for him. Also, it was possible for a member to sell his turn either to another member of the *mol?o* or to an outsider, and then the group worked for the buyer just as it would have for the original member. Finally, some members had to delay their turn because they were not ready in time, while others occasionally needed to jump ahead of the cycle because, for example, weeds were about to choke out their fields.

It was the *mənzi* who kept order in the system, who reconciled, as best he could, competing claims, and who decided when and for whom the *mol?o* would work next. The whole cycle of rotation was constrained by the sequencing of horticultural tasks (see Figure 3), and in the central valley of Maale, *mol?o* usually worked four times a year for each of their members on: (1) clearing *le* fields, December through January, (2) cultivating and planting *le* fields, March through mid-April, (3) weeding *le* fields, mid-April through May, and (4) clearing *silo* fields, mid-June to mid-August. Other tasks in the horticultural cycle (e.g. harvesting) demanded less labor over short periods of time and were accomplished either with small *dabo* or with household labor.

Whereas the kingship of a *mol?o* was best filled by a mild-mannered man who was good at talking, the *mənzi* was required to take a more forceful role. Besides scheduling, he also policed the group during the first half of the working day, punishing laggards and latecomers with whippings to the lower leg. After a rest period if a few men stayed behind to smoke while others began to work, the *mənzi* would take away their water pipe and begin to whip their legs until they ran off to catch up with the others. One elder explained that when a *mənzi* was installed, he was instructed how to mete out punishment:

> When someone arrives late for work and he says some trouble kept him away, then whip him
> a little on the leg and stop. But if he was late because he went to his own field, then whip him

until he bleeds. Afterwards, when the group sits down during a rest period, the affair will be taken up with the king. The king will ask, "Why were you late?" And if the man says that he had some trouble, that he was coming back from a funeral, for example, then the king will excuse him. But if the man says that he went to his own work that morning, then the king will say, "This is someone's work also, isn't it? You just refused to come this morning, didn't you? Because of that, you will have to pay a gourd of beer." The next time the *mol?o* works for that man, he will have to make an additional gourd of beer for the *mol?o*.

The roles of chief *(ziso)* and queen-mother *(gesho)* completed the array of *mol?o* offices. The chief was in charge of providing tobacco for the group (the Maale are avid smokers), and during the last half of the work day, he was in charge of policing the *mol?o*. The queen-mother (often a male since few *mol?o* had female members) played a principal role in the ritual beer drink at midday. Kneeling, the queen-mother offered a gourd of beer to the king. After the king had drunk some, the two of them, with their mouths side by side, drank from the same gourd *(daggane)* the rest of the beer without stopping. The queen-mother repeated the same small ritual with the *mənzi* and then with the chief, after which the whole *mol?o* drank. The union (in Maale weddings the bride and groom drink together from the same gourd) of hierarchically arranged persons (first the king, then the *mənzi*, then the chief, then the others) guaranteed, according to the Maale way of thinking, harmony and prosperity. The crops they were farming, the Maale said, would ripen in abundance.

Since most *mol?o* members were young or middle-aged men (elders retired from *mol?o* work as soon as their sons were old enough to join), all of the offices enumerated above were filled mostly by junior men. Although they had formal control over *mol?o* matters, in the broader context of local politics, junior men were subordinate to elders. The *mol?o* was, in effect, a miniature social system encapsulated in the wider gerontocratic structure of Maale local politics. Elders whose sons worked in the *mol?o* stood backstage, as it were, and *mol?o* decisions often reflected their influence along with that of the official *mol?o* hierarchy.

Days on which *mol?o* worked, particularly those when beer was provided, were highpoints in the day-to-day life of Maale communities. As in *helma* custom, the owner of the field on which the *mol?o* worked could choose to brew beer or not. With beer, the group worked a full day, and without, a half-day. In contrast to *helma*, however, *mol?o* members more often than not chose to provide beer, and that choice required planning and a considerable outlay of female labor. The man's wife or, if he were unmarried, his mother and sisters, had to grind, carry water, and brew—tasks in addition to their normal workload. If malt (sprouted finger millet, an ingredient that took five days to prepare) were on hand, beer could be ready for drinking on the fourth day of preparations. The women in one household in Bola who happened to prepare beer for a *mol?o* of fourteen workers during my labor survey spent roughly twenty-five hours on the entire process.

After beer had been prepared and had fermented, the *mol?o* began work on the appointed day at about 8 or 9 a.m. and continued until about 4:30 or 5:30 p.m. The work group sat down to rest, to smoke their water pipes, and to drink beer usually at about 10 a.m., 1:00 p.m. and at the end of the work day. It was those convivial periods of beer drinking that Maale looked forward to, for such occasions attracted not just *mol?o* workers but members of the wider community. Most in evidence were elders whose sons worked in the *mol?o*. They alternated between lending a hand here and there, shouting advice and supervision to the workers, and retiring to shade trees, companions, and gourds of beer. Also, neighbors who were working in fields close to the site of the *mol?o* came over for the beer drink. Most who came were relatives of *mol?o* members, often of the sponsor of the *mol?o* that day, and those who drank more than once were expected to join in the work. Even herdboys out with cattle or goats for the day often managed to show up when the *mol?o* sat down to drink, edging up to the gathering in the hope that someone would share a gourd with them.

It was almost as if these social occasions were the gathering of a large family to a common meal. In fact, the rules of hospitality at home and at a *mol?o* were the same. A stranger or a Maale who lived some distance away who came to one's house at mealtime should be fed, according to Maale etiquette. Close friends, neighbors, and relatives also occasionally dropped in at one another's houses at mealtimes. It was considered bad form, however, for someone who lived nearby to arrive at another's house at meal time when no special relationship existed between the guest and the host. Then the Maale were likely to say disgustedly, "He came just to eat."

The same kind of rules held for the *mol?o*: travelers from outside the vicinity who happened to come by during the beer drink were given a place to sit and a gourd of beer. Likewise, relatives, close friends, and neighbors of the *mol?o* sponsor occasionally dropped by to drink beer. But it was bad form for someone with no special relationship to the sponsor and who lived nearby, someone who belonged directly (or indirectly through sons, in the case of elders) to a neighboring *mol?o*, to show up when the group sat down to drink beer. Once when I went to the beer drink of a *mol?o* in Bola with a Dofo elder (whose son belonged to the Dofo *mol?o*), the old man said sheepishly as we approached the gathering, "You go first. They may chase us off."

If the rules of hospitality suggest an analogy between households and *mol?o*, Maale themselves said that neighbors who worked together were like "relatives," *iginni*. Whenever a quarrel developed between *mol?o* members, third parties inevitably pointed out reprovingly, "But you two have worked together. Stop quarreling!" "Working together" was more than simply a technical means of accomplishing horticultural tasks; it was a social relationship which established and, at the same time, depended upon closeness, mutual support, and solidarity.

The emphasis on solidarity among *mol?o* members and the automatic intervention of *mol?o* members in quarrels between their work mates was apparently enough to smooth over arguments that otherwise would have led to the rupture of social relationships. An incident that occurred during my fieldwork in Dofo provides an illustration: One morning as cattle were being driven out to pasture, a young heifer from Chore's herd wandered into Sula's house garden. In a temper, Sula ran out of his house to drive the heifer away and threw a rock that happened to hit the cow exactly on the head. She fell down, instantly dead. As in many cases, there were wrongs on both sides. Chore's herdboy should have been watching the cow; on the other hand, Sula should not have lost his head and thrown a rock. When he heard about the cow, Chore was furious—not only about losing the heifer but about the fact that Sula had gone to work that morning instead of butchering the animal. As it happened, Chore's son and Sula worked in the same *mol?o* (they were not kinsmen) and the group was working that morning. What could he do, Sula asked. He had no one to replace him in the *mol?o*; he had to go to work.

An elder tied to Chore's and Sula's *mol?o* intervened and finally managed to sooth Chore's anger and to persuade him not to demand compensation. (Originally the heifer had been given to him by a bond friend, *belli,* and the elder and Chore finally convinced the bondsman to accept the meat of the heifer for which Chore could eventually expect, after making several more gifts, another cow.) When I wondered at the fact that Sula gave no compensation to Chore, the elder who had helped settle the case protested, "But aren't they countrymen? They are neighbors. They work together." He implied that people had to live together; perhaps tomorrow Chore would require Sula's forbearance and goodwill. Had Chore pressed his claim in the court of the *bālābbāt* in Bola (where adversaries are described as "enemies," *bālagārā*, a word borrowed from Amharic), it would have been tantamount to repudiating his long relationship with Sula's family and their common *mol?o*. Chore and Sula's father had worked together for almost thirty years, and after both had retired from *mol?o* work, their sons had worked in the same *mol?o*. With the weight of that history behind them, Sula's killing Chore's cow was finally defined as "a work of God." Chore's legal claim was probably a strong one, but had he pressed it and alienated Sula's family and refused the mediation of other *mol?o* members, he would have isolated himself. He would have had to establish new friends, to gather a new set of work partners, and to curry new supporters in local affairs.

Sometimes, of course, parties to a quarrel became so embittered that they chose to isolate themselves from old work partners. In the case that I related in Chapter 3, when Duno married Kababo against the adamant opposition of her father, Duno's and Kababo's fathers had previously worked together in the same *mol?o*. Kababo's father refused, however, to be placated. He would not even listen to elders who attempted to mediate the dispute. He quit the *mol?o*, and when the time came for spring planting and cultivation, he tried to recruit new work partners in Bola, especially among the traders and *mɜni*. Even so, he was very late in planting his field, and when I left Maale in late 1975 he was talking of moving to another chiefdom.

In the most extreme cases, disputes rankled so long and ramified so far that *mol?o* broke apart and ceased to function. After a period of recovery and realignment, new *mol?o* were organized and the boundaries between the new groups often reflected the new lines of political cleavage on the local level. Thus the relationship between *mol?o* and political solidarity went both ways. From the outset, those with similar political interests and identities tended to work together. Conversely, those who worked together developed bonds of solidarity and a mutual investment in continued cooperation.

To recall the analysis of the last section and to anticipate the next, it was neither residence nor kinship that provided the primary framework for local politics. Among productive groups, the *helma* was small and short-lived while the *dabo* had no permanent membership nor administrative hierarchy. In contrast to these, it was the *mol?o*, a relatively large group from seven to about thirty members, and a relatively enduring group, sometimes as long as about thirty years, that furnished the principal focus for local politics.

The metaphorical identification by the Maale of a *mol?o* with the polity as a whole was not, therefore, fortuitous: *mol?o* were in effect miniature kingdoms, each one a partially sovereign group, each one a relatively solidary social system. And *mol?o* members tended to live in roughly the same local territories. At the edges, fuzzy areas intervened where one household belonged to one *mol?o* while the next belonged to a different one. But toward the cores of *mol?o* territories, almost all neighbors belonged to the same work group, and there, *mol?o* had their distinctive centers of gravity. Also, closely related men of the same minimal descent group (who, of course, tended to live close to one another) nearly always belonged to the same *mol?o*. This "piling up" of relationships based on residence, descent, and (as I will show) *helma* and *dabo* work groups within the primary framework of *mol?o* was a principal feature of local political economy in Dofo, Kaiyo, and Bola.

In the last section, I isolated four social groups in Dofo, Kaiyo, and Bola which tended to form relatively distinct *helma* labor pools. As I showed, ties of descent and affinity along with ethnic identity and caste were all factors that contributed to the definition of boundaries among *helma* pools. As Figure 7 (an elaboration of Figure 6) shows, membership in *mol?o*, in turn, built upon this social substratum and grouped *helma* pools into two larger units focused on two separate *mol?o* work groups. The first, which I shall call Dofo (though it had members who lived in Bola, its center of gravity was located in Dofo) was composed of members from the relatively large Maale *helma* pool in Dofo and

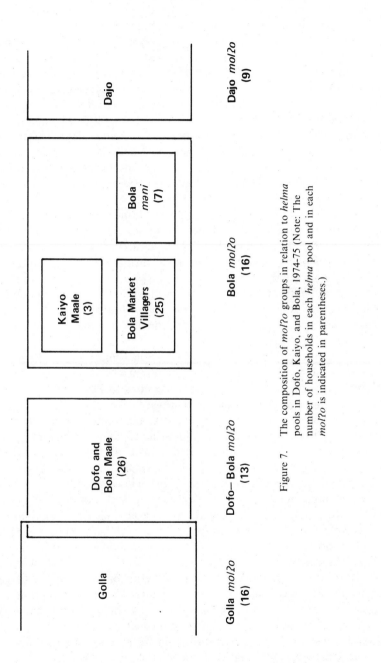

Figure 7. The composition of *molʔo* groups in relation to *helma* pools in Dofo, Kaiyo, and Bola, 1974-75 (Note: The number of households in each *helma* pool and in each *molʔo* is indicated in parentheses.)

Golla

Dofo and
Bola Maale
(26)

Kaiyo
Maale
(3)

Bola
mani
(7)

Bola Market
Villagers
(25)

Dajo

Golla *molʔo*
(16)

Dofo— Bola *molʔo*
(13)

Bola *molʔo*
(16)

Dajo *molʔo*
(9)

Bola. The second, which I shall call Bola, drew together three *helma* pools—Kaiyo Maale, Bola market villagers, and Bola *məni*.

If, as a first approximation, *helma* labor pools provided the building blocks out of which *molʔo* were constructed, a number of qualifications have to be made. Not all of the members of Bola *molʔo* came from the *helma* labor pools discussed so far. As Figure 7 shows, four of the members of Bola *molʔo*, all *məni,* came from Kuile, a community adjacent to Bola (see Map 6). Also, three households that belonged to the Dofo-Bola *helma* labor pool nevertheless chose to work in Golla *molʔo*, not Dofo *molʔo* (hence the overlap between the two groups shown in Figure 7). Finally, the overlap between Dofo and Golla *molʔo* was further increased by the fact that all of the elders' households among the Dofo-Bola Maale with large supplies of domestic labor belonged to two *molʔo,* Dofo and Golla.

A second series of qualifications have to be made as well—mainly, that not all households in the *helma* pools belonged to *molʔo* work groups. Only in the very small, three-household Kaiyo pool did all members belong to a *molʔo.* Otherwise, households headed by women, for example, usually did not have the male labor required to participate in *molʔo.* Also, newcomers to Dofo and Bola and, of course, more established men who had recently quarreled with their neighbors were not members of *molʔo.* Finally, many of the market villagers and, to a lesser extent, some of the *məni* did not cultivate enough to warrant *molʔo* membership.

Of the twenty-six households in Dofo-Bola *helma* pool, ten did not belong to *molʔo* at all. Five of these were households headed by single women, mostly elderly widows; two were the latest newcomers to Dofo, both having come within the last two years; and two had just broken away from Dofo *molʔo* because of quarrels and disagreements. A similar pattern occurred among the Bola *məni*; two out of the seven economic units did not belong to *molʔo.* One was a newcomer, and the other hardly cultivated at all. Finally, the market village was the least tied into the *molʔo* system of all. Twenty-one out of twenty-five households in the market village did not belong to *molʔo.* Seven of these were households headed by single women, and another eight, engaged in trade, hardly cultivated. The remaining six households cultivated fairly large fields, but did not belong to a *molʔo.* For reasons that will emerge in the next section, most of these men preferred to sponsor *dabo* work parties rather than join *molʔo* groups.

To summarize the analysis so far, three major points have emerged: (1) almost all households fully active in horticulture, with the exception of a few market villagers, belonged to *molʔo,* (2) householders who that were not *molʔo* members were linked indirectly through ties of kinship or common *helma* membership or so forth to one *molʔo* group or another, and (3) the boundary between Dofo and Bola *molʔo* was sharply defined.

To understand the formation of the boundary between Dofo and Bola and its political significance requires recourse to local history. The Dofo *mol?o* was founded in about 1964 by a group of young men in their twenties. Previously, the only *mol?o* in Dofo or Bola had been one organized by the young men's fathers in about 1930. In the early 1960s, many of the men in the old *mol?o* (the "elders" in 1975) had begun to retire from *mol?o* work as their sons matured. At first, the children simply replaced their fathers in the old structure—the *mol?o* king's eldest son became king, the *mənzi*'s eldest son, *mənzi* and so forth. As one Dofo elder recalled, "Then we got old and as our children came up, we told them, 'Don't destroy the little *mol?o*. One by one, all of you join.'"

The admonition went unheeded, however, for a group of young men, many of them younger brothers, organized a new *mol?o* with officers of their own choosing. The new *mol?o* prospered and attracted new members while the old one began to work less frequently, becoming increasingly plagued by disagreements. The chief of the old *mol?o* was a man named Doilo, and originally his eldest brother, Sere, had held the more important role of *mol?o mənzi*. Sere died in the early 1960s, and his teenaged son, Gulo, took over the role of *mənzi*. In Maale descent theory, Gulo should have taken precedence in status over Doilo, for Gulo had inherited the headship of the minimal descent group. But in fact Gulo was very young and inexperienced, and Doilo was well into middle age. This contradiction between age and descent group status carried over into the *mol?o,* for there also Gulo had been thrust into a position superior to Doilo.

Doilo apparently resented Gulo's new position and from the beginning maintained that Gulo was too young and inexperienced to fill the role of *mənzi.* But Gulo persisted, no doubt in ways that Doilo found even more offensive, for the conflict between the two of them festered until one day their quarreling led to the end of the old *mol?o.*

Gulo described the last day that the old *mol?o* worked in the following terms: After the *mol?o* had finished one round of work and had sat down to beer, Doilo was dividing up the beer, and he gave a disproportionate amount to his lover, a local widow. Gulo said, "Give beer to the people. What are you doing—only giving beer to her?" Doilo replied, "Sha! That thing [Gulo's public comment on his relationship to the widow] is making me very angry." The *mol?o* got up and worked a second round, and when they sat down to drink a second time, Doilo and the widow, according to Gulo, monopolized the water pipe so long that no one else could smoke. Acting in his role as *mənzi,* Gulo told Doilo's lover, "That's enough. Go on now. Either that or, our father's younger brother, you go on! While you two smoke, no one else can. The people are complaining. Give me the pipe." Doilo refused and Gulo snatched it away by force. When the *mol?o* resumed work, the quarrel continued and even disrupted work. Finally Gulo quit, saying, "All right, after this, you and I won't work together again." The old *mol?o* never worked together again, and by 1975 Gulo and Doilo had not resumed working together. Doilo later helped organize the Golla *mol?o*, and Gulo joined the new *mol?o* in Dofo.

With the old *mol?o* defunct, the young men's *mol?o* became even stronger and larger, and the elders, most of whom were retired from *mol?o* work by then, assumed their place backstage, as it were. As the elders retired from fully active economic roles, they took on more political responsibilities and, as I noted before, elders who lived near the king's residence in Bola traditionally had a special political role to fill as intermediaries between the king and the surrounding populace.

As Chapter 2 described in some detail, the period during which Bola and Dofo elders would have expected to take up their traditional roles at the center of the kingdom—the early 1960s—was a period of political crisis. The chiefs of Makana and Bola in league with influential northern landlords living in Maale went to court, removed the old Maale king, Yebirka, and replaced him by Bailo. For the first time according to Maale memory, the king was chosen by outsiders. The Maale king was no longer primarily a divine king or *kati*; in a critical sense, he was a landlord and a representative of the Ethiopian administration, *bālābbāt*.

With the change in the character of kingship went a change in the political position of Bola elders. Most of the elders had grown up serving the old king, Yebirka. It was to Yebirka that they had looked for favors in the past (help in marrying a girl against her relatives' wishes, a reduction in their rent compared to surrounding communities, the enjoyment of consuming part of the king's tribute, and so forth), and it was naturally to Yebirka that they would look in the future. When the question of who was properly king of Maale went to court, the Bola elders sided with Yebirka (except, as I have mentioned, for the Kaiyo elders). In effect, however, their support meant very little, for the elders had little knowledge of or means of influence in the new political arena of northern courts and administrative offices.

When Bailo was established as *bālābbāt* by court fiat, the elders could do little but acquiesce. They carried out their ritual roles in the installation ceremony for Bailo and their duties like labor tribute, but still there was some tension between them and the new king. The elders had, after all, supported Bailo's opponent, Yebirka, who, it should be noted, was still alive. But perhaps more important than their political disqualifications, Dofo and Bola elders could not fill the kind of intermediary role that was increasingly required under the new king. Collecting rents began to require keeping written rolls; settling local disputes, at least the most serious disputes, began to require written agreements attested to by witnesses; and all of the king's communication with the administration resident in Jinka required a knowlege of Amharic which he himself did not have.

After Bailo had established the market village in Bola in 1964 and after a number of traders had settled there, he began to turn to these men, a few of whom were literate in Amharic, to fill the role of intermediaries. Since the newcomers were outsiders, they were even more dependent on Bailo's good will than the Bola and Dofo elders; the land on which they settled was Bailo's land, and if they displeased the *balābbāt* they were evicted. On a number of counts, therefore, the traders became more useful to Bailo than the traditional elders in Dofo and Bola. As Bailo gradually began to depend on the market villagers to fill support roles, the elders who were being pushed aside increasingly came into political opposition with the newcomers. The cleavage between the two groups developed unimpeded by any history of past cooperation, any common ethnic identity, or any cross-cutting ties of kinship or marriage.

As it happened, the early 1960s not only witnessed the beginnings of the structural changes noted above, but also the onset of missionization in Maale. By the early 1970s, three strong Protestant communities had begun to flourish in the highlands not far from Bola, and a number of young converts had begun to trade in order to finance their schooling. In general, the Protestant communities seem to have taken the lead in diffusing throughout the highlands a more accurate knowledge of prices in markets outside Maale. This, according to the traders who lived in Bola, was the principal cause of the decrease in their profits during the 1970s.

With profits from trade falling, market villagers had to step up their cultivation, and by 1975 probably the majority of the male-headed households in the market village depended more on horticulture than on trade. As market villagers cultivated more, they integrated themselves into local work patterns, both in *mol?o* and *dabo* work parties, in a very distinctive way. A few years before, the *mani* living in Bola had organized a new *mol?o*. Whereas the Dofo *mol?o* had been founded in the regular process of one Maale generation succeeding another, the Bola *mol?o* organized in about 1971 was an innovation. Previously *mani* had not worked in *mol?o*. It was the Bola *mol?o* founded by *mani* that market villagers began to join. And it was also the Bola *mol?o* that Kaiyo Maale finally joined.

What caused such a heterogeneous collection of groups to begin work together? Certainly, it was not ties nor affinity. Nor was it simply spatial contiguity, for the Kaiyo Maale, for instance, worked with *mani* and market villagers but lived closer to Dofo and Bola Maale. In the beginning what all these groups shared was a common political opposition to Dofo and Bola Maale, For the *mani*, the opposition grew out of their long-standing ritual and economic subordination to Maale horticulturists. In 1975 most of the Bola and Dofo Maale still upheld the ritual prohibition against *mani* entering their houses or fields. The second group, the Kaiyo Maale, had previously worked and lived with their Dofo and Bola neighbors as we have seen, but a series of

Plate 10.   The Bola *Mol?o* Clearing a New *Silo* Field

Plate 11.   The Dofo *Mol?o* During a Beer Drink

quarrels had recently separated them. Perhaps more importantly, the principal elder in Kaiyo had departed from his counterparts in Bola and Dofo by enthusiastically supporting the new king Bailo. Estranged from many of their neighbors in Dofo and Bola, Kaiyo people ignored the old taboos against *məni* and joined the new Bola *mol?o*. Finally, the last group, the market villagers, came in collision with Dofo and Bola Maale almost from the beginning, as they began to take over the Maale elders' traditional role as retainers of the king.

If initially political interests were paramount in establishing the composition and boundary between Dofo and Bola *mol?o*, working cooperatively helped to cement both groups into relatively solidary political factions. During the twenty-month span of my fieldwork, the few disputes among Dofo, Kaiyo, and Bola residents that led, despite the mediations of local elders, to accusations before the *bālābbāt* or his representatives involved adversaries from different *mol?o* groups. No court case included opponents drawn from the same *mol?o* or from the same social group (Dofo-Bola Maale, Kaiyo Maale, Bola *məni*, or Bola market villagers) that combined to form *mol?o*.

Exactly how *mol?o* groups in Dofo and Bola provided a channel for local politics, how antagonists mobilized support from their respective groups, and how contests were finally settled are all aspects of Maale political economy best analyzed in reference to a concrete case. The following incident took place in December 1974, and because it was something of a local crisis, a social drama in Victor Turner's words, the case helps to lay bare the lines of cleavage in local politics.

In late 1974, the dry season began early and as a consequence many September fields (*silo*) did not ripen. By December grazing around Dofo and Bola was becoming scarce and people began turning their cattle into their unripened fields. One day two men whose households belonged to Dofo *mol?o*, Chore and Gulo, turned their cattle into the unripened field of Ermo, a young man from Kaiyo who worked in Bola *mol?o*. Now, there is some question whether Chore and Gulo actually drove the cattle through the fence of briars and bushes or whether the cattle got in themselves. And the act, if intentional, may have been a retaliation for some past injury that Chore or Gulo had suffered at Ermo's hands. There was apparently a long-standing uneasiness between the two sides.

During the market in Bola which took place that day, Ermo confronted Gulo about the cattle and demanded that he drive them elsewhere. But Gulo and Chore refused to do anything about the situation, and that night Chore did not even drive the cattle into his corral but left them to graze. As anyone should do who feels himself wronged, Ermo sent three "elders" or intermediaries to Chore. In this case, the "elders" Ermo sent turned out to be three young men, all of whom were Ermo's coworkers in Bola *mol?o*. (In disputes of lesser

magnitude, it was not unusual for younger men to serve as "elders.")
Emboldened and uninhibited by a day of drinking at the market, the
intermediaries, Wobo, Umbula, and Mishke drove Chore's cattle out of the
field and into his corral and came up to the gate of Chore's compound. It was
already late and Chore had closed his compound gate for the night. Because he
was mad, or because as he said later he was afraid of drunken visitors in the
middle of the night, Chore refused to let his guests in. Had the young men—
especially Wobo, a *mani* who had a reputation for unruliness—come "as
elders" or to beat him up, Chore asked.

The next day, Wednesday, Chore went to Bola and in the court of the
balābbāt formally accused Wobo and Umbula of entering his compound after
dark and attempting to beat him. Mishke, the third young man, and a close
relative of Ermo, was left out of the accusation. Wobo and Umbula, both *mani*,
were perhaps more vulnerable.

In the meantime, another more serious dispute was rankling which would
ramify the conflict between Dofo and Bola factions. Aroshiba, a young man
from Dofo *mol?o* (and Gulo's father's younger brother's son) blamed Mika, a
young man from Bola *mol?o* (and Ermo's father's younger brother's son) for
being a part of a group which had beaten him up on an earlier occasion. On
Tuesday night after the market, after the earlier argument between Gulo and
Ermo, Aroshiba, along with three other boys from Dofo, set off to gang up on
Mika. When the four boys reached Mika's house, his family along with Ermo's
was gathering in a clearing outside their compound to wail for Ermo's father
who had died several weeks ago. Mika spotted the four moving in the dark, and
he and the others chased the four boys to find out who they were. Aroshiba was
cornered by one of the men and when he was confronted, he lifted the gun he
was carrying (actually the *balābbāt*'s gun, which had been loaned to Aroshiba's
father). Undaunted, the other man said, "You big sack of flour, the likes of you
won't kill me." And when the man stepped up to try to take the gun away,
Aroshiba aimed and pulled the trigger: the gun did not fire. Whether there was
no bullet in the chamber or whether the bullet was defective was never clear.
Again, Aroshiba pulled the trigger. Again, the gun failed to go off. The man
began to call out for help or, perhaps more precisely, for witnesses: "Father of
Dode, help! Father of Arabo, help! Aroshiba has killed me!" When two Dofo
boys came along, the affair ended. Hurling accusations back and forth, the men
went home.

The next day, Wednesday, while Chore was making his accusation in the
balābbāt's court, Mika and his family formally accused Aroshiba and his
friends of attempted murder. Two days later, on Friday, the parties to both
cases were called to Bola by the *balābbāt*'s scribe. The market village was
buzzing as people grouped and regrouped, entered first this house, then
another (many of the houses in the village had liquor for sale), told and retold

this or that part of the story. Early in the day Chore's and Wobo's case was settled. Elders, emphasizing wrongs on both sides, coaxed the two to drop the case and let bygones be bygones. Chore, Wobo and Umbula agreed, and afterwards, they shared the cost of providing the group of elders involved in the case with three dollars in drinks.

Mika's and Aroshiba's case, however, took all day to settle. Just before noon, Aroshiba confessed that he had pulled the trigger and from that point on, Mika's side seems to have won the day. The fact that the gun belonged to the young *bālābbāt* put added pressure on Aroshiba's side to give in and pay a fine. If the case went to the police court outside Maale—as it would if it were not settled in Bola—the gun would be confiscated. Finally Aroshiba's father agreed to pay 70 Ethiopian dollars (a large fine—about the price of a mature heifer) to Mika's father.

At the end of the day after I had gone home, Aroshiba's father came to my house worried and breathless. He explained that Mika's father had refused to accept his young ox and was demanding cash—would I loan him the money or buy his ox? I gave him twenty dollars and later I heard that with much pleading from Aroshiba's father and the elders in the case, Mika's father relented and accepted the twenty dollars. When I left the field a year later, Aroshiba's father had made no further payment to Mika's father. Elders whom I asked doubted that Mika's father would ever get any addition; they pointed out, however, that if relations between the two families worsened, Mika's father could always reopen the case by accusing Aroshiba in the police court outside Maale where cases involving guns were always treated serioiusly. Instead of the dispute being "settled" perhaps it is more accurate to say that a truce was drawn. Whether, in fact, the case would ever come up again would depend on future relations between the two sides.

The elders in Mika's and Aroshiba's case were carefully chosen to represent Dofo and Bola. They were (1) Chore, perhaps the most respected elder connected to Dofo *mol?o* and a party in the previous case; (2) Lashababe, a *mani* man and "king" of Bolo *mol?o* of which Mika was a working member; (3) Gutse, a man who lived in Dofo but who was a bond friend of Mika's father; (4) Taddesa, a butcher who lived in the market village who nevertheless often worked with Aroshiba's father in *dabo* work parties, and (5) Ino, an outsider, a very old and respected man from Dajo, a community just south from Dofo and Bola. The balanced representation of both groups, plus the intervention of elders with ties to both groups, finally managed to effect a shaky reconciliation.

This case concluded, the division between Dofo and Bolo *mol?o* continued to provide the dominant focus for local political relationships. Membership in one *mol?o* or the other reflected the lines of political allegiances. Working cooperatively in the same *mol?o* strengthened political ties among coworkers while, at the same time, political interests influenced who would work with whom. The net result was that the major community-wide productive unit, the *mol?o*, also tended to be a relatively solidary political faction.

The Maale themselves interpreted the contest between Dofo and Bola in terms that emphasized old enmities, shared opposition to political opponents, ties of kinship, common cultural identities, and common religious affiliations. What none of my informants was entirely conscious of was the wave of historical change that was sweeping these various and different factors into a single, if imperfect, pattern: First of all, the increasing domination and absorption of Maale into the Ethiopian state; the appointment of an innovating *bālābbāt* by administrative fiat in 1962; his local support by *məni*, by a few elders living in Kaiyo, and by immigrant traders who were bringing Maale into increasing economic association with wider Ethiopia; and finally, passive opposition to the *bālābbāt* and his supporters by traditionalist elders in Dofo and Bola, a privileged group in the old order who were being swept under by the new wave of change.

The *Dabo*

In comparison to *helma* and *mol?o* work groups, the *dabo* system of cooperative labor, as I have pointed out, presented two structural contrasts. First, sets of cooperating households were not distinctly bounded. In sponsoring a *dabo*, a household brewed beer and asked a number of its neighbors to come and work. Different households had different circles of *dabo* partners, and workers in one *dabo* were often not the same as in the next *dabo*, even those sponsored by the same household.

The second major contrast was that reciprocity in *dabo* labor given and received was not built into the system of cooperation. In *helma* work groups, each member received back the labor he put into others' fields in a matter of days, in *mol?o* work groups, in a matter of a month or two. But since *dabo* were sponsored *ad hoc* as the need arose, and since there was no set cycle of rotation, a much longer time might elapse before a household recovered the labor it put into others' fields. Indeed, if certain households consistently had motive and means to sponsor more *dabo* than their neighbors, then long-term imbalances in the amount of labor given and received could develop.

To investigate the extent of imbalances requires a relatively self-contained group of households as far as *dabo* cooperation is concerned. That is, most households' *dabo* partners should come from within the sample, not outside. Dofo, Kaiyo, and Bola households turned out to present such a characteristic: in 1975, 91 percent of the workers in the *dabo* work parties in these three communities came from within the collective group. Another requirement for analyzing *dabo* is that the self-contained sample of households be studied for a long enough time that balances within the system could become manifest. On that score, I kept a record of the *dabo* work parties sponsored during the entire span of planting and weeding *le* fields in 1975, a period of four months (see Figure 3). This time period was a strategic choice since it was the season of peak labor demand in Maale, the bottleneck during which about half of all *dabo* were sponsored. Even in the (unlikely) event that imbalances during my study period were numerically balanced by reverse flows of labor at other times of the year, the total effect on yields still would not have balanced since the level of labor input during planting and weeding probably affected final yields more than labor inputs at any other time.

Let me begin with a description of how *dabo* were organized. Like *mol?o*, *dabo* provided highlights in the everyday social life of local communities. Work usually began about 9:00 a.m. and was punctuated every two or two and a half hours by rest stops with beer drinking. (It was impossible to have a *dabo* without beer.) The length of the work day varied according to the number of workers and the amount of beer brewed. When the beer was finished, work finished. Besides workers, a number of others, especially local elders, usually dropped by to share the beer during rest stops.

There was no set cycle of rotation for *dabo* work parties; each household sponsored its *dabo* as the need for labor arose. Also, there was no automatically bounded group from which each household drew *dabo* partners; depending on how much beer was brewed, work parties comprised any number of workers from two or three to twenty-five or thirty. In all cases, it was households and household heads in particular who both sponsored and sent workers to *dabo*, and no household could be expected to send more than one worker to a neighbor's *dabo*. Large households, therefore, (i.e. elders' households) had a definite advantage in maintaining large circles of *dabo* partners.

Compared to the sponsor of a *mol?o* who received the labor of his work group as a corporate right, a *dabo* sponsor was in a weaker position structurally. As the Maale said, a *dabo* sponsor "begged" (*shik'ene*) neighbors to come to his work party. Neighbors when they worked in a *dabo* did the sponsor a favor, as it were. Strangers to a community who had not built up a history of past cooperation had more difficulty than others in recruiting *dabo* labor. In order to break into the system of cooperation, a stranger gave a piece of grass to neighbors with whom he had not worked before. If the neighbors accepted the piece of grass (symbolic, apparently, of a gift, a favor, perhaps even of past labor cooperation) he obligated himself to go to the stranger's *dabo* work party. After the neighbor had worked in the *dabo*, then the obligation lay with the stranger (by then not a stranger but a functioning member of the community) to return the labor.

Plate 12.   A *Dabo* Work Party Weeding

It is not quite accurate to describe *dabo* sponsors as accumulating labor "debts," for the Maale did not keep an exact accounting of labor given and received, at least not publicly. Exact accounting would have been a repudiation of how Maale defined *dabo* cooperation—as a long-term, global relationship of mutual assistance. Nevertheless, informants were explicit on the point that a *dabo* sponsor retained obligations (if not "debts") to return labor to those who had worked for him. Those obligations became particularly evident for households who had other commitments but who were "begged" to work for those to whom they were obligated. In such cases, Maale were expected to explain beforehand why they could not attend the *dabo* in question. Not explaining would have meant breaking off the cooperative relationship. Such breaks did occur, and in Dofo in the spring of 1975, one man was essentially ostracized from *dabo* cooperation. After he had alienated one after another of his neighbors, Dofo households, except for those of his own lineage, refused to work in his *dabo* when asked.

In addition to the fact that Maale described *dabo* invitations as "begging," several other aspects of work party organization indicated the weaker structural position of *dabo* sponsors compared to *mol?o* sponsors. Sponsors of *dabo*, for instance, were expected to provide higher quality beer than *mol?o* sponsors. One elder in Dofo explained to me that no one could sponsor a *dabo* unless he brewed beer with a fair proportion of finger millet, the best grain for brewing. When finger millet was in short supply, as it usually was just before harvest during the strategically important time of weeding *le* fields, a *mol?o* sponsor—but not a *dabo* sponsor—could go ahead and sponsor work made with very little finger millet.

Finally, the sponsor of a *dabo* could depend on less work discipline than a *mol?o* sponsor. Elders present might remonstrate and reprove workers who wanted to rest before they should have, but there was no person like the *mol?o mani* who had authority to oversee the work process and to punish laggards. When the *dabo* beer finished, work finished and no one felt any responsibility (as they did in *mol?o* groups) to stretch beer when it was in short supply in order to complete a work day. All in all, according to one of my informants, less work was usually done in *dabo* than in *mol?o*: "When the beer is getting low, the people leave. One will say, 'I'm sick. I have to go.' Another will say, 'It's late now.'"

What kind of network did *dabo* cooperation establish? In itself, the *dabo* work party system did not automatically establish a series of neatly bounded, discrete groups. If household A worked with B, and B worked with C, then A did not necessarily work with C (as was the case, of course, in *helma* and *mol?o* groups). If, as an extreme case, *dabo* work ties were completely "intransitive" (if, in the example just cited, A and C worked together no more than would be randomly expected), then the web of *dabo* ties would spread out evenly,

Plate 13.   A *Dabo* Work Party Carrying Grain From Field to Granary

incorporating all households in Dofo, Kaiyo, and Bola in a single, continuous network. In fact, the network of *dabo* work ties departed markedly from such an ideal. Table 10 shows that two relatively discrete groups of *dabo* partners formed, and that households in each group worked almost exclusively with members of their own group. So even though discreteness was not automatically entailed by the organization of *dabo* work parties, in practice, fairly marked boundaries resulted.

What accounts for the split shown in Table 10? After the analysis of past sections, it will come as no surprise that the two *dabo* cooperating groups corresponded fairly exactly with the two political factions formed around Dofo and Bola *mol?o*. As in *mol?o*, working cooperatively in *dabo* required a certain amount of political solidarity so that a household's *dabo* partners usually came from its sphere of *mol?o* partners. Although there was some slight overlap, no member of Dofo *mol?o* consistently chose *dabo* partners from Bola *mol?o* nor did most members of Bola *mol?o* take *dabo* partners from Dofo. With few exceptions, *mol?o* membership generally determined who would work with who in *dabo* work parties.

A closer examination of the data allows a more precise analysis. In addition to the broad contrast related to different *mol?o* groups, there is also a finer structure in Table 10 that correlates with descent relationships. For the Bola *mol?o* group, the lower right-hand portion of Table 10, there is little evidence of the influence of descent since very few households are linked by kin ties, but for Dofo *mol?o*, the upper left-hand portion of Table 10, the effect is clear. Households in the same minimal descent group worked together in *dabo* more frequently than with non-kinsmen. The fact that *dabo* work parties involved longer term obligations than either *helma* or *mol?o* and the fact that the obligation to return *dabo* labor was only loosely defined and not built into the system of cooperation may help to explain why close kinsmen (usually one's most dependable neighbors) were chosen as *dabo* partners.[1]

Not all descent ties, however, had the same salience in establishing *dabo* cooperation. Apparently, the frequency of *dabo* work exchanges depended on the stage of development of the minimal lineage. In Table 11, minimal lineages in Dofo and Bola are arranged in order of their phase of development. In the early and middle phases, *dabo* labor exchanges within the group were as much as 37 percent more than if households had chosen their *dabo* partners randomly. As minimal lineages approached and reached segmentation, however, the extent of *dabo* cooperation decreased to only about 15 percent more than randomly expected.

While the saliency of descent relationships decayed over time, in the earliest stages of minimal lineage development, they were probably a "stronger" factor in establishing who would work with whom in *dabo* than was *mol?o* membership. Such a conclusion is suggested by two bits of evidence.

Table 10.   Matrix of *Dabo* Labor Given and Received in Dofo, Kaiyo, and Bola over Four Months in 1975. (The numbers from left to right and from top to bottom refer to households shown in Map 6. Reading across row x, one sees the number of times household x worked for others, and reading down column x, one sees the number of times others worked for household x.)

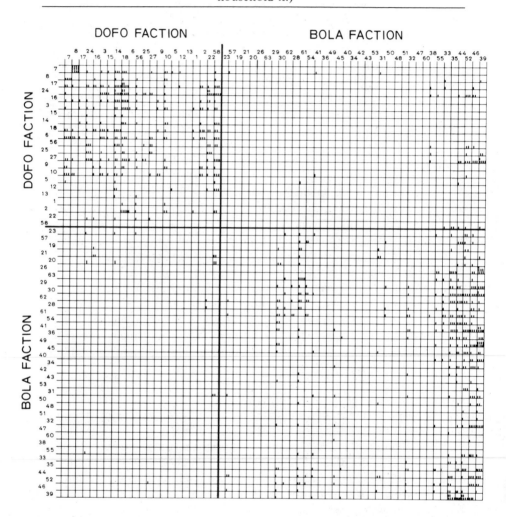

First, there was one example of a man in Dofo, a member of a recently established descent segment, who belonged to a *mol?o* different from that of his lineage mates. He drew almost twice as much *dabo* labor from either of his brothers' households as from any unrelated member of his *mol?o*. The second consideration involves systematic data from the left-hand portion of Table 10 taken as a whole: Most cases of extreme imbalance in labor given and received—probably a good measure of the strength of ties between households in Dofo group—occurred within minimal lineages in the early stages of development. Six out of seven cases of imbalances of four labor days or more between households in Dofo faction occurred within lineage segments in their early phases of development (i.e. phases 1 and 2 of Table 11).

Finally, after descent relationships and *mol?o* membership, residence appears to be a third factor which correlates with much of the remaining variation in the pattern of *dabo* cooperation. Consider, for example, the households located in Dofo that did not belong to Dofo *mol?o*. Excluding their kinsmen, 79 percent of the workers in the *dabo* of these households came from within Dofo. The effect of residence can again be seen in the pattern of Bola *dabo* parties: Bola households who were not members of the Bola *mol?o* and who did not have close kinsmen in Bola still gathered 81 percent of the *dabo* labor from neighbors in Bola.

It is, of course, reasonable that residence or simply propinquity would have an effect on the network of the *dabo* ties. It is much more difficult to ask distant rather than close neighbors to work parties and to remind them as the work day nears. Also, close neighbors are more likely to have fields located near one another. Beyond a certain distance, households did not have daily intercourse with neighbors, and the inconvenience of working together was simply too great.

If residence played a part in establishing who would work with whom, it was apparently a weak, residual factor. Shared *mol?o* membership was clearly a stronger factor, as the case of the four Maale households located in Bola but working in Dofo *mol?o* shows. Eliminating the times they worked with close kinsmen, these households still gave and received 79 percent of their *dabo* labor in Dofo rather than among their closer neighbors in Bola and Kaiyo.

To summarize the analysis of this section, a hierarchy of factors—close descent relationships, membership in the same *mol?o*, and residence within the same community—appears to have been salient in establishing who worked with whom in *dabo* work parties. Going up the hierarchy, each factor is successively stronger and overrides the effect of those below it. As factors become stronger, however, their range of applicability is restricted to smaller and smaller groups.

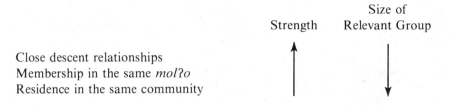

For the great proportion of households, these factors coincided to produce the boundary between Dofo and Bola. As Table 12 shows, many members of the same minimal descent group worked in the same *mol?o* and lived together in the same hamlet. The predominance of these congruent cases, particularly in Dofo faction, accounts for the relatively clean split into two independent *dabo*-sharing groups, one focused on Dofo, the other on Bola.

Table 12.   The Interrelationship of Descent, *Mol?o* Membership, and Residence as They Influenced the Pattern of *Dabo* Cooperation in Dofo and Bola Factions

Combination of Social Factors[a]	No. of Households in Dofo Faction	No. of Households in Bola Faction
D	–	–
M	4	3
R	5	27
DM	1	–
DR	3	–
MR	3	8
DMR	5	–

a. The letter D represents a tie of descent in the early phases of minimal lineage development; M, a tie of common *mol?o* membership; R, a tie of residence in the same hamlet. DM, DR, MR, and DMR are the respective combinations that these factors can take.

At other times or in other places, the hierarchy of factors isolated above might be expected to combine to produce different patterns, variations on the theme of Table 10, in which boundaries between groups are perhaps fuzzier and less distinct. The peculiarity of Dofo, Kaiyo, and Bola resulted largely from their placement at the center of Maale, the major point at which wider economic and political forces, in collision with local ones, were transforming Maale political economy.

Labor Imbalances in the *Dabo* Work Party System

As I have noted, the beer that a *dabo* sponsor provided his work party cannot be considered a wage from the Maale point of view, since the sponsor, besides providing the beer, also retained an obligation to attend the future *dabo* of those who had worked for him. Unlike other forms of labor cooperation in Maale, however, the obligation to return *dabo* labor was not enforced by any organizational sanction but was generalized and fairly loosely defined. Sometime in the future, when asked, one should return *dabo* labor.

If the system of *dabo* cooperation were in fact exactly balanced, then the matrix shown in Table 10 would be exactly symmetrical about the diagonal. Folded along the diagonal, each square of the matrix would touch another square of exactly equal magnitude—i.e., if household A worked twice for B, then B would work twice for A. A cursory inspection of Table 10 shows that the *dabo* system was markedly imbalanced.[2] In order to elucidate the pattern of imbalances in Table 10, I want to consider Dofo and Bola factions separately and then integrate the results; as it happens, different principles appear to provide the main explanation for *dabo* imbalances in the two different factions.

Dofo, to recall the results of Chapter 3, was composed of households with very different supplies of domestic labor. Elders' households were generally large and possessed of ample supplies of labor (low C/W); middle-aged households, in contrast, were typically short of labor since they had many children in relation to the adult workers who supported them (high C/W). Finally, the households of young men and their wives along with those of widows were neither labor rich nor labor poor. Chapter 3 also showed that, contrary to theories of domestic production, workers in households in Dofo faction from all stages of development seem to have worked about the same number of hours a day. That finding posed a paradox: Since elders' households were not marketing nor giving away any consistent surplus, middle-aged households were apparently underproducing, consuming less than others. Such a conclusion, however, was contrary to my general impression.

The solution to this paradox, or at least a major part of the solution, appears to lie in the pattern of *dabo* labor imbalances in Dofo faction. With two notable exceptions, households of low dependency ratio (C/W), predominantly elders' households, consistently gave away more *dabo* labor than they received. Conversely, households with high dependency ratios, predominantly middle-aged mens' households, received more *dabo* labor than they gave away. Finally, young mens' households and most widows' households in the middle range of dependency ratios—experienced neither a large deficit nor a large surplus. In sum, there was a net transfer of labor mostly from elders' households mostly to middle-aged mens' households.

In order to demonstrate numerically that such transfers took place in Dofo faction, a number of preliminaries are required. First, a few households worked in and sponsored *dabo* so infrequently during my study period that their "imbalances" might have been the result only of the time period studied. Consequently, the five Dofo households only weakly integrated into the *dabo* system, whose total of *dabo* days given added to those received was less than twelve, are eliminated from the analysis below (i.e., from Figure 8). Second, three households in Dofo faction were obviously "deviant" cases. One middle-aged man had a very high dependency ratio but managed to draw no surplus labor from his neighbors. According to his neighbors, the man had been thrown out of the Dofo *mol?o* in 1974 for laziness, and in 1975 during the present survey, he cultivated a very small field and was considering moving. The other two exceptions were elders' households with relatively large supplies of domestic labor who yet supplemented them with net surpluses of labor from neighbors. One was by far the richest elder in Dofo, the only exception to the even distribution of wealth among Maale in Dofo-Bola, while the other household was headed by a half-Maale trader of moderate wealth who had married a Dofo woman and who had established close ties with the Dofo faction, rather than to Bola.

Given these qualifications, the correlation of *dabo* imbalances with household dependency ratios (C/W) in Dofo faction is quite striking. Figure 8 shows the least squares linear relationship between the two variables. The correlation coefficient, r, is 0.89; that is, 78 percent (r^2) of the variability in *dabo* imbalance is explained by variation in dependency ratio. And the correlation shown in Figure 8 is significant at the 0.001 level.

In less formal language, Figure 8 shows that households with, for example, as many as three children between two and six years of age (dependency ratio of about 2.8) had reached a critical balance point. They gave out about as much *dabo* labor as they received and still apparently managed to meet their consumption requirements. With less favorable ratios of domestic labor (i.e. more children), most Dofo households depended upon a modest surplus of *dabo* labor drawn from their neighbors. And with more favorable labor supplies, Dofo households consistently gave away much more *dabo* labor than they received.

Figure 9 presents data for all households in Dofo faction on the exact nature of *dabo* labor flows—from whom middle-aged households and others of high dependency ratio received labor and to whom elders' households gave labor. Over the four-month period of study, there was a net flow of 67 work days from Dofo faction to households outside its boundaries, especially to the *bālābbāt* (35 days) but also to various households in Bola faction (a total of 32 days). Internally, there were even greater flows of labor. The seven households in Dofo with low dependency ratios (elders' households in addition to one widow's household) transferred 57 *dabo* days of labor to the nine households in Dofo with high dependency ratios (middle-aged households along with that of one elder who had married a second wife and had small children). Also, the two exceptional elders—the rich Maale elder along with the half-Maale trader— drew 18 work days from other elders and 7 from young mens' households. (This latter pattern which appears to be related to wealth and type of economic activity will reappear in the Bola faction.)

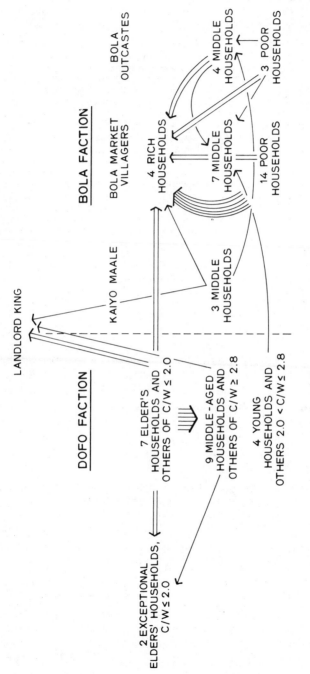

Figure 9.   The pattern of *dabo* labor flows in Bola vicinity (each
arrow is proportional to ten days of *dabo* labor).

Clearly, any theory of noncapitalist production which neglects labor flows between households, as Chayanov's and Sahlin's theories do, cannot realistically describe the Maale case. Middle-aged men's households, apparently instead of working long hours, tended to draw a net surplus of labor from elders' households by sponsoring more *dabo* work parties. If, however, that fact provides a major part of the answer to the paradox raised by Chapter 3 it also raises other perplexing questions: Why did labor flows take place? Why were elders, or at least most elders, willing to preside over the transfer of their households' labor power? These subjects will be discussed in the last section of this chapter after the contrasting pattern of labor imbalances in Bola faction has been presented.

Imbalances in *dabo* work parties in Bola faction were even more extreme than in Dofo. And in contrast to Dofo the phase of household development in Bola did not correlate with the pattern of imbalances. As Chapter 3 set out, household size among the Bola market villagers varied little with the age of household head and there was some (inconclusive) evidence that household size depended more on wealth than simply on the phase of development. Likewise, in relation to the pattern of *dabo* imbalances, the hypothesis that I want to investigate is that wealth was the single most important factor and that rich households consistently enjoyed a large surplus of *dabo* labor while poorer ones experienced deficits.

Chapter 3 classified market village households into categories of rich, middle, and poor; this same classification will be used here to investigate the effect of wealth on *dabo* labor flows. As in Dofo, the *dabo* imbalances of households that worked in and sponsored only a few work parties were more likely to have been the result of the time period studied than the imbalances of those more integrated into the system of cooperation. Accordingly, households that gave and received less that twelve days of *dabo* labor during my study period were not included in the correlational analysis below. Excluded in this were all of the seven households headed by single women in Bola (none of whom had fields) and four middle-level traders (who were away from Bola so often on trading trips that they cultivated very small fields).

For the remaining households in the market village, Table 13 presents the relationship between wealth and net *dabo* imbalances. The variation of *dabo* imbalances between wealth categories was significantly greater than the variation within categories, and an analysis of variance indicates that the null hypothesis—that wealth had no association with *dabo* imbalances—can be rejected at the 0.001 confidence level. In other words, the probability that the above distribution resulted only from chance is less than one in a thousand.

What was the relationship between wealth and *dabo* labor flows in the other components of Bola faction—the Kaiyo Maale and the Bola *mani*? Figure 9 presents the pattern for Bola faction as a whole. As Figure 9 shows, all

Table 13.   The Variation of Net *Dabo* Labor Imbalances with Level of Wealth for Bola Market Village Households

Poor		Middle		Rich	
Household Number	Net *Dabo* Days	Household Number	Net *Dabo* Days	Household Number	Net *Dabo* Days
31	– 4	32	0	35	37
36	–12	33	9	39	54
40	– 6	52	43	44	32
41	–16	54	–3	46	49
45	– 7				
55	6	Average	12	Average	43
Average	– 6				

three Kaiyo households were comparable in wealth to middle-level market villagers. Unlike the latter, however, Kaiyo households consistently experienced net deficits in *dabo* cooperation. As it happened, Kaiyo households were caught in a special situation in the spring of 1975. The past November, the head of the Kaiyo minimal lineage had died, and the funeral had depleted the grain stores of all three households. As a result, none had enough to sponsor *dabo*. Since Kaiyo households did not cease participation in their neighbors' work parties, all showed net deficits in *dabo* labor. By continuing to participate, Kaiyo people hoped to be able to sponsor *dabo* the following year after regaining their economic standing (though it is clear that labor deficits during 1975 only made regaining that standing more difficult).

Like Kaiyo households, Bola *məni* also consistently showed net deficits of labor in *dabo* work parties. There were both poor (mostly young men who were still involved in tanning) as well as households of modest means amongst the Bola *məni*, and as Figure 10 shows, both contributed about the same amount of labor to wealthy market villagers. Middle-level *məni*, however, were able to offset some of their losses by drawing labor from the poor *məni* themselves and from Kaiyo Maale. Wealth affected the pattern of *dabo* imbalances among the Bola *məni*, even though middle-level *məni* were not quite as successful as comparable market villagers in maintaining positive balances. The middle-level villagers' devotion to trading, the limited time they had left for cultivation and their incentive to minimize the amount of food grain they had to buy from the market seem to have combined to provide an impetus for traders to sponsor more *dabo* than cultivators of the same wealth among the *məni*.

As in Dofo faction, there were exceptions to the general level of *dabo* flows that emerge in Bola, but in general, increasing levels of wealth were highly correlated with increasingly positive balances of *dabo* labor. The four richest households in the market village collectively enjoyed a remarkable surplus of 146 *dabo* work days during my four-month study period, while the seventeen poor market villagers and *məni* experienced a collective deficit of 121 *dabo* work days. This flow of labor helped to keep the rich rich and the poor poor, to maintain and reproduce the wealth differences between strata in Bola faction.

Labor Flows and Local Politics

In Dofo faction there was a large net flow of *dabo* labor from most elders' households to most middle-aged mens' households. In Bola faction, there was an even larger flow of *dabo* labor from most poorer to most richer households. When people were free to choose to work in *dabo* or not (One informant explained, "When someone begs me to work in his *dabo*, I go if I want to; if not, then I don't go") why did such flows take place?

The first possibility that must be investigated is that there were in fact no labor flows—that the labor embodied in *dabo* beer tended to balance the amount of labor done by the work party (cf. Sahlins 1972: 107). Unfortunately, this is a difficult question to answer except by approximation, and the only attempt to deal with it in the anthropological literature of which I am aware is Barth's study of Darfur. Barth (1967: 166) estimated that the labor embodied in Darfur beer was about one-third of that accomplished by work parties. For the Maale case also, I have based my calculations on certain estimations combined with other reasonable assumptions (see the Appendix). On the basis of these calculations, it appears that the labor embodied in *dabo* beer was about half of that carried out by the work party. So while the "real" labor flows were approximately half of the simple imbalances in *dabo* days discussed above, they were still sizeable. Also, it should be noted that these labor flows occurred at the principal bottlenecks in the productive cycle when the magnitude of labor input had its greatest effect on final yield.

The question remains therefore: When *dabo* were voluntary forms of cooperation, why did net flows of labor develop? I believe that the answer lies principally in the global nature of labor cooperation in Maale. Working together rested not just on narrowly defined economic relationships but on social and political grounds as well. Obligations accumulated in *dabo* work parties, while discharged mainly by returning *dabo* labor, could apparently be dealt with in a number of ways. Descent relationships within minimal lineages during the early phases of their developmental cycle provided one basis for labor flows. That is, a small number of households contributed a net amount of labor to their relatives just because they were relatives and needed help. But more important for understanding the overall pattern in Dofo and Bola were political relationships. Some politically influential household heads commanded *dabo* labor on the strength of their ability to dispense favors and to inflict punishment. Others, conversely, in different contexts contributed *dabo* labor to their neighbors in order to gather and maintain political support.

Exactly how politics interacted with the organization of *dabo* requires a closer examination of the local political scene, first in Bola and then in Dofo.

The most politically influential men in Bola faction corresponded almost exactly to the richest four market village households that enjoyed such a surplus of *dabo* labor from their neighbors. Their influence and, to a great extent, their wealth, derived mainly from their relationship to the Maale *bālābbāt*. Two of the four had served as the king's scribe, presiding over court cases in the *bālābbāt*'s absence, collecting rents, and serving as the *bālābbāt*'s go-between with Jinka, the subprovincial capital. A third man had served from time to time as the king's representative in collecting rents. All of these three men, much more than middle-level men in the market village or surrounding Maale, were regularly involved in settling local court cases. They acted as guarantors (*wasi*) and as "elders" who tried to reconcile disputes. Only one of four had occupied no position whatsoever in the administration nor apparently wielded any more influence in local affairs than other men.

For a number of reasons already investigated, after 1964 the *bālābbāt* Bailo increasingly relied on this small set of men in the market village to carry out support roles. These men became, in effect, the lowest rung in the Ethiopian state apparatus which reached all the way up to the Emperor. Their position gave them a great deal of influence in Bola, and finally, wealth. When they collected rents, these men were able, within bounds, to set the amount of money Maale paid and it was an unspoken assumption that before passing on what they had collected to the *bālābbāt*, they would retain a portion for themselves. In 1974 Maale pointed out with some bitterness that the king's scribe had arrived two years before with nothing, and since then he had accumulated a herd of ten cows, the largest in Bola.

To determine why this small group of market villagers were able to enjoy such a surplus of *dabo* labor requires examining two questions: To what extent did access to grain and to the womens' labor needed to turn it into beer differ among groups in Bola faction and, second, why were middle and poor market villagers, Maale, and *məni*, willing to contribute *dabo* labor to rich villagers when very little labor was returned to them.

On the first count, the rich market villagers' relative wealth and their control over monetary resources were critical in their *dabo* activities. Roughly half of the beer they employed in *dabo* work parties, I estimated, was bought from the market. Ordinarily beer brought to the market on Tuesdays was sold by the drink for ten Ethiopian cents. The four richest Bola villagers—but almost no one else in Bola or Dofo—regularly bought whole gourds of beer for their *dabo* work parties. This supplement to the beer produced by women of their own households (who were engaged in other tasks such as distilling hard liquor and making honey wine) was crucial in allowing rich villagers to sponsor more *dabo* than they otherwise would have been able to.

A disproportionate amount (about two-thirds) of the net surplus of *dabo* labor that richer villagers enjoyed was drawn from people in the poorest categories, among whom the median household sponsored no *dabo* at all during my study period. While part of that disproportion reflected the fact that households such as those of single women and poor *məni* pursued horticulture to such a limited extent that they had no regular need for *dabo* labor, the limited access of these poor households to surplus grain and to beer was also important. Poor market villagers, in particular, often did not have the extra grain to make *dabo* beer or, alternatively, the extra cash needed to buy beer from the market. When I asked one young man who did not have enough grain to make *dabo* beer why he continued to work in others' *dabo* when he had no hope of receiving help in return, he explained that he hoped gradually to accumulate enough resources to sponsor *dabo* in the future. It is reasonable to suppose, of course, that many of the young men of poor means would be able to move into the middle category as they grew older, but it is also clear that their present *dabo* deficits (labor deflected from their own fields) actually delayed the time when they would be able to recoup their labor losses, Moreover, if the present pattern can be taken as any guide to the future, it is fairly clear that any newly arrived middle villager would not receive labor from those to whom they had previously contributed it, i.e. from the rich market villagers. Indeed, during my study period, middle villagers—while on the average enjoying a small net surplus of *dabo* labor—still showed a deficit in cooperation with richer villagers.

If relative access to the resources needed to prepare beer helps to explain why poor households experienced a greater net deficit than middle ones, still *all* categories in Bola faction contributed a net amount of *dabo* labor to the small group of relatively rich villagers. Given the number of households that worked in rich villagers' *dabo*, it was clearly impossible for the latter group to return the labor they received. Indeed, as I have pointed out above, *dabo* cooperation was more than a simple economic arrangement designed only to exchange labor for labor. Working together, first of all, established and confirmed a comprehensive relationship between participants in which common economic as well as political and even ideological interests were affirmed. Had, for instance, poor market villagers openly refused to work in the *dabo* of their better-offs, such a refusal would have been taken as a social breach, a declaration of social separation. The households in Bola faction that worked in one another's work parties were loosely united by a common opposition to traditionalistic Maale, by support for the Amharized *bālābbāt*, and by varying degrees of identification with national Ethiopian culture.

If poor and middle households did not actually expect labor in return when they worked for rich market villagers, they probably did hope for and expect a variety of political favors. In this regard the rich market villagers' role as the local representatives of the Ethiopian administration was crucial. Goodwill at rent time and help with a court case were the kinds of favors that most of the rich villagers were able to dispense. The flow of labor encouraged by differences in political power in Bola helped, on the one hand, to reproduce and even augment wealth differences and, on the other hand, to give Bola people a clear advantage *vis-à-vis* the surrounding populace. It was commonly remarked upon that rents in Bola were lower than any place nearby.

The case of the *balābbāt* offers a final and clearcut illustration of how differences in power which were sanctioned by the Ethiopian state skewed *dabo* exchanges in Bola and Dofo. During my study period, the *balābbāt* enjoyed about the same amount of surplus labor as the rich households in Bola (though his labor was drawn mainly form Dofo and not Bola). For those who worked in his *dabo* work parties, there was little question whether they would receive labor in return at some future date: no one would have dared to ask the *balābbāt*'s household for such help. In effect, then, the *balābbāt*'s work parties functioned as labor tribute. Although the ideology of balanced equality remained, in situations of marked differences in power and wealth, practice departed considerably from the ideal norm.

The pattern of *dabo* labor flows in Dofo faction was diametrically opposed to those in Bola. In Dofo most politically influential households experienced deficits of labor in *dabo* work parties, not surpluses. As I have already shown, there was a net transfer of labor from most elders' households to most middle-aged mens' households.

The two exceptions to this general pattern in Dofo (elders' households that enjoyed a surplus of *dabo* labor) are revealing. One, Chore, was an ordinary Maale elder, a younger brother who had not yet become head of his own minimal descent group and who was, therefore, under the authority of his eldest brother. Two aspects of Chore's character are notable for the present discussion: First, he was an extremely hardworking and diligent man, and he had managed to accumulate the largest herd of cattle in Dofo. Although, as Chapter 3 explained, Chore could not be said to be the sole owner of the cattle he had accumulated (when his minimal lineage finally segmented, some of his cattle would undoubtedly be claimed by his eldest brother), nevertheless, he was clearly the richest man in Dofo faction. Second, however, Chore was among the least active of Dofo elders in local politics. He gave the impression of one who wanted to mind his own business and to get ahead economically. Everyone respected him. His house was often a gathering place for Dofo people. But, in general, Chore tried to steer clear of political entanglements. He did not take an active role, for instance, in the politicking about installing a new *kati* in 1974 and 1975. (Precisely because he and his family were little involved in the old politics, Chore's eldest son was chosen as a leader of the new cooperative which was set up by the revolutionary government in 1975.)

The other elder's household that enjoyed a labor surplus was headed by a man, Husein, whose father had been a trader from Jimma and whose mother was Maale. The man had assimilated to Maale ways more than to Jimma, and although he continued to trade to a limited extent, he also cultivated. Husein married a Maale woman with many kinsmen in Dofo and had given her male relatives large marriage gifts, even though it was not Maale custom to do so when the woman had been married before, Through his wife's kinsmen, Husein had integrated himself into Dofo faction. He was neither influential nor even very concerned with the issues that animated traditionalist elders in Dofo. And although he was an "elder" in age and although the dependency ratio of his household was in the range of other elders' 'n Dofo, the composition of Husein's household differed markedly. His wife was childless, and Husein's economic unit consisted only of himself and his wife.

The rest of the elders' households in Dofo faction, all of whom experienced large deficit in *dabo* labor, were (1) to varying degrees all involved in local politics, particularly the issue of who should become *kati* and (2) possessed of relatively large supplies of domestic labor including several grown children.

As a result of the economic and political changes that were accelerating throughout the early 1970s, the elders in Dofo faction found their traditional position of special influence in Maale challenged from two sides. On one side, they came into conflict with immigrant traders in Bola who were taking over the elders' old role as middlemen between the king and the surrounding population, Literate traders, not elders, were becoming more effective in dealing with and profiting from the new system of landlords, rents, and local court cases. On the other side, another threat to the elders grew—that of the Maale Protestants. Protestant communities grew up in political opposition both to the old divine kingship to which the Dofo elders were so tied and to the new Ethiopian system of political influence based on land ownership and ties to landlords. In the early 1960s, many of the Dofo elders, mindful of the increasing importance of education, sent a son to schools that Protestants had opened near Dofo. As the friction between the Protestants and the *bālābbāt* grew, however, the *bālābbāt* ordered the Bola elders to take their children out of Protestant schools. By the time of my fieldwork, a great deal of bitterness existed between Bola elders and Protestants. Junior men were more neutral on this issue, and more than one informant pointed out that it was mainly junior men who were converting to Protestant Christianity—in particular, younger brothers who stood to inherit very little when their fathers died. In Protestant communities, junior men with a few years of education were gaining a great deal of influence that they would not have enjoyed under the old Maale system. For the Dofo elders, therefore, Protestant communities threatened to lure away their young men and to undermine the loyalty of their closest following.

Caught between the immigrant traders in Bola and Maale Protestant commmunities, the elders in Dofo faction were fighting to keep alive the old system and their special position in it. It was in this context, I am arguing, that elders—in order to shore up their faction and to maintain political support—transferred labor to households of junior men. Of course, elders themselves did not generally work in the *dabo* of middle-aged men; it was elders' dependents—unmarried adult children as well as married eldest sons and their wives—who actually did the work. Still, it was elders who presided over the labor of their households.[3]

Simply stated, elders appeared to be transferring labor to middle-aged men in return for support and for deference. The greatest portion of that transfer went to middle-aged rather than young households. Middle-aged households typically contained relatively many nonworking children and had a special need for extra labor just to meet their consumption needs. Labor flows in Dofo faction, therefore, did not function to maintain and expand differences in wealth (with the exception of Chore and Husein). Elders were not contributing to their own future subordination as were poor market villagers in Bola. Just the opposite, for elders were obligating and subordinating middle-aged households by providing part of the labor that allowed the latter to keep up normal consumption levels while working normal hours. If middle-aged men did not return *dabo* labor then at least they were under some compulsion no to offend their elders. After all, elders' labor support for junior men could be withdrawn as Wuzare's case shows. (After Chore and Husein, Wuzare was the third "deviant" case in Dofo faction.) Wuzare—after being thrown out of the Dofo *mol?o* and after quarreling with Gulo, his mother's brother's son in Dofo—did not receive any more *dabo* labor than he contributed to others in 1975. As noted before, Wuzare was talking of moving from Dofo in late 1975.

Young households, by contrast, had no comparable need for extra labor. Working normal hours, young men and their wives could apparently meet normal consumption requirements fairly easily. In addition, during the first few years of new households' existence, it may have been difficult for some to accumulate extra grain for beer. Finally, recently married men only just out from under their fathers' direct authority and often recently obligated to their senior relatives and neighbors for help with marriage gifts were probably already more strongly tied to the elders than were middle-aged men.

Of course, if the pattern I discovered in Dofo during 1975 had held over the past generation (a proposition probably impossible to verify) or if the pattern can be assumed to operate over the next generation (an hypothesis even more tenuous), then *dabo* flows would tend to balance out, at least over generations. Whether either of these long-term speculations happen to be true, in the short-term, the inequalities and obligations that I have discussed above would still operate and would still prove, I think, a basic element in the local political economy.

In both Dofo and Bola factions, *dabo* labor flows reflected fundamental inequalities in political power and influence and (in the case of Bola, mainly) inequalities of wealth. As I have mentioned, conflicts within either Dofo or Bola factions—even between those on the top and those on the bottom—were muted and rarely reached public expression. Part of the reason for this solidarity across strata in both groups must have been the strong vertical cleavage, the political tension between Dofo and Bola. It was the increasing incorporation of Maale into the Ethiopian state along with the *balābbāt's* policies to found a market village and to bring immigrants into his administration that established and maintained the vertical cleavage between Dofo and Bola. And if the policies of the *balābbāt* were partly the cause of the cleavage, he himself performed the function of settling the conflicts that were generated. As I noted above, Dofo elders could not conceive how Maale could survive without a king after the revolution in late 1975. "Even bees have a king." In a sense, the elders were correct—correct at least as long as old political realities, old ways of working together were assumed to hold in Maale.

5

Conclusion: Work, Power, and History

Consider for a moment the image of Maale production that would have resulted if I had drawn the boundaries of my study unit differently, as I was initially inclined to do. If I had focused only on Maale households, no doubt the transfer of labors from elders to juniors would have appeared very "traditional." Perhaps I would have concluded that such transfers reflected the traditional Maale mode of production, a natural economy in which the law of profits did not hold, a primitive communism in which the famous maxim held true—"from each according to his ability, to each according to his need." To exaggerate somewhat, the Maale economy would have appeared to have that paradoxical quality that we have come to associate with traditional economies: influential people seem intent on giving it all away rather than getting more and more.

To have ignored the particular historical flow of changes in Maale vicinity would have misled my analysis in other ways. Labor transfers would have appeared as part of an ingenious, clock-like mechanism: elders helping junior households, and junior households finally supplementing the labor of still younger households. In the long run, exchanges would tend to balance. In the short run, the system would be eminently adapted to compensate for temporary labor shortages. Short-term inequalities, as if designed by some unseen hand, would seem to have functioned to reproduce the static system over time.

But, as I have shown, labor transfers in Bola vicinity reflected a response to local social and historical forces, not the effects of a perduring, primordal tradition. Whether such transfers occurred elsewhere in Maale is questionable. Unfortunately, I do not have enough data to document the relevant patterns of regional variation.

At the least, it is clear that Dofo and Bola leaders could have used their household labor resources differently; they could have produced extra grain to trade for cattle, a transaction often carried out within bond friendships (*belli*). Such exchanges were common in Maale (though not in Bola vicinity in 1974-75). In the southern, drier areas of Maale in particular (southern Irbo, Bunka, and Gero in Map 4), horticultural production was precarious, except on alluvial land near major rivers. Whether this land, which was located near the Maale-Banna border, could be cultivated depended on the state of relations between the two peoples. In 1974-75, fighting and cattle-raiding prevented such cultivation, and southern Maale consistently traded cattle (that thrived in the lowlands savannahs) for grain, mostly from northern Bunka.

To produce extra grain in the highlands took labor, of course, and it was generally recognized that an elder with many working children (*wərshado*, "father of a multitude") was often able to produce for such exchanges. When, for example, I asked about buying grain in bulk, my Maale neighbors told me that I should inquire at the houses of *wərshado*.

If labor transfers were not necessarily characteristic of other communities, the fact that elders typically presided over relatively large household labor supplies appears to have been a widespread phenomenon in Maale. Censuses in chiefdoms other than Bola revealed the same pattern of stem family household development. Exactly how in each case elders used their labor resources probably depended on local politics as well as on local ecology; in sum, labor patterns depended upon the position local communities occupied within the wider social system. Bola, located at the political center of Maale, offers one example of local production and a strategic view of the encapsulating social systems of Maale, the southwestern region, and Ethiopia.

A Summary of Forces and Relations of Production in Maale

As far as I could tell, certain relationships were characteristic of Maale as a whole. Everywhere two forms of social relationships upheld an uneven distribution of product. That is, there were two principal relations of production: (1) that between male household heads and their domestic dependents, both wives and working children, and (2) that between landlords, representatives of the Ethiopian state (northern landlords, Maale chiefs, and the king), and their tenants.[1]

The previous chapters have attempted to analyze how these relations of production interacted with the major technical and social features of the production process, i.e. with forces of production, to yield the basic outlines of Maale political economy. In the case of male household heads versus their domestic dependents, the most salient aspect of forces of production was that labor was the relatively scarce factor of production in Maale. Land was accessible (usually for a rent); hand tools were simple and possessed by everyone. In this context, the limiting factor to production was generally labor.

With labor the technical limit to production, the strength of household heads—or the degree of possible contradiction between the interests of elders and their domestic dependents—was interrelated with the demographic development of households, particularly with the relative number of consumers to workers. Household heads, it should be remembered, controlled the disposition of household product (or labor in the case of Bola vicinity) above that consumed. During certain phases of development, households typically consumed all they produced (sometimes more), and in those cases, heads had no surplus with which to politick by becoming bond friends with an influential man or to "reinvest" by marrying another wife. During other phases of development, households headed by elders had relatively great resources to deploy.

If the technical aspects of the production process conditioned the pattern of relations of production, the reverse was also true. Within limits, elders shaped the developmental cycle of their households. The fact that the eldest sons were usually given much the largest share of inheritance was one of the factors that kept them in their fathers' households after marriage. And the fact that all children needed their fathers' consent or assistance to marry gave elders influence over the timing of childrens' exits from their households.

The second major relation of production was that between landlords and their tenants. In Maale there were two rather dissimilar kinds of landowners, each of whom had gotten their land in different ways. The first were Maale who had been given *gabbār rest* after the Italian occupation. As Chapter 2 explained, the Ethiopian government divided land among the Maale mainly as a way of securing a tax base, and it was mainly as tax collectors that *gabbār rest* owners functioned. As far as my knowledge goes, *gabbār rest* owners generally did not collect monies from their "tenants" much in excess of the taxes they themselves owed to the government; in other words, they did not receive rents, and in this sense they were not landlords.[2]

Other landlords, notably northern immigrants with measured land and Maale chiefs and the king who had originally been given *maderia* lands, occupied a distinctly different economic and political position. First of all, they were actually part of the Ethiopian administration of the southwest, waxing more or less influential at different times in the twentieth century. Second, their plots tended to be much larger than *gabbār rest* plots and were often located in strategic cattle-raising areas. Third, these landowners did collect rents. Up until 1974, well after the practice had been declared illegal, the Maale king, the most powerful northern landlord, and at least one of the chiefs even continued to receive labor tribute. The presence of *gabbār rest* plots nearby acted as a brake on the amount of rents that landlords could collect, but all received rents above the modest level of taxes they owed to the government.

Landlord relations of production developed out of the northern conquest of the southwest in the late nineteenth century. Compared with Western colonial governments, the Ethiopian administration was relatively weak; during most periods, it had only a limited capacity to penetrate directly into the countryside. Consequently, governmental aims were circumscribed and limited to keeping a minimal degree of order, to encouraging trade, and to maintaining the flow of taxes. These aspects of administration of the new area required some arrangement in which the costs of government would be borne mainly by southwesterners.

In this context, the Ethiopian administration came to rely on a combination of indirect rule—maintaining the old Maale political hierarchy with grants of land—and the settlement of northern "gun men" in Maale— many of whom were also rewarded with land. As Chapter 2 showed, the nature of the relationship between landlords and their tenants evolved from the *gabbār* system of personal servitude and tribute toward a more specific and limited form of rent collection.

In this evolution, the two segments of the developing landlord class, northerners and Maale, sometimes came into collision; their fortunes tended to wax and wane in inverse proportion. With strong provincial governors, northern settlers in Maale tended to prosper relative to the Maale elite. Strong governors could afford to bypass traditional Maale leaders and to carry their policies directly into the countryside with the help of northern soldier-settlers. By contrast, weak governors, their power circumscribed by the emperor and his central administration, had fewer economic and political resources; consequently, they had to rely more heavily on a policy of indirect rule through the Maale elite. The friction that developed between Maale and northern landlords over these ups and downs of the political cycle, if not actually encouraged by governmental officials, served administrative interests in maintaining malleable and responsive local elites in Maale.

If technical aspects of the Maale production process under northern rule conditioned the development of landlord relations of production, the reverse was again true. Once landlords had begun to consolidate their positions, they blocked further centralization of the government. To reiterate a statistic quoted earlier, by 1967 the agricultural sector of the Ethiopian economy produced 65 percent of the gross domestic product, employed 87 percent of the population, but contributed only 7 percent of state revenues (Markakis 1972: 129). Moreover, landlords in Maale (and apparently elsewhere in Ethiopia) proved an obstacle to the government's objective of developing agriculture and of increasing the marketed surplus of grain to towns to feed workers in planned capitalist enterprises. (Without a relatively cheap source of subsistence goods for workers, the cost of wages would have made capitalist ventures unprofitable.) Landlords, since they were not involved in the actual process of production, apparently took little interest in improving technology. Before the revolution, one landlord in Maale was considering introducing an irrigation scheme, but in general the main aim of landlords appears to have been to collect rents and to keep abreast of the politics of local courts. Repeatedly, aid missions from Western capitalist countries emphasized the fundamental role of land reform in Ethiopian development, but it was not until after the revolution of 1974 that the power of landlords was broken and the land tenure system radically changed.

It was the interaction between aspects of forces and relations of production such as these—combined with Bola's position at the political center of Maale—that resulted in the particular patterns of the production process described above. Of the two principal relations of production, that between landlords and their tenants was dominant not only in the sense that landlords as a category were much more powerful than household heads but also that landlord relations of production in Bola conditioned the way households entered the production process. It was the conflict between segments of the landlord class over succession to the kingship that broadly defined the two labor-sharing groups in Bola vicinity—one focused on Dofo *mol?o*, the other on Bola *mol?o*. And it was mainly the evolution of landlord relations of production toward ever closer conformity with the wider Ethiopian pattern that conditioned the way elders in Bola vicinity deployed their labor resources.

Theoretical Implications of the Present Study

Analysis of the production process in Bola vicinity has shown a web of relationships among aspects of kinship, economics, and politics. A dominant theme of preceding chapters has been the analysis of these connections in concrete detail: the relationship of the developmental cycle to the economic strength of households, of the system of marriage gifts to the political inferiority of junior men, and of work-group membership to political factions. Despite the common anthropological wisdom that systems of kinship, economics, and politics tend to coexist in undifferentiated structures in many noncapitalist societies, theoretical difficulties in formulating the exact nature of the interconnections have persisted.

Consider the problem of the relationship between economics and politics in noncapitalist societies and consider Sahlins' (I would argue, neoclassical) solution (1972). According to Sahlins, Chayanov's rule is the fundamental economic tendency of noncapitalist societies. If systems of kinship and politics somehow did not exist, all noncapitalist societies would conform to Chayanov's rule. But, of course, such systems do exist, and in Sahlins' theory, particular structures of kinship and politics cause "deviations" from the fundamental economic tendency in all societies: Certain households produce more than they "need" and trade the surplus for political influence; others give their surpluses to kinsmen in order to fulfill the norms of kinship and so forth.

Notice that economics and politics interrelate in Sahlins' theory only in the sphere of circulation—certain people trade goods for power, etc. While such processes are undoubtedly important, they hardly exhaust the domain of politcal economy. How are some households able to produce extra goods to make these exchanges? Specifically, what combination of economic and political forces mold households as units of production? These questions cannot be posed or answered within Sahlins' theoretical system. Like all neoclassical approaches, Sahlins' theory assumes a certain institutional framework for production and can, therefore, offer no explanation of it.

Consider the problem of the relationship between kinship and economics. The anthropological literature contains a long series of arguments on this issue that I can consider only very selectively here. Principally, I want to draw attention to the similarity of some important aspects of these controversies to those in economic anthropology and, by contrast, to explain the position of the present study.

A classic stance within anthropology, to state it boldly, has been that kinship is a determining factor of the economy of most "primitive" societies. This position, most closely identified with substantivists, has been widely accepted within functionalist social anthropology:

> ...the Western firm is an association (i.e. contract organization), not importantly affected by kinship, religion, or political affiliation of participants. In Africa, however, production is often undertaken by intimate communities of persons sharing a multitude of social ties and functions, one of which happens to be production of material goods (Dalton [1962] 1971: 124).

> The most general thing about production organizations in primitive and peasant society is that they tend to be derivate. The social organization carrying out the making of goods or the tendering of services is dependent on and derived from other sets of social relations (Nash 1966: 23).

Reacting against this position, other anthropologists have insisted that kinship is no more than an expression of more basic economic and political interests, in particular those involving property. Edmund Leach's study of a Ceylonese village (1961) is paradigmatic of the argument that "economic relations are prior to kinship relations."[3] Leach writes:

> Kin groups do not exist as things in themselves without regard to the rights and interests which center in them. Membership of such a group is not established by genealogy alone. Properly speaking, two individuals can only be said to be of the same kinship group when they share some common interest—economic, legal, political, religious as the case may be— and justify that sharing by reference to a kinship nexus (1961: 6)

A series of issues has arisen in this debate, but perhaps the most basic is the question of individual motivation in noncapitalist societies. Leach and other writers maintain that it is principally "economic" and "political" interests that animate individual action whereas other anthropologists insist that the moral values of kinship—what Fortes (1969) calls "the axiom of amity" or "prescriptive altruism"—are fundamental and cannot be reduced to economics.

Very reasonably, Maurice Bloch (1973) has observed that there is little to choose between these two alternatives. As long as analysis is confined to the question of characteristic kinds of motives in individual action—as was the substantivist-formalist debate in economic anthropology—the only realistic and productive analytical question becomes one of specifying *which* kind of motives operate in *what* kind of contexts. Bloch argues that the moral axioms of kinship offer long-term security in many societies while more narrowly defined economic values come into play in situations where short-term interests are dominant.

Consider the different perspective on these questions that the present study offers. By focusing on institutional arrangements that surround the production process, we have been able to avoid misleading formulations of "economics" versus "politics" or of "economics" versus "kinship." In regard to the Maale household, for example, not much analytical advance is to be gained by asking whether it is a social unit based fundamentally on descent and alliance or on economics. With respect to household organizations, Maale kinship *is* economics and vice versa.

Expressing a view of noncapitalist economies generally, Manning Nash writes:

Peasant and primitive societies do not have organizations whose only tasks are those of production, and there are no durable social units based solely on productive activities. The economic unit and its membership depend upon prior sorts of social relations (1966: 23).

With regard to Maale households, in what sense are other social relationships prior to economic ones?. Temporally? Logically? It might be argued that biological reproduction is in some sense prior, but kinship, a system of reckoning "relatives," can hardly be said to determine household organization. The "demographic squeeze" that I observed in Bola vicinity was not an inevitable consequence of Maale kinship. In the case of stratified villages in eighteenth century Austria studied by Berkner (1972), servants were drawn into and expelled from households to produce a relatively unchanging dependency ratio over the developmental cycle. Similarly, Claude Meillassoux ([1964] 1978) notes other mechanisms that accomplished the same effect for production units in Guro society. Part of the value of the present approach is, therefore, flexibility in following out a train of analysis wherever it leads. To paraphrase Clifford Geertz once again, we have been able to pursue our fox into whichever field the chase took us, whether kinship, economics or politics.

If flexibility is one aspect of the present approach, I would argue that another is specificity. A focus on forces and relations of production has allowed a precise description of key relationships in Maale political economy. Maurice Godelier ([1973] 1977) argues that kin relations in certain contexts play the role of relations of production in many noncapitalist societies. The results of the present study bear Godelier out. For example, the relationship between fathers and their coresident, adult children is a relation of production in Maale. This is not to say, of course, that kinship is some omnibus and dominating structure that functions as relations of productions as a whole. The tie between a man and his father's father's brother's son in Maale, though a relationship based upon descent, is not a relation of production.

Notice finally that the relationship between elders and juniors—contrary to Meillassoux's general model of closed horticultural economies ([1960] 1978 and [1975] 1981)—is not a relation of production in Maale. The relevant relationship is that between male household heads (whether junior or senior) and their domestic dependents. It happens, for reasons explained above, that household heads typically wax strong as they reach elderhood. The general asymmetry between elders and juniors in Maale becomes manifest not within the constitution of productive units themselves but within the circulation of *dabo* labor. Indeed, the direction of labor flow in Bola vicinity from elders to junior would be completely inexplicable if the relationship between the two functioned as a relation of production. It would be as if capitalists worked for proletarians.

The precise specification of relations of production is not just a formal exercise of classification for classification's sake. We expect that relations of production will delineate the major fault lines in a social formation—the cleavages along which tensions build up, are ameliorated by constant and slow slippage, and at times are violently resolved by radical realignments. The present study's focus on the production process has provided, I would argue, an approach to locating these tensions and conflicts within the wider political economy and to assessing their role in its transformation and change. To recall only a few paradigmatic incidents or fragments of the previous analysis, we have noted the characteristic tensions in stem family households headed by elders, the conflict between the king Arregude and his people during the early period of indirect rule in this century, and the violent opposition of Maale to the exactions of northern landlords just before the Italian invasion.

Work and power, forces and relations of production, lead then to a consideration of history. "Men make their own history, but they do not make it just as they please... (Marx [1852] (1966: 15)). Late 1975 was a decisive turning point in Maale history. The postrevolutionary future is open, of course, but as Marx noted, not totally open. Changes will depend, to some extent, on the structure of prerevolutionary Maale political economy. The degree to which the present analysis can serve as a guide for understanding current social transformations is a question still to be answered.

Appendix

Beer for Labor in *Dabo* Work Parties

To calculate the amount of labor embodied in *dabo* beer versus the amount of labor that work parties accomplished, we need to know, first of all, the average number of hours that went into producing a pound of grain in Maale. I did not collect output figures for households in Bola vicinity; however, given the fact that Maale households in Dofo, Kaiyo, and Bola were almost entirely self-subsistent and produced almost no surplus above consumption in 1974-1975, it seems reasonable to assume that output and therefore consumption was approximately the same as in similar economies in Africa. From Clark and Haswell (1970) and from Schneider (1964), I have therefore adopted an approximate figure of 650 lb. of grain per adult per year.

Consider now a household of dependency ratio 2.8. (It will become clear why such a choice is convenient.) Within the household, there is 1 adult worker to support 2.8 consumption units. Assuming that each consumption unit requires 650 lb. of grain a year, then the household would have to produce 1,820 lb. of grain a year.

How much labor would go into producing that amount of grain? From Figure 8, we saw that a household of dependency ratio 2.8 gives away as much *dabo* labor as it receives. Therefore, the labor input into its fields reflects only the work of its own household members. Since the average worker among the Maale works about 4.5 hours per day (cf. Chapter 3) and since our hypothetical household contains only 1 worker, the total labor expenditure for the year would be 1,642 hours. Given these assumptions, therefore, 1 lb. of Maale grain would require 0.9 hours of labor.

In order to have enough beer so that a neighbor can work about 6 hours in a *dabo*, a sponsor must have approximately 2 lb. of grain. According to the figures above, those 2 lb. of grain require about 1.8 hours of labor to produce them. In addition, 1.5 hours of female labor is required to turn that amount of grain into beer. In all, therefore, a household that sponsors a *dabo* has to expend about 3.3 hours of labor in preparation for every 6 hours of *dabo* labor that it receives. In other words, a sponsor receives about twice as much labor in a *dabo* as it expends.

These calculations are, of course, crude. They assume that an hour of labor at any task carried out by any person is equivalent. In addition, the amount of grain in beer was estimated from recipes of women who sold beer in the market. Since market beer was somewhat richer than most *dabo* beer, the figure of 2 lb. of grain for every *dabo* worker is an upper limit. Women's labor time in brewing—a factor that Barth (1967) neglected to include in his calculations on this problem—was estimated from one case which appeared in the labor time survey described in Chapter 3.

Notes

Chapter 1

1.   The terms *bālābbāt* and *c'ek'āshum* were the Amharic names given to the office of the Maale king and chiefs respectively; *grāzmāch* was an honorary military title given by Haile Selassie to one of the wealthy northern landlords living in Maale.

2.   Many anthropologists have grappled with the problem of defining peasants. It seems to me that the usefulness of the concept is not so much theoretical (as in such statements as "peasants do X") as heuristic. In the sense in which I am developing the concept here, the term peasant serves as an image—it poses certain problems and emphasizes certain social relationships that are crucial for understanding stratified agrarian societies.

3.   Sahlins' domestic mode of production has inspired more confusion in the literature than any recent work in economic anthropology. Sahlins himself (1972: xii) proclaims his theory substantivist. David Seddon (1978: 413) lists Sahlins' work in a select bibliography of recent Marxist works, and Maurice Godelier ([1973] 1977: 18) presents Sahlins as one of a group of anthropologists currently developing Marxian concepts. But as I have attempted to show here, Sahlins' theory is in important respects a neoclassical theory—as its derivation from Chayanov's work and as its invocation of Hobbes' ideas would suggest.

4.   Asad (1978) offers a more complete discussion of the effect of colonialism on the development of functionalist anthropological theories. In particular, he stresses the fact that anthropology grew up under routine colonialism, "... an imperial structure of power already established rather than one in process of vigorous expansion in which political force and contradiction are only too obvious" (1973: 115).

5.   I am not arguing, of course, that theoretical propositions in the strict sense are impossible in neoclassical forms of analyses. If, for example, scales of individual values ("revealed preferences") are empirically established for a group of people at a certain time t_1 and if we assume that these values are stable over time from t_1 to t_2, then we may make predictions about the pattern of individual actions at t_2 given change in some variable, say prices.

6.   In fact, the only possible explanation for the transformation of feudalism into capitalism becomes one that maintains that the range of individual choice was somehow widened. Characteristically, this takes the form of an argument that the revival of trade in Europe led to the decay of feudalism. But this emphasis on circulation hardly squares with the Marxian insistence on the primacy of relations of production (cf. Brenner 1977).

7.   Whether Chayanov's theory, by itself, presents an adequate understanding of the Russian peasant case is a debated point. For a negative point of view, see Harrison 1975.

8. Meillassoux ([1975] 1981) extends the arguments cited above but still does not attend to the fact that different sets of relations of production (which cannot be captured by the simple oppositions, seniors/juniors or men/women) appear in the type of societies Meillassoux is analyzing. A closer examination of the production process in Maale will, I think, demonstrate this. It should be added that even as I criticize Meillassoux's formulation, his work seems to me to have been extremely productive in posing important questions.

9. This is not to deny that for certain problems neoclassical and Marxian theories offer incompatible alternative formulations. Such is the case, for example, when neoclassical writers propose that the level of wages in a capitalist economy is determined by the marginal productivity of labor. For Marxists, wages may to correspond to the marginal productivity of labor but they are fundamentally determined by a range of social factors including the state of the class struggle, the size of the reserve army of unemployed, the rate of technical progress, etc.

Chapter 2

1. So vast a generalization has to be qualified in relation to particular periods (Trimingham 1952; Abir 1968; Tamrat 1972; Abir 1975). Nevertheless it does point to what I consider a major overarching pattern in Ethiopian history. Also, it should be noted that I am not arguing that Red Sea trade simply *caused* the rise of northern empires. What I want to suggest is that the trade provided a particularly "rich" environment in which northern political power could and most often did grow and augment itself.

2. The Ethiopian Church appears to have come apart along the same seams. During the "Era of the Judges," the Church divided over the question of the number of births of Christ.

3. Here I am translating native terms for several Omotic languages (Maale, *kati;* Dorze, *kaʔo;* Kefa, *tati*) as "king." By doing so, I am using king in a ritual sense, not necessarily a political one. Some of the kings of the southwest held little political power—they had no "kingdoms." Reluctantly, I have chosen this alternative because it is closest to the usage of the Maale themselves (and I suspect other Omotic peoples). The Maale referred to both Haile Selassie and the ritual leader of the neighboring Bako as *kati,* even though they were quite aware that the two men differed vastly in amount and kind of political power. Actually, English usage is not different in this respect: Great Britain, a parliamentary democracy, is said nevertheless to have kings and queens.

3. To reiterate the previous footnote, by translating the Maale word *kati* as king, I do not wish to imply that nineteenth century Maale was a kingdom. In terms of Elman Service's political typology, Maale was a "chiefdom."

5. At present, many marriages do not conform to the rule of moiety exogamy, and Maale say that they no longer follow the custom. However, almost all elderly Maale (many young people do not know even the names of the moieties) maintain that in the past *karazi* married only *raggi* and *raggi* only *karazi.* When questioned further about marriages in the recent past that did not conform to the rule, some admitted that there had always been legitimate exceptions. Whether these exceptions were rationalizations for the present state of affairs or whether the past system during the nineteenth century was more complex than a simple dual structure is a question that will require more historical research to answer.

6. The camps of northern Ethiopian emperors in the fifteenth century (Tamrat 1972: 269-75) show some interesting parallels to the lion house of Maale. Whether the Maale royal compound was borrowed from the north or whether northern Ethiopians perhaps borrowed their pattern from the south is an open question.

7. The dates for these various phases were slightly different for Maale and for northern Ethiopia. Menilek fell ill in 1906, but it was not until about 1911 and the arrival of *dajāzmāch* Merid that governors in Bako began to wax noticeably stronger. The Italians invaded the north in 1935 but did not get to the south until 1936. Similarly, Haile Selassie was deposed in September 1974, but the Maale *bālābbāt* continued in office for almost a year longer.

Chapter 3

1. The reader should be forewarned that I use the term, household, in a different sense than, for instance, Bender (1967); by using the term, I intend the group of people who combine to form one unit of production under the direction of one head. In the vast majority of cases among the Maale, market villages, and *mani,* this group—the household—was also a residence group (Bender's definition of household) and a unit for the preparation and consumption of food (the other diagnostic trait commonly proposed). The only exceptions were polygynous households. In those cases, each co-wife had her own residence unit in which food was separately stored, prepared, and consumed.

    Even though members of a polygynous household resided separately, they formed one unit of production. The male household head directed the activities of the group as a whole, and he "owned" the grain produced. Sometimes, the whole polygynous household cooperated in planting and weeding a common field, and before the harvest, the husband divided the field between his wives for storage and consumption. Other times, each wife and her children were allocated separate fields. In any case, husbands could transfer children (their labor power and consumption requirements) from the residence group of one wife to another and, on occasions, could call his wife and children in one residence group to work in the field of the other.

2. In Table 2 and succeeding tables, ages of household heads are, of course, only estimated. For young people, the error is probably ±2 years, while for elders, the error probably increases to about ±5 years. Adults are defined as persons 14 years or older.

3. This pattern of town organization is apparently both widespread and ancient in Ethiopia. A western physician, Dr. Poncet, visited Gondor in northern Ethiopia in 1698-1700 and noted, "Mahometans are tolerated at Gondor, but 'tis in the lower Part of the Town, and in a separate Quarter . . . The Ethiopians cannot endure to eat with them; they wou'd not eat even of Meat that is kill'd by a Mahometan, nor drink in a cup they have made use of, unless a Religious Man shou'd bless it by reciting over it some Prayers and shou'd breath into it thrice, as it were to drive away the evil Spirit" (quoted in Trimingham 1952: 102).

Chapter 4

1. Among the Gusii of Kenya, work parties of the *dabo* type appear to have functioned similarly as in Maale. While work parties (called *risaga*) were not simply an epiphenomenon of kinship ties, participation was strengthened by such ties: "*Risaga* cooperation is an essential feature of Gusii economic organization. That this is so, and that cooperation is not merely a function of kinship or lineage ties, is proved by the undiminished importance of the *risaga* in areas of very mixed settlement. The *risaga* bond is one of neighborhood and economic dependence. Coincident descent ties may reinforce it with a closer solidarity, but they are not essential to its formation and maintenance" (Mayer 1951: 10).

2. I am assuming, of course, that all *dabo* parties worked about the same length of time. In practice, the length of *dabo* work days varied somewhat, but most *dabo* lasted about six hours. Those that were markedly shorter often seem to have been the result of miscalculations of how many workers would attend.

3. It is important to note a possible coincidence between the interests of elders' household dependents and those of elders themselves. It may have been that dependents, particularly daughters and younger sons, actually preferred working in the *dabo* of others (enjoyable occasions in any case) to working for their own households (any surplus grain they helped to produce would be converted into cattle which would then likely become the property of the eldest son). For a case where the interests of father and sons clashed with respect to work parties see Goody (1958: 70).

Chapter 5

1. A possible third relation of production in Maale as a whole was that between heads of minimal descent groups, *toidi*, and their younger brothers and the latter's dependents. The power of *toidi* to extract an economic surplus from descent mates (principally through ritual means when younger brothers' cattle were declared ritually impure and therefore appropriated) declined over the twentieth century. Bola vicinity had no large ramified lineages, and it seemed to me that the effective economic power of *toidi* there had mostly lapsed.

2. The potential for *gabbār rest* owners to turn themselves into actual landlords probably did exist. As I have noted before, *gabbār rest* owners were chosen from among the wealthier men in Maale and were often heads of large ramified lineages. In at least one case in southern Bunka, an owner had enough clout to evict a kinsman from his land after a disagreement. Perhaps the main reason that *gabbār rest* owners had not become true landlords in the approximately twenty-five years since they had been given land was their lack of knowledge and expertise in subprovincial courts located outside Maale—the principal state agency that upheld the rights of landlords over tenants.

3. Another line of argument against the special status of kinship is Worsley's reinterpretation (1956) of the Tale case. Although perhaps inspired by Marx, Worsley's arguments are basically functionalist. According to him, the functional requirements of Tale horticulture determine the form kinship takes: "The particular forms which kinship relations will take— corporate unilineal descent groups, cognatic systems without lineages, double unilineal systems, etc.—are largely determined by economic and historical forces" (Worsley 1956: 62- 63). To make his case persuasive, Worsley would have to show that the functional requirements of Tale horticulture can be satisfied *only* by the particular kind of kinship system found in Taleland. This, as Fortes (1969: 221) notes, Worsley does not accomplish.

Guide to Transcription

According to my analysis, Maale contains six basic vowels with the values indicates below:

i	pure vowel in the first part of the dipthong [iy] in "bee"
e	pure vowel in the first part of the dipthong [ey] in "bait"
ə	as in "sof*a*"
a	as in "f*a*ther"
o	pure vowel in the first part of the dipthong [ow] in "boat"
u	pure vowel in the first part of the dipthong [uw] in "boot"

Consonants will be obvious, except perhaps for the glottal stop indicated by ʔ. Malle has a number of glottalized consonants, three ejective ones *k'*, *c'*, and *ts'* and two implosive ones *'d* and *'b*.

Some Amharic words, particularly names, appear in the text with conventional spellings; otherwise, they have been transcribed in the system used by Donald Levine (1965). Glottalization has been indicated as above. The vowel system of Amharic is different from that of Maale and accordingly a different transcription system has been used.

a	as in "c*a*re"
u	as in "pr*u*dent"
i	as in "rav*i*ne"
ā	as in "f*a*ther"
ē	as in "pr*e*y"
e	as in "sil*e*nt"
o	as in "g*o*"

Glossary*

bālābbāt	Amharic name given to traditional authorities in south-western Ethiopia (cf. *kati*) who enjoyed official recognition and titles to land
belli	bond friend with whom gifts, usually including a cow, have been exchanged
c'ek'āshum	"village chief," the Amharic name given to Maale chiefs (cf. *goda*)
dabo	work party sponsored as the occasion arises in which the field owner provides beer
dajāzmāch	"Commander of the Gate," Amharic military title higher in rank than *fitāwrāri* but lower than *rās*
dini	land owned in the preconquest system of Maale land tenure, usually by descent group heads or *toidi*
fitāwrāri	"Commander of the Spearhead," Amharic military title lower in rank than *dajāzmāch* or *rās*
gabbār	"tribute-giver," the Amharic word for inhabitants of a fief who owed tribute and personal service to the fief-owner
gabbār rest	land given to former *gabbār* in Maale during the post-Italian period (Amharic)
gatta	Maale functionary who organized the collection of tribute for chiefs and the king in preconquest times
gesho	mother of the king; also an office in *mol?o* work groups
goda	Maale chiefs, one of thirteen in the nineteenth century (cf. *c'ek'āshum*)
gojo	a figure who functioned in all royal rituals in Maale
gult	fiefs granted mainly during the pre-Italian period with rights to service and tribute of tenants or *gabbār* (Amharic)
helma	a small work group of three or four people that follows a set cycle of rotation

---

*Unless otherwise indicated, all terms are Maale.

karazi	the moiety that includes the king and all but one of the Maale chiefs (cf. *raggi*)
kati	Maale king (cf. *bālābbāt*); also used to designate an office in *mol?o* work groups
k'alad	"measured land" that the government expropriated, usually in unoccupied grazing areas, and sold, usually to northern soldier-settlers (Amharic)
le	the long growing season in Maale from March through August (cf. *silo*)
maderia	fiefs granted to administrators and to local *bālābbāts* originally contingent on their governmental service (Amharic; cf. *rest*)
mol?o	large work group of about fifteen members that follows a set cycle of rotation
məni or *mənzi*	group of endogamous potters and tanners in Maale; also used to designate the office of "policeman" in *mol?o* work groups
raggi	moiety that includes the chief of Makana and that is said to be made up of the original inhabitants of Maale before the coming of the *karazi* moiety
rās	prestigious Amharic title, higher in rank than either *dajāzmāch* or *fitāwrāri*
rest	the general word (Amharic) that indicated land ownership in Maale, both for those who originally got their land through *maderia* grants and those who received *gabbār rest*
silo	short growing season in Maale from September through mid-November (cf. *le*)
toidi	"first" or head of a descent group, the span of which may vary from minimal lineages upwards (though not to the level of clan)

Bibliography

Abir, Mordechai. The emergence and consolidation of the monarchies of Enarea and Jimma in the first half of the nineteenth century. *Journal of African history.* 6 (1965): 205-219.

———. *Ethiopia: the era of the princes.* New York: Praeger, 1968.

———. Southern Ethiopia. *In* David Birmingham and Richard Gray, eds. *Pre-colonial African trade.* London: Oxford University Press, 1970: 119-37.

———. Ethiopia and the horn of Africa. *In* Richard Gray, ed. *The Cambridge history of Africa.* Vol. 4. Cambridge: Cambridge University Press, 1975: 537-77.

Abrahams, R.G. Neighbourhood organization: a major sub-system among the northern Nyamwezi. *Africa* 35 (1965): 168-86.

Ames, David W. Wolof co-operative work groups. *In* Melville Herskovits and William Bascom, eds. *Continuity and change in African cultures.* Chicago: University of Chicago Press, 1959:224-37.

Asad, Talal. Two European images of non-European rule. *In* Talal Asad, ed. Anthropology and the colonial encounter. London: Ithaca Press, 1973: 103-18.

Barth, Fredrik. Economic spheres in Darfur. *In* Raymond Firth, ed. *Themes in economic anthropology.* London: Tavistock, 1967: 149-74.

Bender, Donald R. 1967 A refinement of the concept of household: families, co-residence, and domestic functions. *American anthropologist* 69 (1967): 493-504.

Berkner, Lutz K. The stem family and the developmental cycle of the peasant household: an eighteenth-century Austrian example. *American historical review* 78 (1972): 398-418.

Bloch, Maurice. The long term and the short term: the economic and political significance of the morality of kinship. *In* Jack Goody, ed. *The character of kinship.* Cambridge: Cambridge University Press, 1973: 75-87.

———. Introduction. *In* Maurice Bloch, ed. Marxist analyses and social anthropology. London: Malaby Press, 1975: xi-xiv.

Braudel, Fernand. *La Méditerranée et le monde méditerranéen à l'epoque de Philippe II.* 2nd ed. Paris: Librairie Armand Colin, 1966. *The Mediterranean and the Mediterranean world in the age of Philip II.* Sîan Reynolds, trans. New York: Harper and Row, 1972.

Brenner, Robert. The origins of capitalist development: a critique of neo-Smithian Marxism. *New left review* 104 (1977): 25-92.

Cancian, Francesca M. Varieties of functional analysis. *In* David L. Sills, ed. *International encyclopedia of the social sciences.* Vol. 6. New York: Macmillan and Free Press, 1968: 29-43.

Cancian, Frank. Maximization as norm, strategy, and theory: a comment on programmatic statements in economic anthropology. *American anthropologist* 68 (1966): 465-70.

———. *Change and uncertainty in a peasant economy: the Maya corn farmers of Zinacantan.* Stanford: Stanford University Press, 1972.

Caplow, Theodore. *Two against one: coalitions in triads.* Englewood Cliffs, New Jersey: Prentice-Hall, 1968.

Charsley, S.F. The *silika*: a co-operative labour institution. *Africa* 46 (1976): 34-47.

Chayanov, Alexander V. Organizatsiya krest'yanskogo khozyaistva (Peasant farm organization). Moscow: Cooperative Publishing House, 1925. The theory of peasant economy. Daniel Thorner, Basile Kerblay, and R.E.F. Smith, eds. Homewood, Illinois: Richard D. Irwin, 1966.

Clapham, Christopher. *Haile-Selassie's government.* New York: Praeger, 1969.

Clark, Colin, and Margaret Haswell. *The economics of subsistence agriculture.* 4th ed. London: Macmillan, 1970.

Cohen, G.A. Karl Marx's theory of history: a defence. Oxford: Clarendon Press, 1978.

Curtin, Philip D. *Economic change in precolonial Africa: Senegambia in the era of the slave trade.* Madison: University of Wisconsin Press, 1975.

Dalton, George. Traditional production in primitive African economies. *Quarterly journal of economics* 76 (1962): 360-78. *In* George Dalton, *Economic anthropology and development: essays on tribal and peasant economies. New York: Basic Books,* 1971: 123-42.

_____. Primitive, archaic and modern economies: Karl Polanyi's contribution to economic anthropology and comparative economy. *In* June Helm, ed. *Essays in economic anthropology.* Seattle: University of Washington Press, 1965. *In* George Dalton, Economic anthropology and development: essays on tribal and peasant economies. New York: Basic Books, 1971: 11-42.

_____. Theoretical issues in economic anthropology. Current anthropology 10 (1969): 63-102. *In* George Dalton, *Economic anthropology and development: essays on tribal and peasant economies.* New York: Basic Books, 1971: 70-119.

_____. Peasantries in anthropology and history. *Current anthropology* 13 (1972): 385-407.

Dehérain, Henri. Les katamas dans les provinces méridionales de L'Abyssinie pendant le règne de l'empereur Ménélik'. Ministère de l'Instruction Publique et des Beaux Arts, Comité des Travaux Historiques et Scientifiques, Section de Géographie, *Bulletin* 29 (1914): 239-41.

Donham, Donald L. Beyond the domestic mode of production. *Man* 16 (1981): 515-41.

_____. Culture, contradictions et histoire: analyse des anciens Mallé. *In* Marc Abélès and Chantal Collard, eds. *Aînesse et générations en Afrique,* forthcoming.

_____. History at one point in time: 'working together' in Maale, 1975. *American Ethnologist,* forthcoming.

Dobb, Maurice. *Theories of value and distribution since Adam Smith: ideology and economic theory.* Cambridge: Cambridge University Press, 1973.

Epstein, T.S. The data of economics in anthropological analysis. *In* A.L. Epstein, ed. *The craft of social anthropology.* London: Tavistock, 1967: 153-80.

Erasmus, Charles J. Culture, structure, and process: the occurrence and disappearance of reciprocal farm labor. *Southwestern journal of anthropology* 12 (1956): 444-69.

Evans, Martin. A note on the measurement of Sahlins' social profile of domestic production. *American ethnologist* 1 (1974): 269-80.

Fleming, Harold C. The classification of West Cushitic within Hamito-Semitic. *In* Daniel F. McCall, et al., eds. *Eastern African history.* New York: Praeger, 1969: 3-27.

Fleming, Harold C., and Marvin L. Bender Non-Semitic languages. *In* M.L. Bender, et al., eds. *Language in Ethiopia.* London: Oxford University Press, 1976: 34-62.

Fortes, Meyer. *Kinship and the social order: the legacy of Lewis Henry Morgan.* Chicago: Aldine, 1969.

Gabre-Sellassie, Zewde. *Yohannes IV of Ethiopia.* Oxford: Clarendon Press, 1975.

Geertz, Clifford. Thick description: toward an interpretative theory of culture. *In* Clifford Geertz, *The interpretations of cultures.* New York: Basic Books, 1973: 3-30.

Godelier, Maurice. *Horizon, trajets marxistes en anthropologie.* Paris: Maspero, 1973. *Perspectives in Marxist anthropology.* Robert Brain, trans. Cambridge: Cambridge University Press, 1977.

Goody, Jack. The fission of domestic groups among the LoDagaba. *In* Jack Goody, ed. *The developmental cycle in domestic groups.* Cambridge: Cambridge University Press, 1958: 53-91.

_____. Marriage policy and incorporation in northern Ghana. *In* Ronald Cohen and John Middleton, eds. *From tribe to nation in Africa: studies in incorporation processes.* Scranton, Pennsylvania: Chandler, 1970: 114-49.

Greenberg, Joseph H. *The languages of Africa.* The Hague: Mouton, 1966.

Gregson, Ronald Edgar. Work, exchange, and leadership: the mobilization of agricultural labor among the Tumbuka of the Henga Valley. Ph.D. dissertation, Columbia University, 1969.

Gulliver, Philip H. *Neighbors and networks: the idiom of kinship in social action among the Ndendeuli of Tanzania.* Berkeley: University of California Press, 1971.

Haberland, Eike *Untersuchungen zum Äthiopischen Königtum.* Wiesbaden: Franz Steiner Verlag, 1965.

Halperin, Rhoda, and Judith Olmstead. To catch a feastgiver: redistribution among the Dorze of Ethiopia. *Africa* 46 (1976): 146-64.

Harrison, Mark. Chayanov and the economics of the Russian peasantry. *Journal of peasant studies* 2 (1975): 389-417.

Hill, Polly. *Rural Hausa: a village and a setting.* Cambridge: Cambridge University Press, 1972.

Hodgson, Marshall G.S. *The venture of Islam: conscience and history in a world civilization.* Vol. 3. The gun-powder empires and modern times. Chicago: University of Chicago Press, 1974.

Hopkins, A.G. *An economic history of West Africa.* London: Longman, 1973.

_____. Clio-antics: a horoscope for African economic history. In Christopher Fyfe, ed. *African studies since 1945: a tribute to Basil Davidson.* London: Longman, 1976: 31-48.

Hudson, Grover. Questions of language classification and the Semitic pre-history of Ethiopia. Unpublished manuscript, n.d.

Jensen, Adolf E., ed. *Altvölker Süd-Äthiopiens: Ergebnisse der Frobenius-Expeditionen 1950-52 und 1954-56.* Stuttgart: W. Kohlhammer Verlag, 1959

Jones, William O. Economic man in Africa. *Food Research Institute studies* 1 (1960): 107-34.

Lange, Oskar. Marxian economics and modern economic theory. *Review of economic studies* 2 (1934-35): 189-201.

Leach, Edmund R. *Political systems of highland Burma.* Boston: Beacon Press, 1954.

_____. *Pul Eliya, a village in Ceylon: a study of land tenure and kinship.* Cambridge: Cambridge University Press, 1961.

LeClair, Edward E., and Harold K. Schneider, eds. *Economic anthropology: readings in theory and analysis.* New York: Holt, Rinehart and Winston, 1968.

Legesse, Asmarom. *Gada: three approaches to the study of African society.* New York: Free Press, 1973.

Levine, Donald N. *Wax and gold: tradition and innovation in Ethiopian culture.* Chicago: University of Chicago Press, 1965.

_____. *Greater Ethiopia: the evolution of a multiethnic society.* Chicago: University of Chicago Press, 1974.

Lewis, Herbert S. *A Galla monarchy: Jimma Abba Jifar, Ethiopia, 1830-1932.* Madison: University of Wisconsin Press, 1965.

_____. The origins of the Galla and Somali. *Journal of African history* 7 (1966): 27-46.

Lukács, Georg. *Geschichte und Klassenbewusstein.* Berlin: Malik, 1923 *History and class consciousness: studies in Marxist dialectics.* Rodney Livingstone, trans. London: Merlin Press, 1971.

Mair, Lucy. Tradition and modernity in the new Africa. Transactions of the New York Academy of Sciences 27 (1965): 439-44. *In* Lucy Mair, *Anthropology and social change.* London: Athlone Press, 1969: 135-43.

Marcus, Harold G. *The life and times of Menelik II: Ethiopia 1844-1913.* Oxford: Clarendon Press, 1975.

Markakis, John. *Ethiopia: anatomy of a traditional policy*. Oxford: Clarendon Press, 1974.

Marx, Karl. *Zur Kritik der politischen Ökonomie*. Berlin: F. Duncker, 1859. *A contribution to the critique of political economy*. S.W. Ryazanskaya, trans. and Maurice Dobb, ed. Moscow: Progress Publishers, 1970.

_____. *Das Kapital: Kritik der politischen Ökonomie. Erster Band*. Hamburg: Otto Meissner, 1867. *Capital: a critique of political economy*. Vol. 1. Ben Fowkes, trans. London: Penguin, 1976.

_____. Der 18th Brumaire des Louis Napoleon. Die Revolution, 1852. *The eighteenth brumaire of Louis Bonaparte*. New York: International Publishers, 1966.

_____. Formen die der kapitalistisch Produktion vorhergehen. *In* Karl *Marx, Grundrisse der Kritik der Politischen Ökonomie (Rohentwurf)*. Berlin: Dietz Verlag, 1953. Pre-capitalist economic formations. Jack Cohen, trans. and E.J. Hobsbawn, ed. London: Lawrence and Wishart, 1964.

Marx, Karl, and Frederick Engels. *Manifest der Kommunistisch Partei*. London: J.C. Burghard, 1848. *Manifesto of the Communist Party*. Peking: Foreign Languages Press, 1965.

Maurette, Fernand. État de nos connaissances sur le nord-est Africain. Annales de géographie 14 (1905): 433-55.

Mayer, Philip. Two studies in applied anthropology in Kenya. *Colonial research studies* 3 (1951). London: His Majesty's Stationery Office, 1951.

Meillassoux, Claude. Essai d'interprétation du phénomène économique dans les sociétés traditionelles d'autosubsistence. *Cahiers d'études Africaines* 1 (1960): 38-67. 'The economy' in agricultural self-sustaining societies: a preliminary analysis. *In* David Seddon, ed. Relations of production. London: Cass, 1978: 127-58.

_____. From reproduction to production: a Marxist approach to economic anthropology. *Economy and society* 1 (1972): 93-105.

_____. *Femmes, greniers et capitaux*. Paris: Maspero, 1975. Maidens, meal and money: capitalism and the domestic community. Cambridge: Cambridge University Press, 1981.

Millar, James R. A reformulation of A.V. Chayanov's theory of the peasant economy. *Economic development and cultural change* 18 (1970): 219-29.

Minge-Kalman, Wanda. On the theory and measurement of domestic labor intensity. *American ethnologist* 4 (1977): 273-84.

Moore, M.P. Co-operative labour in peasant agriculture. *Journal of peasant studies* 2 (1975): 270-91.

Nash, Manning. *Primitive and peasant economic systems*. Scranton, Pennsylvania: Chandler, 1966.

_____. Reply to reviews of *Primitive and peasant economic systems*. Current anthropology 8 (1967): 249-50.

_____. Economic anthropology. *In* David L. Sills, ed. *International encyclopedia of the social sciences*. Vol. 4. New York: Macmillan and Free Press, 1968: 359-65.

O'Laughlin, M. Bridget. Mbum beer parties: structures of production and exchange in an African social formation. Ph.D. dissertation, Yale University, 1973.

_____. Marxist approaches in anthropology. *Annual review of anthropology* 4 (1975): 341-70.

Ollman, Bertell. *Alienation: Marx's conception of man in capitalist society*. 2nd ed. Cambridge: Cambridge University Press, 1976.

Olmstead, Judith Agricultural land and social stratification in the Gamu highlands of southern Ethiopia. *In* Harold G. Marcus, ed. *Proceedings of the first United States conference on Ethiopian studies*. East Lansing, Michigan: Michigan State University, 1975: 223-34.

Orans, Martin. Maximizing in jajmani land: a model of caste relations. *American anthropologist* 70 (1968): 875-97.

Perham, Margery. *The government of Ethiopia*. 2nd ed. Evanston: Northwestern University Press, 1969.

Polanyi, Karl. *The great transformation: the political and economic origins of our time.* Boston: Beacon Press, 1944.

_____. The economy as an instituted process. *In* Karl Polanyi, Conrad Arensberg, and Harry Pearson, eds. *Trade and market in the early empires: economies in history and theory.* Glencoe: Free Press, 1957: 243-70.

Rosaldo, Renato. Where precision lies: 'the hill people once lived on a hill.' *In* Roy Willis, ed. *The interpretation of symbolism.* London: Malaby Press, 1975: 1-22.

Rowthorn, Bob. Neoclassicism, neo-Ricardianism and Marxism. *New left review* 86 (1974): 63-87.

Rubenson, Sven. *The survival of Ethiopian independence.* London: Heinemann, 1976.

Sahlins, Marshall D. *Tribesmen.* Englewood Cliffs, New Jersey: Prentice-Hall, 1968.

_____. *Stone age economics.* Chicago: Aldine-Atherton, 1972.

Schneider, Harold K. Economics in East African aboriginal societies. *In* Melville J. Herskovits and Mitchell Harwitz, eds. *Economic transition in Africa.* Evanston: Northwestern University Press, 1964: 53-75.

_____. *The Wahi Wanyaturu: economics in an African society.* Chicago: Aldine, 1970.

Seddon, David, ed. *Relations of production: Marxist approaches to economic anthropology.* London: Cass, 1978.

Seibel, Hans Dieter, and Andreas Massing. *Traditional organizations and economic development: studies of indigenous cooperatives in Liberia.* New York: Praeger, 1974.

Skinner, G. William. Regional urbanization in nineteenth-century China. *In* G. William Skinner, ed. *The city in late imperial China.* Stanford University Press, 1977: 211-49.

Southall, Aidan W. *Alur society: a study in processes and types of domination.* Cambridge: Heffer, 1956.

_____. A critique of the typology of state and political systems. *In* Michael Banton, ed. *Political systems and the distribution of power.* London: Tavistock, 1965: 113-40.

Sperber, Dan. Paradoxes of seniority among the Dorze. *In* Harold G. Marcus, ed. *Proceedings of the first United States conference on Ethiopian studies.* East Lansing, Michigan: Michigan State University, 1975: 209-21.

Stent, W.R., and L. Roy Webb. Subsistence affluence and market economy in Papua New Guinea. *Economic record* 51 (1975): 522-38.

Tamrat, Taddesse. *Church and state in Ethiopia, 1270-1527.* Oxford: Clarendon Press, 1972.

Trimingham, J. Spencer. *Islam in Ethiopia.* London: Oxford University Press, 1952.

Turner, Victor W. *Schism and continuity in an African society: a study of Ndembu life.* Manchester: Manchester University Press, 1957.

Uchendu, Victor C. *Traditional work groups in economic development. Universities of East Africa social science conference at University of Dar es Salaam.* Vol. 5. Kampala: Makerere University Press, 1970: 246-61.

Vincent, Joan. *African elite: the big men of a small town.* New York: Columbia University Press, 1971.

Wallerstein, Immanuel. The rise and future demise of the world capitalist system: concepts for comparative analysis. *Comparative studies in society and history* 16 (1974): 387-415.

Warren, Bill. Imperialism and capitalist industrialization. *New left review* 81 (1973): 3-44.

Worsley, Peter. The kinship system of the Tallensi: a reevaluation. *Journal of the Royal Anthropological Institute* 86 (1956): 37-75.

Index